*The Spiritual Lives of Young
African Americans*

The Spiritual Lives of Young African Americans

ALMEDA M. WRIGHT

OXFORD
UNIVERSITY PRESS

OXFORD
UNIVERSITY PRESS

Oxford University Press is a department of the University of Oxford. It furthers
the University's objective of excellence in research, scholarship, and education
by publishing worldwide. Oxford is a registered trade mark of Oxford University
Press in the UK and certain other countries.

Published in the United States of America by Oxford University Press
198 Madison Avenue, New York, NY 10016, United States of America.

© Oxford University Press 2017

Library of Congress Cataloging-in-Publication Data
Names: Wright, Almeda M., author.
Title: The spiritual lives of young African Americans / Almeda M. Wright.
Description: New York, NY, United States of America :
Oxford University Press, [2017] Identifiers: LCCN 2016042333 (print) |
LCCN 2017017849 (ebook) |
ISBN 9780190664749 (updf) | ISBN 9780190664756 (epub) |
ISBN 9780190664732 (cloth)
Subjects: LCSH: African American youth—Religious life. |
Adolescence—Religious aspects—Christianity.
Classification: LCC BR563.N4 (ebook) | LCC BR563.N4 W655 2017 (print) |
DDC 248.4089/96073—dc23
LC record available at https://lccn.loc.gov/2016042333

1 3 5 7 9 8 6 4 2

Printed by Sheridan Books, Inc., United States of America

To my first religious educators,
my parents William and Lula Wright.
And to every young person for whom LIVING is not
an easy or obvious option.

Contents

Acknowledgments

AMONG MY CIRCLE of colleagues there is a common adage that *it takes a village to raise a scholar.* Throughout this research and book project, that has proven to be true over and over. I owe a wealth of gratitude to my village—the many people who assisted and supported this project in innumerable ways: from trusted mentors who believed in the work to the young people who shared their lives and wisdom.

As I have been wrestling with this project for almost a decade, I have several *villages* to thank for their support and encouragement along the way. First, I am grateful to Cynthia Read and the editorial staff at Oxford University Press.

I am grateful to my Emory University family and colleagues, where the seeds of this research were planted. Most especially to Dr. Emmanuel Lartey and Dean Mary Elizabeth Moore for their leadership and patience in reading the earliest iterations of this project and pushing me to carry on. Likewise, I am grateful to the many young people, faculty and graduate students at the Youth Theological Initiative. I am indebted to Elizabeth Corrie and Brenda Bennefield, for their leadership, as well as Catrice Glenn and Anjulet Tucker for helping to create research instruments and conduct interviews. The youth interview transcription would not have been possible without the generous funding of *the Lilly Endowment* through the Emory concentration on Religious Practices and Practical Theology.

I am also grateful to my faculty colleagues and students at Pfeiffer University. This was one of the first places I got to "try out" my ideas and you will never know how much it meant to have students working in youth ministry giving direct feedback (and challenge) to my ideas for how to help youth and young adults. Thank you for pushing me.

I am also truly grateful to my Yale Divinity School (YDS) village. I am grateful to Dean Gregory Sterling for the generous support and funding for sabbatical research to complete the manuscript. I have also been blessed and often surprised by the generosity of time and encouragement from my faculty colleagues: including the strong junior faculty network; my faculty mentor Mary Moschella; Yolanda Smith who has been a pillar of strength and support even before I came to YDS; and Tisa Wenger who has been a constant source of inspiration and encouragement, as she held me accountable to daily writing and communal support. Thank you to the numerous students who read chapters in seminars and offered critical feedback; as well as various graduate assistants who edited footnotes, pushed research projects forward, and in general took care of other aspects of my academic life so I could focus on this book. A special thank you goes to Eda Uca, who spent most of one summer writing abstracts, creating endnotes, hunting down permissions, reading every chapter, and asking harder questions than most of my reviewers up to that point. Eda's care and passion for my work came at a time when I wasn't sure I would finish on time.

Beyond the institutions where I studied or worked, my village includes an amazing network of racial and ethnic minority scholars. This network has been facilitated and funded by the Forum for Theological Exploration (FTE). So I must give a special note of gratitude to my FTE family first for funding my doctoral work, where portions of this project originated. I am also indebted to FTE for the mentorship and colleagues who believed in me, including Sharon Watson Fluker and Matthew Williams, and for the life-long scholar-friends-cheerleaders who I met at FTE conferences. Truly, without Dr. James Logan and Dr. Monique Moultrie this work might have stayed an idea or might have been discarded after failed attempts to get it "right" or get it published. For the blessings of friendship, humor, and accountability, I am grateful.

To all of my church families, from Sharon Baptist Church to Union, Victory, Friendship and Community, thank you for letting me grow and try out new ideas and progressive pedagogies with your children. I am deeply grateful for the 4:12 Youth Ministry team, including amazing co-teachers Pastor Timothy Jones and Kathryn Bradley. I have never encountered such a "dream team" of creativity, passion, and experience. Thank you for pushing me to *improved practice* during the final stages of writing.

To my family, thank you for always loving me and believing in me even before I knew that writing, critical reflection, and faith in God were part of my life's calling and work. Especially, I am grateful to my parents. To my mom who is no longer physically here, her love of God and me were constant and I am grateful for all the ways she shaped my faith and pushed me to act and believe, at the same time. To my father, who is still a constant support and critic—thank you for always pushing me further than I ever believe I can go. To my sisters, I am still amazed by your love, encouragement, and support. To Angela who has traveled with me from start to finish, showing up first and often to remind me with her presence that she believed in this work. Thanks for printing out drafts and not talking about all the footnotes. To Aletha, thank you for modeling what it means to truly be a champion for young people. I am grateful for the thankless work of taking care of daddy, so that I have the space and energy to work and write. To Anita, thank you for always being my theological conversation partner and my sponsor of the creative arts. Thank you for sending the letters in college that made me think critically about faith; thank you for listening (and not thinking I was a complete heathen) as I went through Harvard; and for coming back years later, after completing your own theological work to let me know that I wasn't crazy. To Anna, Aliyah, Jamie, and Tramaine, thank you for reminding me first-hand of the creativity and wisdom of young African Americans.

And to everyone I have forgotten to acknowledge by name, to all the ancestors who went before me, and to all who unknowing to me, supported this work with their prayers or even their calls for religious communities to be a place where young people are loved and where life is affirmed. Thank you.

Permissions

THE PERMISSION TO reproduce or reprint portions of works included in this text has been granted by the following copyright holders. Permission to publish previously, unpublished works has been graciously granted by the authors.

Youth Poetry

Jalen Kobayashi, "Untitled," Louder than a Bomb Individual Finals, 2015.

Novana Venerable, "Cody," *Louder than a Bomb Documentary,* 2011.

Antwon Funches, "Ouch," Louder than a Bomb Individual Finals, 2015.

Alexis Pettis, "Hush Little Baby," Louder than a Bomb Individual Semi-Finals, 2014.

Tonya Ingram, "Unsolicited Advice to Skinny Girls," College Union Poetry Slam Invitational Finals, 2013.

Sermons

Nyle Fort, "I love you, too," *Seven Last Words: Strange Fruits Speaks,* The Riverside Church in the City of New York, 2015.

Portions of Manuscript Previously Published by the Author

"The Power of Testimonies," in *Children, Youth and Spirituality in a Troubling World,* eds. Mary Elizabeth Moore and Almeda Wright (St. Louis, MO: Chalice Press, 2008).

"Personal Jesus, Public Faith: Cultivating a Generation of Young Public Theologians," in *Faith Forward: A Dialogue on Children, Youth, and New Kind of Christianity,* eds. David Csinos and Melvin Bray (Kelowna, BC: Woodlake Publishers, 2013).

Introduction

OVERWHELMED

THE LIVES OF young African Americans, from their classrooms and churches to the accounts of violence in the news, can be overwhelming— both to live and to observe. While teaching in public middle schools and in African American Sunday schools, I saw the joy and pain of young African American students who had the potential to succeed, but often did not have the support to do so. Often, I saw the smiles (coupled with trash talking) when a student won a jump rope contest (which we were using to generate data for our math lessons) or the pure joy when members of their youth group showed up to see their high-school theater production. I also had numerous conversations with middle-school boys who bragged of selling drugs and how that life was much better than the reading and math remediation I was offering. There were young girls who told stories of having to fight off advances from city bus drivers and other adult men as they were struggling just to make it to summer school or walking to church. I constantly listened for the places of hope or transformation in their stories. In particular, I listened to see if or how faith entered their narratives. Surprisingly, even among Christian youth, there were significant *silences*.

Listening specifically to the narratives of young African American Christians, I heard stories of young African Americans who regularly experience racism, poverty, sexism, violence, and other affronts to their humanity. And these same youth were *silent* about the possibility of God working to address these injustices in their lives. I had to wrestle with why they could profess such a strong faith in God and yet fail to describe God as empowering them to combat the cycles of oppression around them?

Could they trust that God would or could do something to change their current reality? Had they been taught that God did not care about these things? Or were their problems just too overwhelming for them that "taking it to God" did not seem sufficient either?

I soon understood that the disconnect between the issues young people face and their understanding of God is quite complex—pointing toward a "fragmented" concept of God, and at times toward a fragmentation in their own identities and lives. Religious educator Evelyn Parker first identified a "fragmented or fractured spirituality" among African American youth. She gives examples of African American youth who boldly proclaim God's ability to change their lives and to empower them for personal success, yet notes that these same youth are silent about God working in the realm of communal oppressions and injustices. Parker's language of fragmented spirituality helped to illuminate my observations of African American youth. For example, young people revealed that God is very important and active in certain areas of their lives, but God appears limited or non-existent in other areas. God, for these youth, is a very personal reality. However, it seems that for them resolving societal ills and systemic problems have nothing to do with God; instead they are something that belongs in some "utopia." They are things that one can wish for but never expect to happen.[1]

The concept of fragmented spirituality among African American adolescents also points to and reflects trends within society at large. A coherent and unifying self is no longer the norm. Instead, multiple selves and narratives constitute a person's identity. Discussing fragmentation and the multiplicity of human identity enables us to understand how African American youth can espouse seemingly disparate spiritual beliefs and practices.[2] Similarly, fragmented spirituality connects with many trends lingering from modernity that separate our lives and society into public and private realms—and that develop divergent expectations for what takes place in each realm. In particular, exploring sociological trends, which view religion as personal and private, helps us understand how some youth lack the expectation that their religious convictions or practices should concern or affect anyone beyond themselves.

While I find it problematic that African American youth do not conceive of God or their Christian spirituality as responding to the larger, systemic ills that they experience and name in their daily lives, there is in fact something "highly functional" about fragmented spirituality. Fragmented spirituality helps youth function in a society where individualism is rampant and absolute truths are not part of the contemporary lexicon. For example, African American Christian youth, characterized as having a fragmented spirituality, are often the ones most involved in their church or school communities and have positive outlooks on their personal success, based on their personal relationship with Jesus. Many of these youth passionately respond that they can do "all things through Christ who strengthens them" and do not find it contradictory to exclude working toward social and systemic change in the list of "all things."[3]

At the other end of the spectrum, I have also encountered African American Christian youth who are actively engaged in their communities, even working as social activists or trying to figure out how to respond to social justice issues (via protest, social media, etc.), but who also do not see this work as remotely connected to a larger history of Christian social witness or to any Christian community. In other words, regardless of whether youth are enamored with a personal Jesus or actively protesting injustices, there appears to be a chasm between these arenas for them, such that neither informs the other and their spiritual lives remain fragmented or compartmentalized.

African American youth with fragmented spirituality are not necessarily *at risk*; however, the African American community and church are at risk if they perpetuate youth participation in the mythology that the personal and the communal are separate; or that the spiritual and political are separate. While I assert that youth who experience a fragmented spirituality are not necessarily *at risk*, I do not an attempt to downplay the seriousness of this phenomenon. Youth who exhibit a fragmented spirituality are highly functioning in our current society; therefore the bigger issue is whether merely functioning in a corrupt society is enough? Instead, should the church help youth live fully into their God-given vocations? Religious educator David White writes, "While youth seem outwardly comfortable with such distortions of human life, they risk never finding authentic selfhood or Christian vocation described by Jesus as love of God, neighbor, and self."[4]

The issue is not simply expanding the minds of African American adolescents. Instead, the issue is, How do we ensure that Christian theology, African American religious education, and ministry with youth are relevant to the particular needs of youth (both the personal and systemic) and offer youth the tools for integrating the seemingly disparate arenas of life?

To this end, the purpose of this research is twofold. First, I further explore and clarify the experience and components of fragmented spirituality among African American youth. Second, I explore alternatives to fragmentation, and I propose a pedagogy that fosters a more integrated spirituality. I begin this exploration of fragmented spirituality among African American youth asking these questions:

- How and why are African American Christian adolescents experiencing fragmentation in their spirituality? In what ways are youth not connecting their belief in God with a call to work for change or even a hope that change in their communities can take place?
- What can we do to foster an *integrating* spirituality? What type of theological claims and pedagogical frameworks will help adolescents develop a more integrated spirituality? What spiritual practices or disciplines empower youth to attend to the myriad dimensions of youth life and societal concerns?

I approach these questions by offering a practical theological analysis of fragmented spirituality among young African Americans. I explore my definitions and rationale for a practical theological methodology and analysis below.

Earlier Research on Fragmented Spirituality among African American Youth

In this research, my preliminary conversation partner and the theorist responsible for the language of "fragmented and integrated spirituality" is religious educator Evelyn Parker. Her work, *Trouble Don't Last Always: Emancipatory Hope among African American Adolescents* gives voice to the spirituality and spiritual concerns of African American adolescents. Parker also offers the only explicit treatment of fragmented or fractured spirituality among African American youth that I have encountered.

Parker encountered fragmented spirituality in looking at the interview data of African American youth in the 1990s in the Chicago area. Her interviews gave examples of youth who passionately described their understandings of God and how they saw God working in their lives. But when she prompted conversations of their experiences of racism, the youth switched to language of "wishful thinking." They did not exhibit the same confidence, or even see God working in their lives regarding racism, as when they talked about God working in their personal lives. Parker notes, "Deeply held religious beliefs and issues of race and violence are bifurcated.... These teenagers express little or no expectations regarding racial injustice and no beliefs of God's activity in ending racism."[5] Parker's work was somewhat startling because she was not simply articulating the occurrence of disillusionment or hopelessness in youth without a core faith or faith community; instead her research pointed to the disconnection between beliefs about God and expectations of change in the world among some of the "most faithful" youth.

With Parker's work in mind, I interviewed and observed African American youth to get a better understanding of the "fragments" of their spirituality, to better understand why and how youth are experiencing fragmented spirituality, and to explore strategies for working toward a more integrated spirituality. Just as the narratives of contemporary society have expanded, so have our discussions of the lives and spirituality of young African Americans in the decades since Parker began her research. In particular, this work explores the experiences of African American youth for whom Christianity is still significant, but who are attempting to navigate Christianity, social media, and communal violence in a world where there is a naïve but growing expectation that racism and violence against youth of color is not (or should not be) prevalent any more.

My work focuses on the interconnections of youth beliefs and practices, and their engagement in their communities. I look at what spiritual practices, theology, and pedagogy are able to attend to, and integrate, youth understandings of God, humanity, community, society, and themselves as individuals, African Americans, and Christians.

In this text, the goal is to help youth integrate each of these areas, without prioritizing one over the others. Growing up in a church that espoused individual salvation and a personal relationship with Christ reminds me of the value and sustaining dimensions of those beliefs. I also know that, at times, my current efforts to effect change are thwarted when I do not have a spiritual grounding and personal disciplines (such as prayer, scripture reading, meditation, and communal sharing about God's goodness) to sustain the "work of justice." In other words, my hope is not simply that all African American Christian youth will embrace a social-justice-oriented Christianity, but that these youth will be empowered both by a "personal relationship with Christ" *and* be compelled by this relationship to see and respond to systemic and communal injustices. Likewise, my hope is that youth who are already involved in activism and community engagement will get a stronger sense of the religious heritage that affirms this type of work.

Each of the aforementioned dimensions—of personal piety, spiritual discipline, faith in a powerful God, pride in one's self and one's ancestors, and working for social justice—is part of the complex legacy and history of the African American church.[6] I reflect on contemporary adolescent spirituality in light of this legacy. The complexity of African American Christianity is that these dimensions are not equally emphasized at all points or at all times (arguably it should not be). However, part of helping youth navigate a complex and ever-evolving world is inviting them into conversation with the communities and traditions that have influenced their faith and action, directly or indirectly. Part of this work includes inviting youth into an experience of the complex and *integrating* nature of African American and Womanist spirituality.

Integrating Spirituality

The "spirituality" of a people ... [is] the animating and integrative power that constitutes the principal frame of meaning for individual and collective experiences. Metaphorically, the spirituality of a people is synonymous with the soul of a people: the integrating center of power and meaning.

—PETER J. PARIS[7]

Spirituality ... arises from a creative and dynamic synthesis of faith and life, forged in the crucible of the desire to live out the Christian faith authentically, responsibly, effectively, and fully.

—ALISTER E. MCGRATH[8]

Building on my research on the spiritual lives of African American youth and on several definitions of Christian spirituality, I assert that fragmented spirituality is problematic and that youth should work to embrace an *integrating* spirituality, and I suggest how. *Integrating spirituality is spirituality that empowers youth to hold together the seemingly disparate areas of their lives, to tap into the resources of their faith communities and learn from historical and current faith exemplars, in order to see themselves as capable of living abundant life by effecting change on individual, communal, and systemic levels.*

I intentionally call for an *integrating* spirituality because spiritual formation and living out one's spirituality are ongoing processes. Given the ever-evolving nature of the world and the ever-expanding areas to which youth will be exposed, there is a need for a spirituality that is open to and inherently built on making sense of change. I also hold to the idea of an integrating spirituality because I understand the difficulty of living out a spirituality that must hold together so many tensions. It would be easier, in response to the pressures of social saturation and the deconstruction of master narratives, to cling to only one narrative or one dimension of our spirituality and lived experiences. However, a pedagogy that offers supports for the ongoing process of integration is essential for thriving in contemporary society.

In general, Christian spirituality works to heal fragmentation and is inclusive of the "whole person." For example, William Stringfellow writes,

> Spiritual maturity or spiritual fulfillment necessarily involves the *whole* person—body, mind and soul, place, relationships—in connection with the whole of creation throughout the era of time.... Spirituality encompasses the whole person in the totality of existence in the world, not some fragment or scrap or incident of a person.[9]

Though he does not explicitly consider the lives of African American youth in his research, Stringfellow reminds us that Christian spirituality should speak to the whole person, which includes our experiences of race (and racism), gender (and sexism), emotions, bodily needs, and expressions—all within a social and relational context.[10] With Stringfellow and other scholars, I affirm that experiences of God should include elements of transformation, such that experiences with God should *not* leave youth feeling disempowered or limited in how they can act in the world. Further, Peter Paris, looking specifically at African and African American spirituality, affirms that "African spirituality is never disembodied spirituality but always integrally connected with the dynamic movement of life.... The goal of that movement is the struggle for survival.... [And] it is the union of those forces of life that have the power either to threaten and destroy life ... or to preserve and enhance it."[11]

These definitions affirm the integrating nature of spirituality. Paris, however, explicitly names the power of spirituality to destroy or preserve and enhance life. This understanding of spirituality is particularly poignant in light of the death-dealing forces in which many African American youth live. Therefore, the call for an integrating spirituality is not simply about spiritual health and vitality; it is also about wrestling with how communities of faith empower youth to resist and survive in a world that does not value their lives.

In essence, fragmentation is antithetical to most understandings of Christian Spirituality. Similarly, my understanding of integrating spirituality emphasizes that there is or should be a connectedness to Christian life; and youth will need to discern how they work and live this out. Christian spirituality, under the best of circumstances, does not call for or include fragmentation of the person or of their lives. Instead spirituality is often defined in terms of its integrative role or power.

My understanding of an integrating spirituality and pedagogy is one that empowers African American adolescents to make sense of and use the myriad resources they already have and to be open to including the experiences that will come as they continue to live. Revolutionary educator Paulo Freire notes that "integration [as opposed to simply adapting] results from the capacity to adapt oneself to reality *plus* the critical capacity to make choices and to transform that reality."[12] Likewise, youth need to be able to handle their lived realities and feel empowered to be agents of transformation in their lives. An integrating spirituality is essential to this work.

A Word on Methodology
Practical Theological Interpretation and Methodology

I approach the spirituality and concerns of African America youth as a practical theologian. My methodology attempts to carefully interconnect the experiences and wisdom of youth with the wisdom and traditions of scholars and theologians, often far removed from the experiences of these youth, such that both are enhanced. For many scholars and practitioners, "the term 'practical theology' strikes the ear as an oxymoron."[13] Dale Andrews writes,

> The chasms that stretch between the discipline of theology and our ordinary lives of faith exist because theology does not frequently appear very practical. . . . Indeed, while theologians go to extraordinary lengths to reconceptualize and articulate the life of faith, the

actual struggle to find theology practical wrestles with the meaning of life and the daily experiences of living.... Practical Theology
attempts to bridge these chasms.[14]

Even though the term *practical theology* has lost some of its oxymoronic character in many academic circles since Dale Andrews published
his *Practical Theology for Black Churches*,[15] his assessment of the chasm
between the academic discipline of theology and the lived realities of faith
communities, particularly African Americans communities, still rings
true. There is also an urgent need to bridge the chasms between the religious academy, communities of faith, and youth. Specifically, I am mind-
ful of the need to attend to the continued chasm between Black churches
and African American youth. Historian Albert G. Miller argues that
"rather than fissures or small cracks, a more accurate description is the
biblical metaphor 'breach.' The chasm between Black youth and the Black
church is as wide as the Grand Canyon."[16] Miller observes the "scarcity of
youth" in the Black church, recounting the difficulty Black pastors name
in recruiting and keeping teenagers and young adults,[17] and goes so far
as to say that the Black church is "irrelevant" to the concerns of Black
youth.[18] Anne Wimberly, in a more recent discussion of "disconnected"
Black youth, echoes Miller's observations and notes that this "breach" has
not gotten smaller.[19]

In response to many of the claims about the irrelevance of churches
and the disconnections between the religious academy and youth, several
scholars have begun the work of affirming the ways that youth ministry is
practical theology and are pushing practitioners (youth ministers, youth
workers, and others) to participate in the process of ongoing practical theological reflection about and with youth.[20] Ongoing practical theological
reflection is necessary for effective ministry with youth in order to begin
bridging the chasms between youth, theology, and their faith traditions.

Bridging these chasms emphasizes the responsibility and work of practical theologians to attend to and take seriously the "ordinary lives of faith";
and to do so in such a way that is responsive to the ongoing struggles
and questions of communities. The task of bridging the chasm remains
daunting because the "messiness" of lived communities often eludes easy
analysis, and thinking constructively with communities can be consum-
ing. In particular, when thinking about what it means to take seriously
or pay attention to the "daily experiences" of African American youth, the

scope of what practical theological analysis entails can vary widely and can often require multiple processes.

However, given my attention in this text to the fragmentation of the spiritual lives of African American youth, my methodology must also attempt to integrate seemingly disparate areas and bring together the best of the lived realities of young people and the most robust theories and praxis. A practical theological methodology allows us to do that, and models for youth and youth workers an approach to a more integrated spirituality.

The practical theological tasks I conduct in this book build upon Mary Elizabeth Moore's definition of practical theology in our edited volume on the spirituality of children and youth. For Moore, practical theology is

> the study of God and the world by engaged reflection on action (past or present practice) and reflection for the sake of action (future practice). Practical theology, thus, originates in the world of practice, moves into engaged reflection and construction, and returns to praxis as the goal.[21]

These movements (from the world of practice through engaged reflection and construction, and returning to praxis) provide the organizational structure of this text and push me to honor the primary role that religious practices and communities of practice play in my work. The questions that emerge in these contexts guide and come into conversation with theory in a critical and mutually reflective manner, and eventually press for a constructive response. In other words, this practical theological method makes young African Americans equal conversation partners with theologians and scholars, such that their narratives push us toward a better understanding and articulation of theological truths (instead of attempting to simply apply theology to the lives of youth).

A Practical Theological Approach to Fragmented Spirituality among Young African Americans

My practical theological approach to fragmented spirituality among African American youth includes three movements: (1) attending closely to the lived realities of African American adolescents and their spirituality; (2) engaging in constructive critical reflection on this reality by placing the experiences of African American youth in relation to theories of adolescent spirituality and religious education, identity development, sociology of religion, and African American history, Womanist and Black theology; and (3) returning to the concrete realities of youth by offering proposals for improved practice with African American adolescents. To be certain, these are not discrete movements; they overlap such that the reader will see hints of proposed practices in earlier movements or may see a continued discussion of the current realities of youth and African American religion in later movements. More generally speaking, in these three movements of the text, we are attempting to explore the following questions: What is the current reality of African American youth spirituality? How did we get to where we are? (What has happened historically?) And how do we go forward?

Attending to the Lives of Young African Americans

In order to understand the spirituality of African American adolescents, I begin by documenting and analyzing their articulations of core beliefs about God, humanity, community, society, and themselves. Alongside this, I analyze the educational curriculum that African American adolescents are taught in churches. I start with and give priority to the voices and understanding of African American adolescents. I interviewed eight African American Christian youth and conducted online surveys with another fourteen youth. The interviews and surveys allowed me to listen carefully to the youth and to offer some accounts of how African American youth are thinking about and experiencing fragmented spirituality. While a sample of this size is not large enough to predict trends for the entire population of African American Christian adolescents, these interviews give "texture" to theories about adolescent spirituality and serve as the starting point for further empirical research, theorization, and exploration of the spiritual formation of African American adolescents.[22]

In this first movement of *attending to the lived realities* and voices of African American adolescents, my methods of both collecting and sharing the youth narratives are influenced by the work and methods of Black and Latina feminist anthropologists and other scholars of color, who strive to give voice to the complex realities of historically marginalized communities. For example, I borrow from the methodology of Ada Maria Isasi-Diaz in *En la Lucha*. In her text, she uses the tools of ethnographic interviews and introduces "meta-ethnography" as a way of making sense of the multiple accounts and interviews with her research participants. She begins by presenting the interviews, mostly as the women have articulated them, but then begins the process of bringing "together the single accounts by pointing out some of their commonalities and differences."[23] The process of *knowledge synthesis* in meta-ethnography

> is not to establish norms and values—though they may be deduced quite easily—but to elucidate the self-understanding of Latinas in order to contribute to the enhancement of their moral agency.... The purpose of knowledge synthesis is not to examine what the women say to the point where the analysis and not the lived experiences of Latinas becomes central to the theological enterprise, but to allow the voices of Latinas to be heard because they have a right to be heard.[24]

Isasi-Diaz's understanding of knowledge synthesis directly influences my methodology in collecting and presenting the youth interviews in the next chapter. In particular, my larger goal in interviewing youth is to enhance their self-understanding and agency. Likewise, I foreground the voices of youth because they "have a right to be heard"—not simply to support the theories I present about spirituality.

Chapter 1 introduces us to each of these young people and gives us a glimpse of how young African Americans understand the role of religion and the church. These youth explore tough issues, including their understanding of God's role in addressing systemic oppressions. Their narratives point to the ways that adolescents are feeling pulled in myriad directions by competing loyalties. The youth describe fragmentation within their identities, spiritualities, and actions. However, we also see glimpses of how these youth are holding these *fragments* and *tensions* together.

A second dimension of the current realities of African American adolescent spirituality includes what youth are taught and what theologies are influencing their spirituality (and contributing to fragmentation). Chapter 1 also explores a national sample of African American Sunday school curricula and sermons. The current curricular and pedagogical approaches within African American churches reveal several unsettling trends, both in the topics addressed and the types of actions the authors expect from God and African American adolescents. While the purpose of the chapter is not to place blame for fragmentation, the curricula and sermons reflect the fragmented worldviews of youth. For example, the absence of discussions of systemic oppression in this sample of sermons and curriculum parallels the narratives of young African Americans who failed to name God's presence in their experiences of oppression or injustice.

However, the truth is that fragmented spirituality is not simply a product of theology or youth perspectives; it also reflects the larger US context. Therefore, in chapter 2, I review the various dimensions of fragmentation and the larger contexts that shape the experiences of fragmentation for youth and adults in American society. In particular, I explore the psychological and psycho-social dimensions of fragmentation, from discussions of navigating racial ethnic identities, such as W. E. B. Du Bois's early twentieth-century articulation of "double consciousness" to postmodern experiences of plural and saturated selves. Likewise, I explore theories affecting the larger sociopolitical and religious context, including theories of the privatization of religion and religious individualism. The current reality of African American adolescent spirituality parallels trends in the religious lives of American youth in general; thus I explore Christian Smith's theory of *Moralistic Therapeutic Deism* as the prevalent religious worldview of American youth, and I discuss the ways that African American youth both express these worldviews and complicate this depiction of youth spirituality.[25]

Critically and Constructively Reflecting on African American Adolescent Spirituality

The second movement of practical theology calls us to reflect critically and constructively on the primary texts of adolescent lives, the curricula in African American churches, and the larger US context in order to ascertain patterns in what the youth are saying individually and in order to more fully ask, *How did these patterns emerge, and out of what historical and religious realities did they emerge?* More specifically, in this movement it is imperative to reflect on the youth interviews in conversation with theorists or figures who offer alternatives to fragmented spirituality. Inherent in naming the "problem" is the assumption that there are different, less problematic, more holistic forms of spirituality. In this section, I explore the complex legacy of the Black Church and African American spirituality. I argue that there is a need for youth to reconnect with the liberative and integrating elements of this tradition. Therefore, in chapter 3 I pay attention to the nascent theologies of youth as I explore theological norms that can expand upon their nascent theologies and foster theological understandings that are more holistic.

However, reconnecting youth with African American religious traditions and spirituality is not a naïve suggestion that these traditions alone will correct the fragmentation youth are experiencing. There are both resources and limitations within African American Christianity and spirituality. In particular, in chapter 4, I further explore youth fragmented spirituality and the often-unspoken question of theodicy at the center of African American youth fragmented spirituality. For many youth, it is easier to have "no expectation" that God should work in particular areas of their lives than to wrestle with the question of how a good God can fail to respond to the concerns of Black youth. I outline several attempts to address theodicy within Black religious and Womanist theological thought, and I place these attempts in conversation with the questions and experiences of African American youth. This chapter also serves as a reminder that a good theodicy may not be sufficient for the religious lives of youth. Instead, it may be insulting. A better response invites youth into this conversation, without the expectation that simple theological state-ments will be a corrective. In other words, an alternative or response to fragmented spirituality among African American youth emerges not in a rigid, orthodox perspective, but in enlarging the process by which youth come to wrestle with theological complexities at the center of their lived experiences.

However, theodicy and other theological questions should not render youth inactive or hopeless. Therefore, reflecting on the traditions and resources available within African American Christianity and history requires us to lift up models of integrated spirituality and action. Chapter 5 focuses on the work of young African American Christian activists. Their narratives and examples push for a better connection between the legacies of Black religious leaders and communal and political activism. In par-ticular, this chapter asserts that public theology is an essential corrective for much of the individualism of American religion and fragmentation among Black youth. It is here that I reflect more on contemporary and young exemplars of faith, who model for other young people and adults ways of connecting social change and African American religious life. In exploring contemporary and historical strategies, I begin pointing toward the final move of this text and toward creating a bridge for these issues.

Proposing Improved Practice with African American Adolescents: Toward a Critical Pedagogy of Abundant Life and Integrating Spirituality

In the process of critically reflecting on the lives of young African Americans and their experiences of fragmented spirituality, practical theological meth-odology also includes a constructive step of proposing both a vision and practices that can help shape and invite young people into an integrating spirituality. In some ways, each of the earlier movements crescendo in the third step, in that it is here that an alternative vision is offered. Throughout the text, the narratives and realities of ongoing oppression in the lives of African American youth begs for a voice or vision of something beyond their current struggles. I propose that proclaiming a vision of *abundant life* with African American youth does this. A theology of abundant life is not without its historical precedents or limits, but it is robust enough to speak to the struggles of youth, for whom life is an increasingly fragile idea and death is a more prevalent reality. I argue that a vision of abundant life (a historical idea with renewed traction in the lived realities of Black youth) is what we are striving for.

This naturally raises the question, How do we get there? How do we teach youth to embrace this vision of abundant life and integrating spirituality? Thus, in chapter 6, I also offer a critical pedagogy of integrating spirituality, which helps youth realize this vision of abundant life. To clarify, my hope is not that all youth will have a spirituality that centers on only one strand or goal. This is neither desirable nor achievable. Neither is my goal for African American adolescents simply to add another voice or expectation to their already-fragmented realities. However, I assert that a fractured spirituality—one that does not allow for the many dimensions of a young person's life to inform one another and interact in such a way that youth feel empowered to work for change on all levels—is insufficient. I argue that a spirituality that does not encourage youth in their striving for the abundant life, which Jesus offered, is also insufficient. Fragmented spirituality is incompatible with an abundant life.

Overwhelmed by Promise

Throughout this book, we encounter the narratives of African American young people as they attempt to make sense of the world around them and their roles in it. At times their narratives are heart-breaking, and at other points they will inspire us to persist in the journey of life and faith. At each turn, we will hear echoes of my beginning assessment that their lives can be and feel overwhelming. It is my hope that this book and the practices with youth that it inspires will offer much more than a catalogue of the struggles that young African Americans face. In reality, the spiritual lives of young African Americans entail much more than struggle! What follows is a reminder that God also offers young people a way of abundant life and we must wrestle with whether we are open to seeing the complex-ity of God and empowering youth to work alongside God to care for and make a difference in their world. In other words, this book pushes us to explore with young people how to resist being immobilized by struggles and to embrace the promises of God through young African Americans.

I

Talking Fragments

FRAGMENTED SPIRITUALITY IN BLACK
YOUTH AND CHURCHES

I MET MARISSA in Atlanta, while working at Emory University's Youth Theological Initiative.[1] Marissa came to the three-week academy exuding an "I can't be bothered" attitude. She was a young artist in the making, and yet somehow she found herself studying theology and living in a dorm with other teens who where "more religious" than her and who, in her opinion, really lived "the Ten Commandments and stuff." Underneath Marissa's surface demeanor were rich reflections, which truly helped me articulate the ways that young African Americans were experiencing God, church, and faith and connecting (or not connecting) it to other areas of their lives. Over the course of her interview, Marissa spoke candidly of the shortcomings of her church as well and pushed me to further explore the potential causes of this fragmented spirituality that I was observing in her and many other young African Americans. For example, when asked if her faith or faith community helped her deal with struggles at her school, Marissa did not hesitate to call her church ineffective in helping her see or make sense of things going on in the world. She also explicitly rejected the idea of talking to a church leader about the issues she sees going on around the world. She responded quite adamantly,

> A: I don't think my church does very much because my church is constantly begging for youth and when they have them in the church, they like run them off. They are constantly, "you can't do this." And it violates our youth. So I don't think the church does much to open our eyes to see the struggle or anything.

Q: Are there particular practices that help you make sense of the turbulent situations of the world, like prayer, meditation, Bible reading?

A: No. I don't think it helps us see things going on around the world.

Q: Do you have specific people that you take your questions and struggles to?

A: My therapist. It's all the rage in my area, so yeah it would be him.

Q: Can you talk to a leader in your church?

A: I could, but would I want to? No.

Marissa's candor is a wake-up call that churches and religious leaders need to heed in order to better attend to the lives of young African Americans, as well as to listen to the places where young people are offering churches and communities a chance to "do better." In this chapter, we hear more of Marissa's story, as well as the stories of many young African Americans as they discuss their joys and struggles, as well as their understandings of God, Church, spirituality, and the world that they inhabit. Listening to these narratives also pushed me to question how churches were influencing or shaping their spirituality. Therefore, we also explore the ways that African American Christian churches and educational curricula also reflect this fragmentation in understandings of God and how young people might integrate their spirituality into their daily concerns.

Fragmented Spirituality and African American Youth

Fragmented or fractured spirituality is spirituality in which youth subconsciously or consciously relegate God to the realm of personal transformation and place societal change and systemic transformation in the realm of "utopia," as things that one can wish for but never expect to happen. In this chapter, I continue building upon the research of religious educator Evelyn Parker and further explore "fragmented or fractured" spirituality among African American adolescents.[2] In order to better understand the religious practices and worldviews of African American youth, I conducted surveys and interviews with Christian youth from across the United States. All of the young people attended or were affiliated with the Youth Theological Initiative Summer Academy at Emory University (YTI).[3] We interviewed and surveyed youth of African, European, Asian, and Latin American descent; however, this work focuses only on youth of African descent. The youth were affiliated with historically Black denominations, as well as mainline and non-denominational churches.[4] The research data include survey data from fourteen youth and in-depth interviews with eight youth. The survey included ten females and four males, while the interview data included six females and two males.[5] All youth who took the survey were rising high-school seniors, ages sixteen or seventeen; the youth who participated in the open-ended interviews ranged in ages from sixteen to nineteen; the majority were rising high-school seniors at the time of the interview, and one student was a freshman in college.[6]

Given the size of this sample, as well as the self-selecting nature of youth who chose to attend YTI, what is offered in an exploration of fragmentation among *this sample* of African American adolescents; it does not generalize to the entire population of African American Christian youth.[7] However, their responses enhance our knowledge of the ways that some African American youth are making sense of their spirituality and their concerns about their communities.

Snapshots of Youth Concerns and Spiritual Lives

In this chapter, I introduce the young people who helped me begin my exploration of the spiritual lives of young African Americans by exploring the narratives of five youth who participated in the in-depth interviews. Their narratives add texture to the theories we explore in later chapters. Here, I attempt to let the youth speak for themselves—noting that the process of editing already reflects my influence and interpretation. In describing each youth, I attend to their autobiographical narratives and to the stories that they explored in the most detail; I explore how these narratives interconnect with their responses to questions about their communities and concerns, their experiences of church and God, and their action in the world. I also look collectively at all the interviews, and survey results to point toward generative themes in the ways that these young African Americans are thinking about their community, their agency, and their spiritual lives.

Marissa

my church is constantly begging for youth and when they
have them in the church, they like run them off.

Marissa is a young woman from New Jersey. Her parents are both profes-sionals and immigrants from Jamaica. Marissa associates herself with the culture and trends of New York City. In her interview, she described her frequent trips to "the city" with her friends. She is also very proud of her hometown, a suburb of New York City with a legacy of progressive civil rights work and early movements for social change. Marissa expresses her appreciation for the sacrifices her parents have made so that she can live in her upper middle-class community and go to excellent schools. Beyond discussing her hometown and family, in her interview Marissa focused on her friends and her school. Marissa also discussed, but was less enthusias-tic about, her experiences in church. For example, when asked to describe a powerful or significant religious experience, Marissa honestly noted that she did not remember ever having a powerful experience in her church. However, when asked how her faith community has helped her become who she is today, Marissa described how winning a contest made her more religious and confirmed her understanding of God's plan for her life:

> So, I won a contest with Nike, because I want to be a sneaker designer when I grow up and after that, I totally knew that this is what [God] wants me to do. Ever since then, I was way more religious than I was before, because I realized He did this for me and if He didn't do that for me, then I would not have known and I probably would have been like bummed. But since He put me in that position, He really wants me to go forth with who I am and wants me to be me.

Her understanding of God helping her figure out her path is a direct reflection of her understanding of her father's theology too. She describes her father as always talking about how God has blessed him to do so much and be successful.

Despite her belief in God and her assertion that God blessed her, Marissa describes questioning her Christian identity. She knows that her church community would claim that she is because she attends every Sunday; but she questions church attendance as the standard or definition of being a Christian. Thus she wonders what being a Christian means. When asked if there were any questions that she was currently exploring or working through, she stated,

> I think, whether I'm a Christian. I don't know if I would consider myself that. I guess my church can easily say that I'm a Christian

only because I show up every Sunday, but I don't know if I would. There is this quote that is one of my favorites that says "I'm a citizen of the world and my religion is to do good," and I think that's exactly what I am. I think my question every night would be if I'm a Christian and what is that.

In following up, Marissa revealed that this question had not been at the forefront of her mind until she came to YTI and encountered other youth who expressed their Christianity in different ways:

> Coming to YTI opened up the question for me only because I see so many people that are religious and so many people that like actually follow the Ten Commandments and stuff like that, to a point that I don't, and I guess I'm shunned . . . but I don't put myself [down], I don't make myself feel bad for it. I think that God likes me the way I am.

Marissa also spoke candidly about the social struggles and concerns of youth. In particular, Marissa discussed interpersonal relationships as a concern of many youth. Specifically speaking about her experience at YTI, she said that "many people still only feel comfortable with their own race" and that they form cliques around race. However, she also mentioned similar concerns about her hometown and school. Marissa recounted her experience of inconsistency in student-teacher relationships. She described this discrepancy in terms of the racism in her school:

> I guess [a concern] would be relationships from teacher to student. Some have that and which is really weird because our school is very diverse, but you can totally tell that some teachers prefer keeping a more personal relationship with white students than they do blacks. They always say I'm here after school and I can help you, but they want to keep it. . . . When it comes to white students, it's a more personal relationship. My best friend, who is white, would see her teacher after and before school, and it got so personal to the point where she was invited to her wedding and she would text her. So I don't think it's fair that you are allowed to do that.

Marissa's discussions of the interactions between teachers and students based on race indicated that she is not hopeful that things can get better or that she can do anything to respond to or change these interactions. She states, "I don't think you can change it because it is something that will always occur whether you try to stop it or not."[8]

In addition to her experience of racism in relationships with teachers, Marissa also described the dynamics of racism within her larger community. For example, Marissa described "white flight" in her community, which she defined in stating,

> Our school experiences . . . white flight, and what that is, is that a lot of white students will leave the schools where they know there are a lot of blacks getting into honor classes . . . and AP courses. So our town itself, . . . [it is] predominately white, but our public school is majority black . . . and the white people they get upset because they don't want to pay taxes for public schooling when their kids are in a whole different school.

While I did not probe further to find out how she learned or became familiar with the term "white flight," she spoke of it in a matter-of-fact manner and further described her experiences of getting harassed and stopped for jay walking when the Black students from her public high school left campus each day for lunch. And as noted above, Marissa adamantly rejected the idea that her church or even practices such as praying or reading the Bible or talking with anyone but her therapist could help her address her experiences of bias and racism at school.

However, juxtaposed with Marissa's belief that she could not respond to the biases of her teachers and the ineffectiveness of her church, she expressed more hope, inspiration, and agency in responding to global concerns. For example, Marissa named sex trafficking as a global concern, which she desires to respond to "when she gets older." Also in contrast to the ineffectiveness of her church or faith in responding to her struggle at school, Marissa named online communities that raise awareness about sex trafficking as supporting her:

> There is a blog on sex trafficking and these graffiti artists from France, and I graffiti too, and they do it as a movement. It's really awesome. They graffitied on a bunch of little trailers and they showed a story of the life of someone who has been sex trafficked, and it's amazing because they traveled everywhere. . . . It's like an exhibition where they just put it in a lot of political areas so they can

get the word out, and I just keep up with that a lot to see what I can do in the future.

Marissa's ambiguity about her identity as a Christian and her assertion that the church does not help her respond to the concerns of youth and other global issues parallels her reflections on the role of God in government or politics. When asked about how or where she experiences God working in the government, Marissa voices her uncertainty about the role that God plays in the government and her concerns about the ways that religion and politics have been converging recently. Her concerns focus on the self-identification of particular politicians as Christian and actions that seem incongruous with such identifications. However, moving beyond these concerns, Marissa talks about particular occurrences of injustices in the government. She states,

> Our society does not think that God is in the government because of . . . cases where people have been shot and killed by the police and there is nothing you can do about it. I think that people give up that God is there, and that's probably why I'm on the fence whether He is there or not. I think He is, but people don't pay attention.

Throughout her reflections on God's work in government, Marissa talks about what "people" think. However, only at the very end does she mention that she is really uncertain as to whether God is working in government—her firmest reply is that she thinks God is present in government, but people do not want to pay attention to God's presence there.

Kira

People get used to hearing about death, especially young death. . . . It wasn't no remorse, it was nothing like "let's come together."

Kira is an African American young woman from Florida, who lives with her mother and two older siblings. She also spends time with her father often and animatedly recounts the days when she explored new places in her hometown with her father. Kira spent the majority of her interview talking about her church and her school. Kira's church is a small apostolic church, which her mother started in their home when Kira was a baby. Her mother continues to serve as pastor today.

Kira and her siblings also participate in the worship services and church programs at least three times a week. As a result, Kira sees church as an integral part of her life. While Kira estimates that they have less than thirty members in their church and describes the process of members transitioning in and out of the congregation, she is very proud that they have their own building now and is optimistic that God will provide for their spiritual growth. Kira also relayed her beliefs about how Christians should interact in the world. She described times when she went "witnessing" in her community and how exciting it was for her to see other young people walking through the neighborhood sharing their faith in Jesus.[9]

When describing her school, Kira notes that her school had been labeled failing. In part, when asked to describe the size by estimating the number in a graduating class, she candidly responded, "Not too many graduate. . . . And when it's seventy-five, that's like a big deal." She also shared many of the concerns she has for youth and her community. She initially named her concern that many young people are struggling with image—or reputation, personality, and living up to preconceived standards in a culture that shuns "being a punk." And while Kira described all the drama associated with trying to maintain this image, she knew that it was something that boys and girls dealt with in her school.

Kira also expressed concern about youth violence and shootings in her community. She talked about worrying even during the summer academy, when she was away from her community, because of the very real possibility that she could go back to school and hear that one of her classmates had been shot while they were on vacation:

> Things that I worry about (and something I forget I need to pray about it), is like to come back to school and . . . oh, you heard where so-and-so got shot during the summer or something like that. Because during the summertime the biggest thing is gun violence. I mean it's been ridiculous bad.
>
> A girl that was sixteen years old, who went to my high school, got shot in the head running away from the club. And then somebody else ended up getting shot. And then everybody was scared because it's like they're going to come to my high school and shoot it up and everything. So everybody was like, "y'all ready to die, y'all ready to die?" So that's like my biggest fear is to come back to school from summer here, like, oh, you heard so-and-so got shot during

the summer or was found somewhere or something like that. That's my biggest fear. It's crazy.

She also talked about her desire for the youth in her school to come together in response to gun violence. She stated that underneath all the conflict, they all really just want to be loved. In seeing this common need, she remains frustrated by their inability to "come together." In the interview, I also asked her about the types of resources (people, religious practices, writing, etc.) she used to help her respond to the violence in her community. Kira describes feeling called to respond. She states that as a Christian she witnesses to people at her school because she wants them to understand the value of life and the severity of the violence around them:

> Being a Christian I feel like it's a need for me to do something and that's why I started a Bible study in the classrooms after school. And sometimes during lunch, we go out in the cafeteria witnessing, and people be like, *are y'all playing?* No, we are really serious. So I do feel like it's a need just to let them know that their life is nothing to play with. Once you're dead, you're dead. I do feel the need to respond.

Her response through "witnessing" exemplifies her theological convictions and demonstrates that her perspective on youth violence is one of ultimate concern. She believes that if these young people die and "have not been saved," they will go to Hell.[10] Her theological convictions are further shown in her assertion that God can help her overcome anything, even this type of random youth violence. She articulates her understanding that she is not struggling against "physical things," but against "spiritual things." Kira asserts that "knowing God" empowers her because she knows that she has God to help her. Kira's response pushes us to consider why she is connecting her understanding of witnessing with the social concerns in her school. Because Kira is one of the few youth interviewed who were taking action (spiritual or otherwise) to respond to the violence around her, I explore her narrative in greater length later in chapter 6.

However, in spite of her actions, Kira's response also demonstrates that she does not see many tangible resources in her community for responding to her concerns about youth violence. For example, she points out the ways that her school and her principal did not help young people grieve after the deaths of their classmates. Kira discusses how her principal attempted to silence any response to the violence and deaths:

> We sometimes feel like we're in an F school, so if anything bad happens it's all over the news. I think that's why they don't make too big an issue—like the gunshot thing, because they don't want it to be a big issue. Because that might bring some more bad media.... The principal didn't say anything about it, [and] if she overheard me asking somebody about the girl that got killed, she was like ... don't even talk about it because we already got a bad reputation.

In other words, Kira does not see the necessary resources to respond to violence and sees the ways that her teachers are prevented by racism and prejudice from fully acknowledging the systemic problems in her community.

Jackie
I'm concerned that each generation is getting worse....
I just hope that they realize that life's not all about gangs
and drugs and being ghetto and stuff like that.

Jackie is an African American high-school senior from California, where she lives with her mother. As she begins her interview, Jackie quickly rehearses the events of her day and spends less than a minute describing what she does during a typical day. However, Jackie becomes more expressive as she talks about her city and school. Jackie describes her school as a diverse and high-achieving public school, which attracts substantial monetary gifts from local businesses. Jackie is also aware of the ways that her school works hard to "keep things hidden"—in that the administrators are reluctant to discuss negative activities that take place at her school. Jackie describes this saying, "We have issues at our school every now and then, riots and certain things, but you would never know because it's a little city, so you wouldn't know a lot of stuff that goes on."

Jackie becomes most animated when she discusses her friends and family. She lists each of their names, how she met her friends, and even chats about losing her phone, which limited her ability to keep in touch with them over the summer. In particular, Jackie describes her admiration for her mother and father. She eagerly talks about their commitment to education and knows that education is one thing that they value for her life. She notes,

> My parents both had trouble when they first went to college and then they both finished. My dad is getting his PhD right now. My mom graduated from college when I was about in fifth grade. And they both graduated with honors, straight As. My mom's really like the hardest worker I've ever seen like in my life.

Jackie also describes her extended family and recounts memories of summers with her father and grandparents. Both her father and her grandfather are pastors, who influenced her religious formation; however, Jackie also talks of the way her church affiliation changed and how she became more self-directed when she moved to a new city.

> My grandpa is a pastor. He has his own church. My dad's a reverend. So every summer if I visit them, I go to their church. They're Baptists. But my grandparents in Seattle don't go to church. My mom used to always take me to a Baptist church when I was little. Then when we moved and we lived right down the street from a Presbyterian church that had good Bible study classes that my neighbor went to, so I started going there.
>
> I used to not like church until about high school maybe. I got into the youth group and so now I go to church on my own every Sunday. My mom doesn't really go to church anymore because she's really busy. So I just have her drop me off and I go to youth group and do whatever they do together and that's it.

Jackie is clear that she enjoys going to church because of the types of relationships that she develops there and describes the most important aspects of her faith community as their openness:

> I like people to see how open my church is and my faith, how we don't push stuff on each other. Like it's not read the Bible every Sunday. I think we barely pull out the Bible. We'll read one verse. Then we'll like relate it to our everyday lives and how we can incorporate it and stuff like that.

Jackie's positive experience of youth group and her faith is expressed in an implicit response to perceptions about church as separate from the concerns of youth. Instead, Jackie says,

> My church isn't just about God all the time. We've had Sundays where we had to sit in a circle and just talk to each other about the problems we're having with each other. Like we had one Sunday, they were looking at our social media pages, and the youth leaders were like, "We see a lot of stuff on that you never tell us. All this hurt, all this pain." So they made us all just talk about everything that we've had problems with. And then they just prayed over us and everyone was crying. It was crazy. So we do a lot of stuff like that. We're really like a second family. And I want people to know that's what church is. It's not just about studying God all the time. It's about making your lives better for God.

Despite Jackie's excitement about the relationships she develops in her youth group, she has also experienced tensions between the youth group and the larger congregation. She shares both that she finds the worship services boring and she has felt unwelcome when her youth choir had to sing in the larger worship services. She is well connected with her youth group, but her youth group is disconnected from the rest of the life of the church:

> When we had a choir, I remember them saying, hinting at things like they didn't want us to sing in the church. My youth group is predominantly black. Well, it's all black. And we've had gays and bisexuals in my group, just a lot of stuff like that. And my pastor is white. He's really cool, though. But from the way it seemed, they didn't want us to really perform in church. They wanted us to get involved. They always come in every year and talk to us about tithes and offerings and stuff. But everything else is kind of like whatever. It always seemed like they didn't really care about us. But we always had our youth pastor. So that was like our church in that church. And so it kind of seemed separated.

Jackie's voice trailed off, as if she was reliving the feelings associated with this tension. But then she continued talking about her concerns for young people in her school and community:

I'm concerned that each generation is getting worse, like in my school I can see it getting worse. Each grade is full of more people that don't care about school and stuff, and just don't really care about their grades. And there are a lot of gangs. There are a lot of drugs. A lot of people smoke and stuff. So my concern is that everyone is going to let that type of life get in the way of the life they should have. I live in a pretty good community. My school is a good school. They're not awful people or anything. But I just hope that they realize that life's not all about gangs and drugs and being ghetto and stuff like that.

While she was emotionally invested in what was happening for young people at her church and school, she was somewhat tentative in naming the types of concerns she saw when she looked more globally, in politics or on the news. She asserts that she never watches the news, because of the way that it reminds her of tragedy that is taking place in her community:

The one time I did watch the news, it was around the time that everyone was getting shot for some reason ... and they're both really personal to me. One—they were shot right next to my house, like my mom heard it. It was at the bank. That night we went to the memorial service and it was really sad. ... What was even more sad to me was that the person that shot the guy was with someone else that didn't know what was going on at all. She just thought he was going to get money. So now she's in jail for being with him. And that's really sad to me, too. And then the other kid that got shot, he got shot because he wasn't part of a gang at all. And so they killed him. And that was right next to a friend's house. And she lives like in a really nice part of our city and everything. I just don't like people getting shot. I wish that would change.

Jackie voices her concerns for her community, pointing both to the underlying changes in attitude that she hopes for and her "wish" that shootings would cease in her community.

Elliot
I'm into activism. . . . I fight for a lot of different things
even if I don't necessarily include myself in that group or
whatever.

Elliot is a nineteen-year-old college freshman from the Southeast. Elliot was one of the few youth interviewed who did not attend YTI. Elliot was also one of the older youth interviewed. He was interviewed after his senior year of high school as he was transitioning to college life. In his interview, he talks about his experience growing up and living in the same community for the entirety of his life, including college. Elliot begins his interview recounting the endless list of activities that fill his days. He commutes between campus and home with his parents. He also balances his love of music, three jobs, spending time with his friends, and his recent activism work. Elliot talks extensively and proudly about his activism. He states that beyond his love of music,

> I'm also into activism. I've gotten a lot into that lately. I represent a lot of different demographics and I fight for a lot of different things even if I don't necessarily include myself in that group or whatever. I do African-American, urban development, homelessness, LGBT issues, pretty much a wide array of things that I'm involved in. There is Social Justice Project, which I helped found, which I think is pretty big for a freshman.
>
> Being a political science major has attracted me to all those. Wanting to get out and meet people, wanting to actually have something to stand for and leave your mark. Especially since I want to get involved in politics someday, it's definitely a good starting point.

He notes that his activism work emerges primarily from his academic environment and his aspirations to get into politics one day.

Elliot also describes some apprehension about attending a large state school, with a very diverse body of about forty thousand students. However, instead of feeling lost in such a large population, Elliot saw student activism organizations as helping him "stay afloat."

> Definitely the organizations that I've gotten involved in, they have kept me from, you know, being that person who just goes to class and goes home. I have a reason to stay down there, and that's mainly what has kept me excited about going to school there.

During high school he had aspirations of attending a smaller, private, liberal arts college; however, because of a lack of scholarship money, he had to attend a larger public college in his hometown. So while his public college was not his first choice, it became a place where he could combine his interests and commitments to social justice.

In addition to his academic motivations for his activism, Elliot describes being actively involved in his church family and the influence of the church on his current community involvement. In many ways Elliot understands himself as a "church baby"—because he grew up in his church and has remained a member of the same church since birth. When asked to describe a time when he felt passionate about being involved in his church community, Elliot recounts examples of singing in the children's choir and then the youth choir, and going through the process of becoming a "Jr. Deacon" at the age of thirteen or fourteen. The experience pushed him out of his comfort zone and encouraged him to be more visible and actively engaged in the life of the church and the community, and to grow in his expressions of his spirituality and practices of worship: "I had to pray for the first time in front of a lot of people. I had to speak in front of large crowds and just be so much more involved." Elliot also describes other experiences that helped him become closer to God—such as singing in the choir:

> With the choir, it's like you feel something when you're actually up there and you're singing. At my core is music, and so it's like you're doing something that you love to do, but you're doing it for even a higher purpose. You have to recognize who you're singing for and what you're singing for, and it's easy to realize it when you're around people who love the same things that you love.

Elliot is also able to name the many ways that his church's teachings have evolved overtime, because of his long-standing participation in this church. In particular, he describes a process of the church becoming more welcoming to and affirming of gays and lesbians. While Elliot states that he was not old enough to fully grasp the details of the changing beliefs, he remembers the effects it had on his relationships at church. Some of his closest friends and their families left the church. However, he names his parents' decision to stay at the church as having a tremendous effect on what he understands about God.

> I know we started as [a] Baptist Church and had a lot of Baptist traditions and we still do there—definitely they're at our core. However, I think the message has changed more so that God is still speaking.

I know if you go to a lot of different Baptist churches and more traditional churches, it's like this is the Bible, this is what that is and
this is what we go by. However, there's not really anything saying
that God is still around. . . . You have to have your own realization of
what God is within yourself.

Building on his assertions about God still speaking, Elliot also states that
his church teaches him that God should have a very active role in the
world. Elliot includes an array of areas where he understands God to work,
but summarizes his understanding of God as being like a personal therapist at times:

God is definitely active, like in every single aspect of your life, in
every single aspect of everybody else's life, politics, economy, international affairs, your personal affairs, definitely, you know, seeking
God in every—for every problem that you may have or even a solution that you may have. I think about God's role like consulting,
kind of like a personal therapist at times, you have a question, sit on
the couch and ask, you know.

Related to his understanding of the different places that he sees God working, he also names a variety of concerns that young people are struggling
with. While he is grateful for very supportive parents, he describes the ways
that many of his friends, some of whom were struggling with their sexual
identity, did not have family or other adults to talk with. Looking at society
at large, Elliot is also aware of the ways that the economy is affecting young
people, as they struggle to find part-time jobs or feel the effects of parents
getting laid off. Elliot also mentions many political concerns, such as legis-
lature on same-sex marriage and hate crime laws, which he wants changed.
Elliot confidently speaks of feeling a need to respond and know that he will
do something "big" in his own community at some point in the future:

I know I'm going to eventually have to do something within my
own community that's going to be big. I don't necessarily know at
this point, because there are so many different things that I'm passionate about; whether it be gay rights or something within music
or something with somebody on the street or something like that,
but I just know that eventually it's going to come a time where I'm
going to have to step up and play my part.

However, he is uncertain about the catalyst for his need to work for change; he states, "I don't know where it comes from. It's...it's...it's just...it's just there."

Elliot concludes his interview stating a final concern of youth and how youth are engaged. He simply asserts that youth are all different and youth should not be pigeon-holed or stereotyped:

> We're just all different. Like for instance in court, it seems like all people are approached—all young adults are approached the same way, as a criminal, when in actuality we all have different situations. We've all been in different things and this situation is most likely definitely different from the other situation.

Danielle

my community ... it's ... not really a community where
you can gung ho go out and do community service and ...
change something.

Danielle is a seventeen-year-old who lives in Georgia. She was born in Jamaica and moved to the United States when she was in elementary school. In her interview she described fond memories of Jamaica and her experience relocating to a predominately African American suburb in Georgia. Danielle began her interview animatedly describing her typical day at school and emphasized the central role of her friends and running track to her life at school. While she is aware of what she calls "typical high school drama," she offers an overall positive perspective on her school. She describes her school, saying, "I love the classes.... They do a really good job of picking teachers that are really passionate about what they want to do, so you get a really good education." On the other hand, Danielle's description of her school is complicated by stereotypes of predominately Black schools; for Danielle notes that her school is diverse *and* a very good school. She illustrates this tension in her understanding of her school as she states,

> We have 51 percent black I think last time I checked. 30 percent Latino or Indian and then about 20 something white, I think, something around there. And so it's like a good mix. *I guess I wouldn't say it was like a black school because the administration runs it like a really good school so I live in suburbia and so it doesn't really have too much of*

like the problems that they associate with like black, predominantly black schools, so it's doing pretty good.

Another primary influence in Danielle's life is her family. Danielle describes her close relationship with her parents and older siblings. She describes her parents, who have been married for thirty years and are both teachers, as "traditional Jamaican"—in that they require particular manners and ways of addressing adults. She also explains how her parents' struggles in Jamaica shape their priorities for her. Danielle describes her parents as constantly encouraging her to work really hard and warning her about "wasting her potential."

Another key component in Danielle's life is her United Methodist church, which she describes as another family. She recognizes that her church is very supportive of her; and she understands the core of their teachings as love. She feels proud to be part of her church when they go into the surrounding communities and serve others.

Although Danielle's interview is overwhelmingly positive, she does not hesitate to name things in her community that concern her or that she struggles with. For example, Danielle is concerned that her community is too apathetic. She points to their apathy as more pressing than any one particular issue like crime or violence, stating,

When I look around my community and my school I feel like we're too laid back. I see it in myself, because I presently feel like I want to change the world but I feel like I don't have all the tools yet. I'm furthering my education, and when I'm finished with my education, then I'll have all the tools that I need. So, I still feel like I'm in the wings, but I still don't feel right just waiting. I feel like the environment I'm in is kind of like this waiting stage; like they are all waiting for something. My community, it's not really a community where you can gung ho go out and do community service and change something. It's more like we're going to stay in our home, and if we each individually make our little homes better then it will work out better. But I don't feel like that. I don't feel like that's how it's going to work. I feel like we all have to come together ... [but] we're all trying to make ourselves better. We're not really worried about too many other people and that's hard for me.

When pushed to reflect further, Danielle talks about how she responds to this concern. Here she expresses a complex response of both hopelessness and agency—stating that she talks to friends, but she still feels hopeless at times in the face of these issues:

> I kind of get this sense of hopelessness like what am I doing or I don't know what to do. Like I'm saying I'm in this community and it's not like there is a stall you can walk up to that they have planted out on the sidewalk like "send money to. . . ." So it's like I feel like I don't know what to do and I feel hopeless, like what is the point of being here if I can't help anyone, and I guess talking to [my friends] helps me remember that I can do something and maybe I'm not in the right position now but I will be, and so that makes me feel better and usually we talk about global issues in class, so I get different viewpoints. When I hear other people's hope I take from that and I bring it to me and I send it back out.

Danielle's interview points to her search for hope and strategies to respond constructively to all that she is concerned about. Danielle's narrative also exemplifies the ways that she is a young person with a vision for how her community should unite and affect change, but who also feels constrained by the expectation that she has to wait until she becomes older or finishes her education to make a difference. Danielle is further constrained by her communal environment that focuses on individual achievement and development. In spite of feeling frustrated about the supports that are available in her community, Danielle still affirms that she feels "called" by God to do something, and she has a plan for later, after she gets her education. However, the question remains of what should she or can she do now—as a young religious person.

Collective Themes

In addition to exploring the individual narratives of these five African American youth, here I look at the collective responses of all the youth surveyed and interviewed, regarding their communal concerns, experiences of church, understandings of God working in their lives and the world, and their agency or communal involvement.

Communal Concerns

Concerns about Their Hometowns

In describing their hometowns, schools, and primary groups of friends, the youth named an array of concerns. For example, in the survey questions about their hometowns, 75 percent of the youth named homicide, violence, or crime as an issue of concern. Over 40 percent talked about divisions among different groups (racial, ethnic, or religious groups); included in that number, 25 percent of the youth named concerns about racism. Their discussions of racism pointed to examples of "white flight" from the public schools and the failure of their communities to welcome newcomers, particularly Hispanic immigrants. Depending on the specifics of their communities, youth also named concerns about the economy, poverty, the relocation of victims of natural disasters, overcrowding, and STDs.[11]

A few youth (16 percent) include in their descriptions of their communities the numerous churches there; however, the youth did not describe the churches as enhancing their communities. For example, one young woman noted that she was concerned about her community's violence and crime, and she saw it as a direct reflection of the communities of faith's "failure to fully unite and expand our spiritual movement." She offered a harsh critique of the misplaced priorities of the religious communities in her area:

> There is literally a church on every corner.... However, because of our failure to fully unite and expand our spiritual movement, there has been sadly a lot of violence and crime. I have heard many say that there seems to be some type of "hold back" for growing ministries. This may be due to the idea of success being 100,000,000,000 and something members. When really success is spiritual promotion and empowerment from God.

Concerns about School

The young people surveyed described many positive aspects of their schools. One student was proud that her school was ranked in the top 5 percent in a *Newsweek* article, and another student wrote about his level of enjoyment at school and the many caring teachers. However, in describing their concerns for their schools, the youth once again related exposure to myriad problems in their schools. Over 40 percent expressed concern about the violence and fighting in their schools. Another third of the youth named racism and race-based cliques as a major problem. The students wrote both about the negative changes that "increasing diversity" brought in their schools and noted the underrepresentation of minority students in AP or honors classes.

Almost a fifth of the youth described their schools as failing, or were aware that their school boards had labeled their schools as such. These same youth described being worried about the negative perceptions of their schools because they were predominately Black and lower-income schools; alongside this concern they named a fear that many of their class-mates had internalized the negative stereotypes about them and their schools.

As noted in their individual narratives, both Kira and Marissa experienced schools that did not always provide the supports they sought or needed. For example, Kira turned to her school community and her principal in particular to help address the onslaught of youth violence and homicides in her community. However, instead of finding a community of support for grieving students, she encountered a school principal who gave an insufficient response to the students' tremendous grief and who, in Kira's opinion, was more concerned with downplaying the possibility of negative publicity. Marissa also encountered prejudices in her school that limited the types of relationships students of color could have with their teachers. In both instances they looked to their schools for support and left disappointed.

Primary Group of Friends

Unlike their discussions of their communities and schools, the youth were overwhelmingly positive in describing their friends and did not name many issues or concerns with their primary groups of friends. However, their responses also illustrated some of their processes of making friends and the challenges they face in determining who their authentic friends were. For example, three youth wrote that they were very selective of their friends—some said that they were only friends with people who "have a personal relationship with God" or that "most of their close friends are also their church family." Other students noted that they were most often friends with people on their sports teams or in the band, and one student explicitly stated that his closest friends were the ones from his public middle school because "the rich private school kids are weird and fake so I keep the friends I know have got my back."

Even their interpersonal relationships become overlaid with structural issues and dilemmas.

Experiences of Church

The youth articulated a significant interest in their religious communities, with over 64 percent selecting that they were regularly or very involved in a faith community. Over one third of the youth were regularly involved, and almost 29 percent said that they were very involved in church. The other 36 percent stated that they were occasionally involved in a religious community, with no students responding that they were not involved in a church or religious community.[12]

For most of the youth, their involvement in church also related to practices with their family: Several youth wrote about experiences when they were growing up of their parents "forcing" them to go to church. Other youth also noted the influence of a particular family member who was either a clergy person or simply very significant in taking the young person to church. For example, in their interviews, Jackie recounted memories of going to church with her grandfather, who is a pastor, and Kira spoke of the ways that she interacted with her mother, who is also her pastor. Additionally, Charles, a young man from Northern Virginia, described in detail how his family served as a key link for his involvement in church:

> So my grandparents and my older family members they were really into church. So we have a church in North Carolina and that's where I grew up with my uncle Charlie. He basically established all the kids in Christianity. He told us, "You gotta read the [Bible], you gotta have the Bible in your life." I grew up on Bible study every day until fourth grade. I did youth ministry. We did the choir ... everything.

Charles's interview also points to the way that changes in family structure impact the lives of the young people. For example, he also states, "After my uncle died I think that's when I just was like I don't believe in this anymore and it just all went downhill from that." While he later discusses his process of becoming involved in the church community again, he is clear that his family members played a significant role in his early involvement.

However, church as family is not the only image relayed by the youth. For example, Marissa's experience of her church does not invoke images of family; instead she describes her church as being laid back, non-vocal, and full of older people. Even her description of her church includes only the logistics of the service and not the warmth of the people. She states, "You walk in and you'll sing a couple of hymns, you'll hear the sermon, do offering and it's all just smooth sailing. There is nothing in particular that makes it any [more] special than any other church, it's just there for you to worship." Marissa describes her experience in church in a very dispassionate manner. Muwasi, a young Roman Catholic, offers a similar description of her experience of church. While she notes that she does not attend her church very often, she says that those who attend regularly are "the elderly so there's not that much to do there as far as youth activities."

Thus, in looking at the experiences of these youth in church, two trends emerge: (1) youth either saw church as an extension of their family life, where they felt integrated into the culture of going to church and the life of the church (even if they were forced to go), *or* (2) youth felt that their churches were not really oriented toward them.

God's Activity in Personal Lives, Community, Government, and World

Experiencing the Presence of God in Their Lives

While some youth struggled to articulate the core of their Christianity or the essential teachings of their church (answering "I'm not sure" or "I don't know"), most of the young people surveyed and interviewed were very clear in their understandings of how God was working in their individual lives.[13] For example, looking at the survey data, when asked to describe a time when they felt the presence of God in their lives, the overwhelming majority of the youth surveyed (86 percent) were able to name an experience of God's presence in their lives. They either gave an account of a time when they felt the presence of God or described their practices of "getting into" the presence of God. The youth described experiencing the presence of God in their lives when they were having family issues (25 percent), when they were in a worship service or during particular religious events (such as baptism), and when God "blessed them" or did something for them.[14] The majority of the young people equated feeling the presence of God with God doing something for them (over 41 percent). While one young person named a material blessing, such as God blessing her to get a deal with a company, the other responses ranged from God blessing them on a test, to God helping them in the midst of their parent's custody battle, to God comforting them when they were lonely and felt like running away, to God blessing them to survive a car accident. However, two youth wrote of experiencing God multiple times, as if experiencing the presence of God was an everyday occurrence. In particular, one young woman wrote, "Anytime I significantly clear my mind of most worldly things and focus on God I can often feel his presence surrounding me."

God's Work in the World and Politics

On the other hand, moving beyond their discussions of God working in their individual lives, the vast majority of young people surveyed and interviewed were less certain about God's role or work in their communities, the world, or government. Most youth were vague or ambiguous in their responses to questions such as "what does your church see as God's work in the world?" Some youth replied with statements as "God wanted them to be light in darkness," and others spoke more generally about "helping others." These responses also were peppered with the phrases "I don't know" or "I guess."

The responses became more complex, but even more uncertain when the youth described how they saw God working in the government or politics. Jackie, for example, responded,

> Politics, I don't pay attention to politics so I really wouldn't know. I don't think so. Well, I mean I think He [God] might try but I think politicians for—some of them are harder to reach, like your little communication with God gets farther as you push Him away. So I think those politicians, a lot of them really have their minds set on what they want, so it's harder for them to communicate with God than it is for people who are actually going through a struggle and going through stuff like that.

While not arguing that politicians have a harder time connecting with or hearing God, Marissa also asserted that she is on the fence about whether God is involved with politics. She responded saying,

> I don't know if I see God working in my community. I don't know if He's in the government. It's really obnoxious because our forefathers were all Christian and they created this country, or the Pledge of Allegiance wouldn't have under God in it, or our dollar bills wouldn't say In God We Trust. And it's really, really sad because George Bush was a Christian, at least that's what he claims, and he

had people fighting in a war and we didn't know what we're fighting over. I think God is in the government, but I don't think that people fully recognize that He is because then there wouldn't be so many unjust situations. Our society does not think that God is in the government because of the cases where people have been shot and killed by the police and there is nothing you can do about it. I think that people give up that God is there and that's probably why I'm on the fence whether He is there or not.

Similarly, Elliot describes the problematic ways that religion shows up in US politics and government. He states,

We're a predominantly Christian country. However, we try to act like there's no other religion in the country. Like with the stories about Guantanamo Bay, people get taken to Guantanamo Bay just because they're Muslim. Even back in religious battles of yesteryear, I'm like can we really justify something like murder and genocide and things with religion? So it's hard to say whether you see God in government, because government can be so corrupt, and they can try to base their views and their actions off of religion. So personally speaking I can't necessarily say that I see God in every single action that we take as a country or in any government. A lot of it is just ego and wanting to be the big dog.

Kira, in contrast, moves beyond the particular actions of politicians and casts the discussion in terms of a larger plan at work in the world. Kira expresses an understanding of political events as connected with the fulfillment of divine prophecies and as consequences of sin. Kira responds,

I feel like God is allowing things to happen in politics. Divine prophecies are going to have to be fulfilled. He's setting things in order to prepare for His Son to come again. I feel like because of sin there will always be tragedy. But I feel like, yes, He is working and He's just setting the table, and He's doing something big.

The youth responses represent an array of perspectives, but point toward historical connections (real or perceived) between Christianity and the US government *and* a sense of hypocrisy or inconsistency among political leaders and governmental structures. These observations fuel the youth's complex understandings and uncertainty about God's work in government. This complexity and uncertainty about God's (and their religious community's) role in their communities and government is not surprising, for scholars of religion continue to research and explore the role that religion should or should not play in public life. Thus the youth responses parallel the complexities and tensions in society at large about God's work in the world, government, and politics.

Youth Communal Involvement

Contrary to the myths that portray adolescents as apathetic or overly complacent, all of the youth surveyed and interviewed through YTI, in addition to naming things they were concerned about, participated in community service and other forms of communal involvement. Whether connected to high-school requirements or on their own, the majority of youth spoke of being involved in community service as a matter of fact—as if their involvement was normal or what all young people are doing.

In the survey we also asked youth to check the types of activities they were currently involved with in their communities. We offered a range of activities from serving in a soup kitchen or homeless shelter, to peer education around sex or tobacco use, to tutoring, and picking up trash. We tried to offer a range of activities including those classified as community service, as well as civic engagement activities—such as writing letters to politicians, registering voters, poll watching, and participating in town-hall meetings or mock governments.

The most popular activity was recycling, with almost 60 percent of the youth recycling or pushing their families to recycle. The next popular was peer tutoring (53 percent) and volunteering at a shelter or soup kitchen (46 percent). However, we noted that much smaller percentages of youth were involved in civic or political issues. For example,

· only one youth worked to register voters;
· only one youth had signed a petition or letter addressing a communal concern; and
· only one youth had ever written a letter or called an elected official regarding a communal concern.

Youth also had an option of writing in other ways that they were involved in their community. While our research list did not include church-based youth groups, about 17 percent of the youth wrote in this activity—pointing to the ways that they view church-based youth groups as a significant part of their community involvement.

In addition to responding about their individual community activities, the survey asked youth to think about the "ways that young people are making a difference in their communities." Almost 80 percent of the youth surveyed believe that young people can and are making a difference in their communities. While a few responses talked generically about what youth *could* do, others gave specific examples of organizations in their communities that youth were involved with. For example, one youth wrote, "Young people in my community really know how to get everyone pumped up and involved in what they stand for. They help raise money, help the elderly, and are doing a Habitat for Humanity type thing soon."

Motivations to Work or Act in Their Communities

We also asked the youth if they had ever learned of a "problem in the world" that prompted them to change something about how they lived. Almost 62 percent of the youth responded affirmatively. Youth named issues such as sex trafficking, genocide, raising money to cure little-known illnesses and AIDS, responding to animal cruelty by becoming vegan, and being motivated by their experience of salvation or watching the lives of others who have not lived up to their gifts. And even though each of the issues they raised was unique, with only two youth naming the same issue, their responses to this question reveal that youth are both concerned about things that are going on in the world around them and are motivated to change and encourage others to change in response to things that are of concern to them.

Youth also responded to questions about people they admired for making a difference in the world and people they knew personally who were making a difference in the world. Youth named parents or a family member most often as someone they admired for making a difference in the world (31 percent); youth also said they admired celebrities for their humanitarian work around the world (23 percent) and pastors (15 percent). However, when we asked about people they actually knew, half of the youth named a pastor, and others named friends (20 percent), a community worker (20 percent), and one young woman named herself.

We also asked youth to discuss if there were barriers or supports to the ways that youth can become involved in the community. When discussing barriers to youth community involvement, five of the twelve youth respondents (42 percent) were very optimistic, asserting that there were no barriers that limited youth. Youth drew upon scriptural references of "we can do all things through Christ who strengthens us"[15] and gave examples of how youth were involved in various ways. For example, one survey respondent wrote, "In my faith community there are no barriers other than your own self. If we are led by God, we are able to give a sermon, prophesy, or operate in the gifts of God. Most people are aware that God can speak through even the mouths of babes."

The rest of the youth were less optimistic; they offered pragmatic responses that youth are often limited by age, finances needed to execute their plans, and their dependency on parents for transportation. Only one respondent commented that youth are limited in their communal involvement by their own lack of knowledge or fear of voicing their opinions. On the other hand, in discussing the supports available to youth, all of the youth who answered the questions offered concrete examples of supports in their community. Youth named community organizations (50 percent), churches (42 percent), and schools (25 percent) as supporting their community involvement. Absent from the list was an explicit mention of the ways that parents encourage their youth; whereas youth were clear that a lack of parental support (finances or transportation) can hinder their progress.

God's Calling to Work for Change

Along with our discussions of practical motivations, supports, and barriers to youth involvement in their communities, in the interviews we also asked the youth if they "felt called" by God or their church to work for change or make a difference in their communities. Most of the young people interviewed resonated with the language of "God calling them" to work for some kind of change or to respond to some of the concerns they named. As noted earlier, Kira named a sense of calling to respond to the youth violence in her school, because she was a Christian and she wanted her classmates to recognize that there was more to life than violence. Both Danielle and Jackie stated that they not only felt called by God, but went further to discuss that they were drawn to a particular profession in response to what they saw going on in their communities. Danielle expressed frustration with her own community because it was not as open to working for change as she wanted it to be. However, Danielle named feeling called by God to respond and to become a lawyer:

Q: Do you have a sense that God is calling you to work for change?

A: Yeah. My personal battle like, why I'm doing law and I want to represent rape victims. Yes there are people that help them, but I don't think they give them emotional support, and I think if you can mix it all together— emotional and legal—I think a lot more people would actually want to report.

Jackie also connected her career path with a desire to help people and what she saw as a calling. In response to the question, "Do you feel a particular calling to respond to some of the social concerns that you see in the lives of other teenagers?" she stated,

> I like to listen to people, about their problems and stuff. My best friend has this one friend who cuts her arms. I don't know her that well, but I want to get to know her just to know what could she possibly be going through. Because she's the happiest person— like when you meet her, she's just so excited and always jumping around. So I wonder what could she be going through to make her do that. I want to be a psychologist when I get older. So when I see stuff like this, I really think I want to help her.

However, when asked if she felt that becoming a psychologist was explicitly a calling by God, Jackie resisted. Her resistance in part arose from the narrow association of calling with pastoral ministry. Jackie stated that at one point she felt that she was called to be a pastor, but she now feels that she can combine religion and psychology.[16]

It is also important to note some major differences between the way that Kira, Danielle, and Jackie respond to the idea of "calling." Jackie and Danielle relate calling to a vocation or occupation, and see it as something that they will respond to in the future. Kira sees her calling as something that comes with being a "Christian," and thus she feels the need to respond right now. Kira also names her work with the Bible study and witnessing at school as meeting this urgent need to get her classmates "saved" or to see that there is more to life than violence. Thus, while Jackie and Danielle are attempting to put off their response until their future careers, Kira is attempting to make an immediate response for the futures of her classmates. Both responses are admirable, but they seem limited in the ways that they are responding to the conditions in their communities.

In contrast, Marissa did not explicitly connect her vocational goals with the concerns she saw in her community. She instead used "wishful thinking" language, noting the difficulty and trends of not responding in her hometown. She stated,

> Living here, we are very one sided. We are just very like "I'm sorry, I can't do anything about it." Like if you're poor, then I'm sorry and there's not much you can do about it. But I work in the Bronx and seeing so many people with Medicaid and gentrification and it sucks and hopefully if I ever get to that point where I have enough money to help other people, I hope I can use it to the best of my ability and just make more resources for other people like the same resources I've had.

Marissa was more pessimistic[17] about feeling called and revealed her opinion about her church and school's role in helping her understand a calling to work for change:

> Q: Do you sense God, through church or family, friends or school calling you to work for change?
> A: No. I don't see that in my church or my school or any of that. It's a personal option for me, and I think that just being in areas or affiliating with certain people have really opened my eyes, and that's why I choose to help other people.

Elliot's response is quite similar to Marissa's. As noted above, Elliot, while he is not pessimistic, is uncertain about his motivation to work for change; he states, "I don't know where it comes from, it's just there." Thus, he neither ascribes nor denies an understanding of God or his church calling him to work for change—even as he insists that he must.

Connecting the Fragments

Looking collectively at their responses to the survey questions, we see that 100 percent of the young people named some issue in their schools, communities, or core groups of friends that they were concerned about and wanted to change; 100 percent of the youth who responded described a positive experience of God's presence in their lives; and 100 percent of the youth were involved in some way in their communities.

While the young people were able to name concerns in their communities and were involved in their communities in many ways, it is important to note that most of the ways that they were involved in their communities did not address or relate directly to things that they were worried about. This disconnect could simply indicate that if youth are working on a problem, then it was no longer a major concern to them. However, this disconnect may point to a larger problem among young people (and people in general)—that youth do not feel empowered to ameliorate things that concern them. The youth interviews and survey responses do not demonstrate a clear connection between these three dimensions of the young people's lives. The young people's concerns about their communities and their personal experiences of God do not translate into reflective and focused action in the world.

In other words, reviewing the youth interviews and surveys, we see examples of fragmentation in the lives of African American youth. The data reflect trends similar to those named by Parker in the 1990s, in that youth have very clear and lively understandings of God's active presence in their individual lives; however, they are not certain of God's activity in their communities and particularly in political and governmental arenas. Their language also indicates fragmentation in terms of how youth understand themselves as agents of change. Thus, looking across the youth interview and survey data, I see indications of fragmented spirituality among the youth as well—in that despite their assertions about a transformative and active God and religious communities, youth are not currently acting in response to that which concerns them, nor are they clearly indicating an expectation that God will work in the areas that concern them.

However, the question of *why not* remains.[18] Why is their understanding of a personal experience with God not fully connected to or integrated with their concerns about the community, their understanding of how God is working or should work in the world, and with the types of actions they are taking in the world? In the second part of this chapter, I continue to explore this question looking at trends within current educational resources with African American youth and at trends in the larger society.

From Sunday School to Sermons
African American Churches and Educational Ministry with Youth

Attending to the spirituality and spiritual formation of African American youth requires listening to the voices of young people, *and* attending to the religious and educational contexts of their young lives. The second part of this chapter analyzes the educational curricula in African American churches to explore what is emphasized in the spiritual development of African American adolescents. To be sure, churches are only part of the spiritual landscape and only one of the influences on adolescent spirituality and formation; however, the Black church remains a significant source for many African American Christian youth. The Black church's complex history and persistent presence in the African American community makes it a critical community to examine in order to understand and redress the prevalence of fragmented spirituality among African American adolescents.[19]

In African American churches, there is not often a paid, professional youth minister or stand-alone youth ministry. Instead, for many African American churches, youth ministry includes an assortment of opportunities to participate in the life of the larger church. Among the majority of African American churches (which typically have memberships of less than two-to-three hundred), the primary forms of youth ministry include a youth choir, youth ushers, monthly-to-quarterly youth fellowship opportunities, Sunday school classes, and Sunday worship services led by or dedicated to youth. In addition to these structured opportunities, youth across regions find ways of sitting together in the back of churches, in the balconies, or with their families—again getting the majority of their spiritual formation alongside of the adults in the congregation.[20] While I advocate and affirm this integration into the main religious life of the congregation, this model of religious formation requires a different level of attention to ascertain the complex narratives taught to most African American youth. It requires assessing content, which is both directly and indirectly geared to youth.

Thus, in order to understand the explicit and implicit "on the ground" theology African American churches present to adolescents, I analyze Sunday school curricula and sermon content. Each of these educational resources offers a unique picture of the theology of African American Churches; however, by analyzing both through the same lens and questions, we get a better picture of the overall perspectives conveyed to adolescents, including which theological themes are significant, what images of God are most prevalent, as well as the types of practical actions and changes a life of faith calls forth. (See Appendix B for the specific analysis questions and details of the curriculum selection process.)

Why Sunday School Curricula?

Long before the expansion of multimedia in ministries and the proliferation of online Christian resources, each of the historically Black denominations organized publishing houses to print educational pamphlets and Sunday school curricula. If one traces the history of the many African American Baptist denominations, one finds that the development of publishing houses or educational boards runs hand in hand with the growth and division of the many denominations. For example, the National Baptist Convention of the United States of America (NBC, Inc.) was successful from its formation in 1895 until 1915, when internal conflict arose around the National Baptist Publishing Board.[21] The result of the conflict was the incorporation of the Publishing Board, the forming of a separate Black Baptist convention, The National Baptist Convention of America (NBCA), and the subsequent forming of another Black Baptist Publisher, the National Baptist Convention, USA, Inc. Sunday School Publishing Board.[22]

Similarly, in tracing the history of African American Methodists, religious educator Kenneth Hill notes the interconnection of the establishment of the denominations and a mission to provide education. The education included literacy for newly freed persons and instruction in the Christian faith.[23] Richard Allen, who founded the African Methodist Episcopal church in 1787, organized both a church and a school for the instruction of youth and adults. Similarly, the African Methodist Episcopal Zion church formed both a church and school in their first church building.[24] Across each of the historically African American denominations, there is a strong connection between their development, the formation of educational ministries, and the formation of the publishing boards.

This work addresses the educational content and curricula used *across* denominations with African American youth. Therefore, I began paying attention to the curricula I observed in churches, across denominations. Most consistently, the churches I observed used the Urban Ministry, Inc. Sunday school curriculum (UMI) for their youth Sunday school classes. UMI, unlike the other curriculum and publishing boards, was *not* started as a denominationally based curriculum, nor has it been historically associated with a single African American denomination. Instead, UMI was founded on the idea that there was a need for literature published by Black people that addresses the specific social and cultural needs of African American youth. The hallmark of the UMI curriculum is both the attempt to design lessons that connect with the historical, social, and spiritual experiences of African Americans and the prevalence of African American images. UMI Sunday school curriculum teacher packets also include spotlights on African American history.

Why Sermons?

From some of the earliest accounts of the religious practices of the descendants of enslaved Africans in the United States, contained in classic texts such as W. E. Du Bois's 1903 *Souls of Black Folk*, to more contemporary works on the influence of televangelism in the African American Christianity, the significance of preaching and sermons in African American Christian worship is repeatedly underscored. In describing his first "Negro Revival," Du Bois characterizes it by the "preacher, the music and the frenzy."[25] Whereas Du Bois's account depicts the performance of preaching in the revival service, his work also addresses the significance of preaching for the moral and religious instruction of the Negro community.[26] Du Bois's description and critique of Negro preachers reiterates the central role that preachers play in the African American church and community. This central role of preachers also underscores the significance of the content of their sermons for the lives of African American adults and youth. In many cases, pastors and preachers offer models of leadership and authority—thus their words not only reflect *a* theological perspective, but carry the weight of being the *Word of God* for that community.[27]

Similarly, in their seminal study, *The Black Church in the African American Experience*, Lincoln and Mamiya write,

> The sermon assumes a degree of importance in the black worship service which cannot be matched by its institutional counterparts in other religious communities. Throughout the historical development of the Black church over the past two hundred years, the sermon has served a wide variety of functions and purposes: its primary purpose has been to glorify God but it has also served as *theological education and Sunday School*; ritual drama and show time; singing and humming; encouragement and political advice; and moralizing and therapy—all rolled into one.[28]

Honoring the importance of preaching within the African American community, I also attend to this vital source of Black religious thought in an effort to uncover the theology presented to African American youth and how this theology fosters and/or ameliorates fragmented spirituality. In some ways, sermons play a greater role in the religious development of African American youth than Sunday school curricula. Sunday school and youth groups are attended less frequently than Sunday worship in the majority of Black churches, and often they are attended by very different segments of the church's youth.

The sample of sermons offer only a snapshot of Black religiosity, but they reflect the diversity of African American Christian traditions, including historically Black Baptist, Methodist, and Pentecostal denominations, as well as an increasing prevalence of non-denominational churches. (See Appendix B for the breakdown of sermons by denomination, geographical location, gender of pastor, as well as membership sizes.)

Theological and Practical Themes

The UMI Sunday school curriculum includes an introductory narrative and practical application sections to help youth connect with the biblical lesson. Most often, the narratives address personal and interpersonal situations, such as struggles with personal success, utilizing one's individual gifts, romance, or spending time with family. Fewer lessons addressed communal situations or even described youth working in their communities. The communal themes included sharing with those in need, talking with a homeless community member, and using the news and print media as a means of affecting communal issues, such as racism and bias.[29] Figure 1.1 summarizes my understanding of personal, interpersonal, communal, and societal themes and actions. I have included this chart because of the varied and imprecise ways of defining each of these terms.[30]

In addition to thinking about the practical themes in terms of whether they address primarily individuals or communities, it was also informative to look at the context and locations of each of the practical narratives. For example, the majority of the narratives and practical situations were set at home (44 percent) and school (28 percent), while only 6 percent addressed or took place in larger community settings (such as on the street or in their neighborhood), and only 12.5 percent of the narratives were set at church.

Overwhelmingly the curriculum did not include social justice issues in the discussions. Only three lessons included discussions of racism, two lessons included discussions of homelessness, and only one discussed

Category	General Description
Personal	The *personal* addresses the actions of individual people to change, tweak, or reflect upon their lives. This includes actions and individual behavioral changes such as eating better, exercising, dressing a certain way, being honest, studying, aspiring for personal success like getting a good job, not having sex, abstaining from alcohol, drugs, and so on.
Interpersonal	The *interpersonal* addresses the interactions between two individuals. This includes actions that affect relationships, such as learning to respect parents or teachers, treating a neighbor well, learning to get along with friends or to be in romantic relationships, learning how to deal with the loss of a relationship, and even dealing with issues of popularity or acceptance and many other actions related to one-on-one interactions that impact individuals directly.
Communal	The *communal* addresses actions or themes that take place in and are geared toward a larger community. The *communal* can include communities such as churches, schools, local governments, neighborhoods, and local organizations.
	The communal can involve the actions of individuals that impact a wider community, and it can include the collective action of an organization. (E.g., the communal can include both an individual city council person working to get better afterschool programs, and it can include a group of youth from the Boys and Girls Club working to raise funds for a family in need or to do a neighborhood cleanup.)
Societal	The *societal* includes actions that are targeted toward society at large—issues that affect individuals and the entire society. This includes public policy decisions and efforts to advocate for social and systemic change. These actions can include involvement in the political and legislative process. Actions typical of this level include lobbying, working with organizations that go to the state and federal law-making bodies, protesting, writing, voting, registering people to vote, running for office, campaigning, and so on. However, the *societal* can also include a global component—of working to affect international systems (such as protesting wars or working on human rights campaigns).

FIGURE I.I Curriculum and Sermon Analysis Schema

sexism. The discussions of homelessness also did not offer any type of social or systemic analysis. Instead, the narratives focused on one individual showing compassion to a homeless person or a youth group serving homeless people, without ever questioning why or how homelessness exists in their communities.

The lack of engagement with social justice issues in the curriculum parallels trends in Black Christian education during other historical periods. Kenneth Hill describes the "de-radicalization" of Black church education in the early twentieth century:

> When I sifted through samples of the Sunday school materials written in the twentieth century by African Methodist Episcopal, African Methodist Episcopal Zion, and National Baptist Publishing Board, I discovered the literature failed to address social justice issues such as war, hunger, racism, and Black Power until the 1960s. Much of the Sunday school literature prior to the 1960s focused on knowledge of scripture, self-help, and a place of warmth and acceptance in which the love of God could be experienced.[31]

Hill notes that within the African Methodist Episcopal Church, during the 1970s and early 1980s the Sunday school curricula had an added emphasis on "Blackness," and he found that more than fifty lessons during the years of 1975–1985 dealt with issues of racism and prejudice.[32] However, Hill's research does not describe the trends in Sunday school literature after 1985 and thus leave opens the possibility of another wave of "de-radicalization" in Black Sunday school curricula within the last thirty years.

Additionally, the curricula included theological themes ranging from the *promises* of God to the *images* of Christ. Across the lessons, God's concern for humanity was underscored in the frequent language of "God cares for us" and "we matter to God." Faithfulness or "remaining faithful" also serves as a theological touchstone of the education curriculum—where youth are encouraged to see the value of their faith and the need to remain faithful in times of disappointment or discouragement. Faithfulness in the lessons further includes the need to draw near to God and to persist in godly living.

Similarly, the sermons address a variety of theological and practical themes. Preachers often offer stories and give analogies to help "make the scripture plain" and to help the hearers apply biblical principles to their daily lives. They draw from the rich resources of African American culture, community concerns, news events, and even from issues in the church. They tell stories from their personal lives and the lives of their children; and they often offer examples of struggles and problems that humans have to deal with on a regular basis. However, instead of simply cataloguing the richness of the narrative style and resources among African American preachers, these narratives also illustrate the many areas that the preachers, and in turn the hearers, recognize as the areas and methods in which God works.

The sermons focused on three major themes of transformation, overcoming, and warning/correction. At the heart of each sermon the preachers are admonishing people to have *faith in God* and to *live according to God's way*. Each preacher presents his or her own understanding of *God's way* and makes the case based on biblical texts as to why we should trust that God's way is correct or will lead to the desired outcomes.

In spite of this diversity of themes, it is always important to ask, "What is *not* presented?" or "What is given the least attention?" In particular, when thinking about fragmented spirituality, I most often question if or how the sermons hold together a strong faith in God *and* a strong commitment to act in personal, communal, and social realms, motivated by God. Looking across the sermons, I found that none included each of these elements in the first sample of sermons from 2009 and only one did from the 2015 sample of sermons.[33] The sermons encouraged the hearers to put their faith in God and to follow God's way or plan; however, only one of the sermons tied this faith in God to acting beyond the personal and interpersonal level (even if they named issues taking place in the community). In one sermon, the preacher catalogued many of the issues facing Black families and Black communities. He offered hope of a better future, but did not give them an example of what working for that hope, beyond waiting on the blessings of God, will look like. The few strategies offered were addressed at interpersonal dynamics within the family, even as he named larger systemic issues taking place in the wider African American community.

Similarly, in an analysis of the language employed in each sermon, the words *justice, injustices,* and *oppression* came up in only twenty percent of the sermons reviewed. During the 2009 sample, the words only occurred as the preacher was offering the background for the scripture text of the sermon. In 2015, there were more discussions of injustices as related to issues confronting the people, including the prison industrial complex and injustices within the church (such as sexism and homophobia). While it was hopeful to review sermons in the later sample that were pushing for more integration of faith and social concerns, even in the sermons that offer some understanding of injustice and oppression, the discussions did not always move to a fuller development. Overwhelmingly, the theological themes presented in the sermons tend more toward faith in God and do not expand to demonstrate how God pushes humanity to address communal and societal issues. Thus, it becomes evident that while the sermons offer tremendous resources and encouragement to individuals dealing with personal and familial concerns, to a large extent they do not address communal or societal issues, theologically or practically.

Understandings of God and God's Action in the World

At the core of theology is human talk about God. Thus, the various understandings of God in the UMI curricula were carefully analyzed, including the numerous images, attributes, and actions of God and ways God is expected to act. God is most often described as *offering guidance* to God's people (individually and communally); as *creating life*, by speaking things into being, opening wombs, and impregnating Mary by God's spirit; as having *requirements* for the people's lives, actions, and worship; and as having *consequences* for human disobedience. The curricula also describe God as being with humans, forgiving humans, and challenging the status quo—by reversing the order of who inherits blessings and by pouring God's spirit out on all persons.

My analysis takes into account the scripture texts for each lesson and the UMI editors' exegesis; therefore, it is difficult to say definitively that the curricula emphasize God as acting mostly in relation to our personal lives or communal lives. For many of the biblical texts, particularly from the Hebrew Bible, depict God addressing the entire nation of Israel and calling the nation or community of people to collective repentance and communal action. However, most discussions of the text describe God's work in the personal lives of youth. Therefore, in holding the texts and exegesis together, we see the potential in the UMI curricula to paint a picture of a God who works both on a personal and communal level. Thus in the curricula, God is described in diverse ways and places, not particularly limited to one realm or arena of action. Despite the richness of the biblical images of God, the exegesis in the curricula exemplifies fragmentation, in that that the biblical texts offer one image and the interpretation moves God's action to the personal or interpersonal.

In the sermons, the understandings of God are also varied and numerous. Each sermon includes descriptions of the actions, attributes, images, or metaphors of God. In general, God is very active. God is described as actively *giving* blessings, favor, instruction, confidence, power, and authority; *calling* humans to particular actions; *using* people to accomplish various goals; *knowing* the actions and plans of humans even before they were made; making *plans* and promises; offering protection and *covering* the sins of humans; and *changing* lives, situations, and names. I found that the most popular understandings of God referenced God's *love* and God's ability to *give* all manner of things to humankind. God is referred to as almighty, strong, compassionate, and at times silent.

However, one must still ask the question, "What is missing from this list?" In many ways, God is not political. Even though God is sovereign and understood to use the Babylonians to teach the children of Israel a lesson, the implications are not that God is really involved with politics. It is interesting, however, that while the content (as we will see in our discussion of the actions, changes, and themes of the sermons) does not focus on political or societal issues at great length, the understandings of God presented in the sermons are robust and tend to transcend even the limited examples that the preachers explicitly name for God to work in. The preachers present very strong and complex images of God. God in this sample of sermons, and in Black preaching in general, is fierce, sovereign, and active in history and in all aspects of life; but the preachers are not pushing this image or applying it, for the most part, beyond spiritual and personal themes. On the one hand, God is presented as being able to do anything, but on the other God is not being asked or expected to do these things. Essentially, the images of God presented are not explicitly pressing the hearers to think about God's action in every area or dimension of life, including personal, communal, and societal liberation and struggle; but they do not limit that either.

Response: Actions and Change

Each UMI lesson includes a final section designed to encourage youth to apply key principles from the lesson, entitled "Do It" and "Jam On it." Somewhat surprisingly, the most prevalent action was reflection and prayer. These are significant practices—however, I question if reflection and prayer that do not serve as catalysts for other types of action can cultivate a substantive spirituality. This also raises the question of whether educational resources (and by extension the church) encourage youth to treat religion and God as simply as something to think about, or as something that has very limited influence. The absence of more concrete, communal, and societal action, in addition to reflection, forces us to ask the question, "Can religion be a resource for broader, more strategic action in the world and community around youth?"[34]

Similarly, the concept of change, in terms of a break from or challenge to a normative form of behavior, belief or attitude, was not explicitly included in each lesson. It also became evident that my presumptions about change, which build upon theological understandings of conversion and repentance, as well as social and systemic understandings of change as social and personal reform, are not evidenced in the curriculum. After reading closer for the implicit calls for change, I found that over one third of the lessons did not include any call for change.

However, the curriculum lifts up "change" in terms of renewal of religious commitments and practices. Half of the samples included language, if not a direct call, which points toward the need for new, or a return to particular religious practices and perspectives. The lessons included language encouraging youth to embrace God's power within humans by being creative, to remember God's faithfulness in bad or lonely situations, to remain strong in their faith, looking for examples of others to encourage their faithfulness, and even calls to act more like God and to understand the great gift of salvation from Jesus.

On the other hand, about 15 percent of the lessons reviewed contained a call for communal or social change. Despite the limited number, these lessons included calls to meaningful engagement in the youth's communities, churches, and neighborhoods. One lesson included encouragement to "tell the whole story" in addressing the systemic misrepresentation of communities, particularly African Americans, in the mainstream media. Youth were invited to review current media stories to observe how African Americans and other ethnic groups are addressed. Another lesson also included a call for youth to correct injustices and "stand for what is right" by looking around their communities to identify an injustice or concern and to take specific action to correct it. In another lesson, which I would classify as communal religious change, youth were both encouraged to see the unique role that each can play in the community of faith and asked to reflect on how they could use their gifts or talents for the benefit of the community, and to think about how they were going to work in their churches and neighborhoods.

Although all of the sermons reviewed called for some spiritual or religious response, the preachers varied in the particular responses they call for. Paralleling the practical and theological themes emphasized in the sermons, over half of the sermons called the hearers to *trust God* to work on their behalf, to change their circumstances, to lead them in the correct direction, and to act in due time. Similarly, a third of the sermons also invited the hearers to *see God in a new way*—to see God as loving, to see God as capable of wrath, and to see how God is going to do things differently. Other sermons also enjoined hearers to *connect with God*, by "getting saved" and joining the church, and to *praise God in advance* of seeing improvements in their lives or of seeing the blessings of God.

In addition to responding in their spiritual practices and faith in God, some sermons called for personal responses, which are not explicitly spiritual in terms of the language used by the preacher.[35] These preachers call for personal self-improvement, such as calling the hearers to take better control of their emotions and to take responsibility for their part in the process of transformation and growth.

Again, the majority of the sermons call for spiritual responses—to simply trust God or connect better with God. And the sermons that call for more practical responses and action focus on individual growth and development. Thus, from this sample of sermons, I see very limited examples of communally or socially active spirituality. Similar to the ways that action and change were called for in the curricula, the sermons call for very limited actions.

Perspectives on Adolescents

Along with attending to the theological content of the curricula, the presentation and images of adolescents in each lesson reveals a great deal about the ways that youth development is affirmed or supported in curricula. The *Inteen* and *JAM* curricula are designed specifically for lower and middle adolescents; thus youth are the key actors and the target audience of the lessons. However, the curricula include some limitations in the types of behaviors and responses that adolescents are portrayed as making. For example, youth are most often depicted as struggling with issues in their lives: Youth in the opening narratives are portrayed as struggling with health and body issues, as struggling with loneliness and finding real happiness, and as getting in trouble at school.

Even though most of the opening narratives had a religious undertone or implication, only a few included explicit or primarily religious concerns or actions in their discussion of adolescents. In some lessons youth were portrayed as struggling to trust God or to figure out how to serve God everywhere; in other lessons youth were portrayed as "feeling the spirit move," as being blessed by God, and as actively witnessing to other youth about God.

The lessons also include many positive portrayals of youth as actively involved and working. For example, one lesson describes a young woman giving her old clothes to a family in need, another describes a young man showing compassion to a homeless man, and others depict youth as organizing events in their schools and churches. Overall, over 40 percent of the lessons portray youth as taking positive action in the world around them and lift up young people as capable of action. In this way, UMI is making tremendous strides in empowering youth to take action and to see themselves as capable.

One of the major concerns with fragmented spirituality and adolescent development in general connects with young persons' abilities to see themselves as capable of acting and working for change (on their own behalf and in their communities). The presence of positive examples of young people participating in acts of compassion, service, hospitality, and charity is significant. However, according to some of the interview narratives and earlier research on African American youth spirituality, it may not be enough. These examples are still often limited to the interpersonal arena—given these limitations, we must further ask how or if we can build upon these to offer youth examples and strategies for working in different ways as well. How do we connect stories about youth showing kindness to a friend with stories of youth participating in activism or protest rallies to work to end violence against all youth?

In contrast to the curricula, the sermons do not address or even reference adolescents for the most part. The sermons do not lift up adolescents as active agents or address their concerns. If we look more broadly, few address *children* as part of larger family units. For example, one preacher refers to "kids" and speaks generally of struggles that children and youth are facing, as part of his discussion of the need to reform African American families. Another pastor only mentions children in passing, stating, "Our children are acting crazy." He includes children in a list of problems and situations that the congregation needs God to work out. Yet another pastor names children as the objects of parental disappointment and the cause of some of the hurt that many parents experience.

Children are portrayed as victims of broken villages and as problems that parents have to struggle with; in each example youth are portrayed in a negative or at best problematic light. They are not presented as capable agents or actors in their own lives, but as parts of families that need repair or as causing problems for the presumed adult listener. While the trope of children "stressing out" parents is not uncommon, it is noteworthy that the only mention of adolescents in the sermons I examined is negative. From this sample, one has to wonder about the prevalence of this practice across African American churches and about the larger effects on the self-concept of youth, as well as the ministry possibilities for youth in churches that primarily view or present youth negatively and in need of miraculous intervention. This lack of positive discussion speaks to the gap between adult-led congregations and youth (and echoes the narratives of several of the youth interviewed above). Discussing larger concerns about the lack of the church's involvement in the policies that affect children and youth, Luther Smith writes, "Fundamental to closing the gap [between children/youth and adults] is building relationships.... Children cannot be reduced to statistics, issues and problems. Such a reduction makes children an abstraction, and presenting children as an abstraction is a form of dehumanization."[36]

Discussions of Race and Ethnicity in the Curricula

Black churches historically were one of the few social institutions owned and controlled by Black people, and as such they were expected to be places where African American youth could learn about the history and practices of Black people, as well as Christian doctrines. Scholars continue to debate whether this expectation was ever fully realized. However, at different historical moments explicit discussion of race or ethnicity within Black churches, theology, and educational materials has varied from fully integrated into the materials to almost non-existent. Further, given the historical emphasis of UMI, I analyzed each lesson attending to the ways that the editors address race or ethnicity. While I argue that the presence or absence of discussions of race and ethnicity in religious educational materials can determine how youth think about their racial and ethnic heritage in connection with their religious identity, it is not guaranteed that a curriculum designed primarily for African American youth models ways of connecting one's African American and Christian identities.

In the review of the sub-sample of lessons, I found that less than one-fifth of the lessons explicitly mention race or ethnicity. In one lesson, the opening narrative mentioned the presence of portraits of significant Black scholars like Mary Bethune, W. E. B. Du Bois, and Howard Thurman lining the walls of the principal's office as the protagonist talks with the principal, and the principal commends him for the way he treated a homeless man in their community. Similarly, the other lessons that explicitly mention race or ethnicity do so in ways that lift up the positive accomplishments of African Americans—with only brief allusions to the major struggles of African Americans throughout history. For example, the remainder of the citations comes from one unit where the editors highlight the work and accomplishments of African Americans as writers and publishers in print media. In this unit, the lessons offered a discussion of race and struggles for equality. The authors described ways that African Americans had to create alternative forms of media (including the Associated Negro Press) in order to have fair and equal treatment in the media and to have access to issues of concern to African Americans.

In addition to the discussions of race or ethnicity in the actual student lessons, the Teaching for Success kits offer posters and brief biographies of three African American figures. However, the information is not included in the student and teacher workbooks and thus *does not* necessarily factor into the lessons each quarter. Therefore, it is possible to use the UMI curricula without including African American history. In other words, most often there is no direct integration of the history of African American people with the biblical lessons.

In contrast to the Urban Ministry, Inc. curricula, with a founding mission to create culturally relevant educational resources, sermons in the African American community do not *explicitly* have this as a central purpose.[37] Whereas one might assume that preaching and teaching in an African American context affects the content of the messages, in terms of an explicit discussion of race or ethnicity, the sermon sample does not directly support this assumption. Twenty percent of the sermons (in both samples) explicitly mention race or ethnicity. The limited role of race and ethnicity in this sample of sermon content remains perplexing and warrants further investigation. For example, my sample may both parallel trends *and* indicate some divergence from an earlier study of African American religious practices conducted by Lincoln and Mamiya.

Lincoln and Mamiya, in their discussion of "black consciousness" among African American preachers since the civil rights movement, noted that 64.3 percent of the clergy surveyed in the 1980s responded affirmatively to the question, "Do your sermons reflect any of the changes in black consciousness (black pride, black is beautiful, black power, etc.) since the civil rights movement?"[38] However, they also note correlations between the age, denomination, and educational level of clergy and their inclusion of Black consciousness material. The most significant difference was between denominations—for example, Lincoln and Mamiya noted that Methodist clergy showed a slightly higher positive response than Baptist clergy (72.5 percent versus 64.2 percent); however Pentecostals were significantly less positive in their responses (46.2 percent).[39]

Lincoln and Mamiya surveyed preachers across a range of historically Black denominations (including Baptist, Methodist, and Pentecostal), and thus their sample may not reflect the more recent preponderance of non-denominational charismatic movements within the African American community. In contrast, a third of my sample includes non-denominational churches, newer African American denominations, such as Full Gospel Baptist, and churches affiliated with mainline protestant denominations. My sample also represents clergy and sermon content twenty to thirty years after Lincoln and Mamiya's seminal work. In light of this, one can only begin to predict the differences that may be inherent in non-denominational churches, which often have roots in charismatic, evangelical traditions (often associated with Pentecostal denominations). However, even in noting the impact of the Civil Rights movement on the consciousness of Black preachers in the 1980s, Lincoln and Mamiya were careful to note that "this should not obscure the fact that an evangelical gospel largely unconcerned with racial matters still has a strong following among at least one-third of the pastors of the historic black denominations."[40]

Learning More and Less Than Black Churches Intended

Reviewing sermons and Sunday school curricula cannot tell us everything that is shaping the spiritual lives of young African American Christians. However, these educational resources, in conjunction with our interviews with youth, provide an important starting point for further exploration of the spiritual lives of Black youth and for the ways that African American churches are currently influencing (positively or negatively) their lived realities. In truth, the majority of African American Christian youth are exhibiting the faith that is being modeled and presented to them. Their faith most closely reflects the faith of the adults around them. In light of this, our exploration of the curricula of Black Churches reminds us that African American youth are not simply experiencing a spirituality that does not adequately address every arena of their lives, but they are being taught that their faith should *only* address their personal or spiritual lives. While this is the current reality, Black Churches do not have to teach this to young people (and I will point to ways that this can be corrected). The remainder of this text will further develop this conversation—offering complexity to the data presented here. However, it is important to sum-marize here the contours of fragmentation observed in these educational resources.

Personal Theology: Recipe for Fragmentation

Across the curricula and sermons, a theology focused on the personal and interpersonal prevails. These trends persist in spite of and in the face of reviewing curricula targeted toward a range of African American denominations. The trends also persist inspite of intentionally selecting sermons from both popular ministers and from voices who heretofore had been overlooked because of gender, sexual orientation, or the rela-tively small number of African Americans in their denomination. The theological and practical themes of the UMI curricula focus on personal and interpersonal issues—emphasizing the ways that God cares for individuals and calls humans to remain faithful. However, the curricula do not emphasize engagement in communal and social justice issues (practically or theologically). Similarly, the sermons covered a variety of theological and practical themes, but also tended to emphasize personal, interpersonal, and religious themes over and above communal and soci-etal issues. While the sermons tended to be more theologically complex than the UMI curricula (offering a wider variety of theological themes and subthemes), the curricula offered more examples of practical com-munal issues than the sermon sample. This skewing toward the personal and religious indicates a tendency to limit the understanding of what is important theologically, and underscores fragmentation. In other words, if youth take to heart the core theological themes of this sample of cur-ricula and sermons, it is not surprising that their understandings of how theology connects with larger societal and communal issues is limited. In truth, the youth interviews are direct reflections of the limited range of issues addressed in the curricula—and the disconnection between faith and justice is part of the theology they are receiving.

Understandings of God: God Acts in Many and Varied Ways

Similar to the variety of practical themes presented in the sermons and curricula, these resources offer myriad examples of how God acts and relates to humanity and the world. Both the curricula and sermons offer a strong emphasis on scripture, and as a result there is a wealth of biblical metaphors and descriptions of God. God's action is not limited to any one arena in the scriptural texts; however, the exegesis of the scriptures and the connections between how God is acting in scripture and in the lives of contemporary humans is not a direct one. Holding the scriptures and resources together, God is active in the lives of individuals and communities. And given the heavy incorporation of Hebrew Bible texts, God is described as acting in and through nations and governments. However, the curricula and sermons noted above did not equally emphasize the diversity of God's actions. Instead, God was described as primarily involved in the lives of individual persons—calling, correcting, transforming, and using individual people. Thus, the understandings of God presented are complex—drawing upon the complicated resources of scripture *and* skewed toward the personal in the applications. In other words, the sermons and curricula offer youth examples and images of a very active and demanding God who works in many ways and areas. However, the youth in many cases will have to interpret the scriptures for themselves in order to apply or see practical examples of how God can move in arenas beyond the personal or communal.[41]

Change and Actions Called For: Exercise Your Faith and Think about Acting

In general, one assumes that educational resources implicitly and explicitly connect with and elicit some type of human action and responses. However, in the UMI curricula, I found that the concept of change in action or behavior was absent. The exception to this was in calling for religious and reflective action. Likewise, the responses called for in the sermons were also religious. The sermons and curricula called people to trust God and to better connect with God. The few sermons that called for practical changes only called for individual growth. A small minority of the lessons encouraged youth to act in their communities. However, across these resources, for the most part the religious education resources and sermons are not pushing for active responses to the lessons beyond individual religious growth. If this sample is any indication of the trends in the larger African American church community, then it shows a definite lack of emphasis on a spirituality that balances or integrates both personal, individual development with communal and societal action. In other words, one should not be surprised when young people do not connect their understanding of faith with work in their communities or for justice, when the core of the religious education does not offer this model either.

View of Adolescents: Youth as Active Agents of Change or Youth as Problems

One of the major factors in empowering youth and ameliorating fragmentation among adolescent spiritually is connected with the ways that youth are encouraged to act (their agency) and to see themselves (their identity). For example, it would be easier for youth to imagine God calling them to work to affect change in the political arena, if youth were invited, encouraged, and offered role models of young people working in public and political arenas (participating in protests or acts of civil disobedience, starting campaigns, raising funds, making phone calls for a local candidate, etc.). The UMI lessons include many positive portrayals of youth as actively involved and working. Over 40 percent of the lessons portray youth as capable and taking positive action. However, the sermons are in direct contrast with the primarily positive portrayal of youth in the Sunday school lessons. For the most part, the sermons do not discuss adolescents at all; and when discussions of children as parts of families are included, the sermons present children and youth among the many things that adults have to struggle with or that the adults are constantly praying to God to help them with.

Looking collectively at the educational resources, we see that within the African American church's educational traditions youth are potentially receiving mixed messages—depending on the setting. While it is encouraging for youth to see and receive positive feedback about who they are in age-appropriate Sunday school classes, it undermines this work if in the primarily adult spaces, youth are only seen negatively, as passive or reluctant to act in ways that benefit themselves and their community. This limited agency attributed to the youth in sermons is problematic and can potentially lead to negative or limited conceptions of what youth are capable of accomplishing in their communities. And it can also hasten the alienation that many predict between adult religion and adolescents.

Race and Ethnicity: Do We Need to Talk about Race in Black Sermons for Black People?

Similar to the images and perceptions of youth, the educational curricula send mixed and insufficient messages about race, ethnicity, and racism. Building upon Evelyn Parker's earlier findings that youth did not talk about race or racism in the same ways as they discussed their relationships and understandings of God, I looked at the discussions of race and ethnicity to ascertain what models of discussing race and racism youth were receiving in the educational resources of African American churches. The majority of the sermons did not include a discussion of race, ethnicity, or racism. Only two of the sermons mentioned race and ethnicity. While race and ethnicity are evidenced in some of the style and structure of the sermons, in looking solely at the content of the sermons, youth find minimal emphasis on race or ethnicity. In this way, one can presume that discussing race or ethnicity in sermons is either not done, not acceptable, or not important. On the other hand, this lack of discussions of race not only points to the possibility of sundering issues of race and racism from religion (as presented in sermons), but it also leaves youth to develop methods for thinking and talking about race, ethnicity, and racism outside of the religious arena.

Even as the Sunday school curricula offer more inclusion of race and ethnicity because of the inclusion of Black imagery and historical figures in the lesson materials, only 16 percent of the subsample included an explicit discussion of race, racism, or ethnicity. Unlike the sermons, where ethnicity and race were only mentioned in passing or in descriptions of the community, the lessons included African American history and accounts of dealing with racism in the media and publishing, and they called youth to reflect on how racism in aspects of the media was still prevalent. Therefore, the educational resources do not discuss race or racism the majority of the time. However, it appears that the UMI curricula are doing a better job of offering youth models of discussing race, racism, and ethnicity in relationships to their faith.

Evidence of Fragmentation?

In this chapter, I briefly analyzed a sample of two educational resources within African American churches: sermons and Sunday school curricula. While neither sample is large enough to offer statistically significant results or to predict trends for the entire African American Christian religious community, the samples give us a snapshot of some trends within educational resources in some Black churches.

The combined sermon and curriculum data demonstrate that, among this sample, African American churches are offering youth limited theological and practical diversity, in that there is an overwhelming silence with regards to communal and societal issues and understandings of how God currently is involved in these areas. While the inclusion of such issues does not in and of itself signal an integrated spirituality, the exclusion of such emphasis raises several flags. Similarly, the resources do not encourage youth to respond in diverse manners or arenas; again the primary emphasis is on the spiritual and the personal.

The emphasis on the religious and personal/interpersonal in terms of explicit content, coupled with inconsistent images of African American youth and a lack of engagement of race and ethnicity (let alone tough social justice issues such as racism) pushes me to believe that the fragmented spirituality of African American youth is not simply a symptom of adolescent development or choice, but may be a byproduct of the educational resources presented in African American churches.

2

Fragmentation in Context

PSYCHOLOGICAL AND SOCIOLOGICAL
DIMENSIONS OF FRAGMENTATION

FRAGMENTATION IN RELIGIOUS identity is not limited to African American adolescents. Our human reality (even before postmodernity) is one of multiple influences and identities, where we must operate in an increasing array of spheres and roles. It is a reality where simple identities based on "what we do" or "who we marry" are not sufficiently stable or consistent; neither are they constitutive of all that we understand about ourselves. Reflecting on fragmented spirituality or the diverse aspects of our lives and the places where we expect our spirituality to function pushes us to consider why or how fragmentation, in general, is problematic and how it specifically effects the lives of African American youth.

In this chapter, we explore the larger US context in which African American youth spirituality is shaped. As noted in the previous chapter, the theology of churches is only part of what influences spiritual development, but in addition to the multiple sources of belief, young people are born into societies and systems that are already structured to pull or push them in particular ways. Spirituality then, by definition, should offer openness to the holding together of the complexities of their lives and not simply a condemnation of the diversity. What is problematic is not that youth or adults experience fragmentation, but rather the problem emerges when they are unable to faithfully navigate the fragments of their lives. Hence, I review the societal influences on fragmentation. I also begin to articulate how increasingly there are resources and theories that underscore the move beyond one essentialized core or even beyond an almost schizophrenic dance between each part of our lives and identities toward models of relational selves and identities as crucial to navigating a plural world.

Psychological Dimensions of Fragmentation and Fragmented Spirituality

Fragmentation in relationship to spirituality, identity, and selfhood is evidenced in early psychology of religion texts. Looking at the early twentieth century writings of William James and W. E. B. Du Bois, there are discussions of many elements of fragmentation or a division within what these scholars refer to as the *soul*. For example, William James in his lectures on the *Varieties of Religious Experience* outlined the religion of the "healthy-minded," the "sick soul," and the *"divided self."*[1] James argued that the sick soul, also characterized as twice-born, had a psychological basis of "certain discordancy or heterogeneity ... an incompletely unified moral and intellectual constitution."[2] James saw the sick soul as an example of the *divided self* in that there was a split between the natural and the spiritual lives in the sick-soul temperament. James gave examples of this divided self in religious terms and figures such as St. Paul when he wrote, "What I would, that do I not; but what I hate, that do I."[3] James saw the divided self as a type of self-loathing or inability to get one's passions and intellect in line, but he also argued that the divided self could undergo a process of unification.[4]

Emphasizing more social psychological dimensions, in *Souls of Black Folks*, Du Bois traced the evolution of Negro religion in America and named two distinctive social psychological and religious temperaments. He articulated this as a dichotomy between the slave's religion and the freedman's religion, or later as the southern and the northern Negro's religion.[5] For Du Bois, the slave's religion was a Christianity of submission and resignation, which suited the inner struggles of slaves and pointed toward otherworldly freedom. On the other hand, Du Bois characterized the freedman's religion as a darker, radical, more intense religion with a note of revenge.[6]

Du Bois describes the northern radical and southern compromising temperaments as responses to the social conditions in America and as responses to the Negro's social psychological experience of "double consciousness":

It is a peculiar sensation, this double-consciousness, this sense of always looking at one's self through the eyes of others, of measuring one's soul by the tape of a world that looks on in amused contempt and pity. One ever feels his two-ness,—an American, a Negro; two souls, two thoughts, two unreconciled strivings; two warring ideals in one dark body, whose dogged strength alone keeps it from being torn asunder.[7]

Discussing the psychological and religious implications of the double consciousness and living the double life, Du Bois writes, "Such a double life, with double thoughts, double duties, and double social classes, must give rise to double words and double ideals, and tempt the mind to pretense or to revolt, to hypocrisy or to radicalism."[8]

Du Bois's concept of double consciousness is informative in thinking about fragmentation in general, for he illuminates how fragmentation permeates from and creates a duality in terms of not only identity (how African Americans saw themselves), but also in terms of loyalties and actions. His example of fragmented consciousness explores the way that African Americans attempted to make sense of and hold together difficult and conflicting visions of the Black self in light of their experiences of injustice and thwarted efforts. My understanding of adolescent spiritual fragmentation also notes the struggles of Black youth to hold together dueling notions of their selfhood, and dueling understandings of God. Youth are often in a subconscious struggle to make sense of (or not think about) the ways that what they *believe* about God is not fully addressing the situations they find themselves in. Although I would not describe any of the youth interviewed as struggling in the negative extremes that Du Bois and James describe,[9] Du Bois's concept of double consciousness and the resultant variations in religious responses pose the question of whether or how fragmentation among African American adolescents also exhibits a response to and a critique of the world around them.

While the language employed by James as well as categorizations regarding religious temperaments have been drastically expanded and challenged, it is helpful to note that questions regarding the interconnection between our selves/souls and the world around us have abounded for generations. Even as the youth interviewed do not demonstrate any type of psychopathology (as James might espouse in discussing the sick soul or divided self) or any tendency toward extreme hypocrisy or radicalism (as Du Bois describes the extreme religious responses of double consciousness), their interviews highlight other examples of fragmentation. Their interviews offer examples of the ways that what they believe *should be* true about the world does not fit nicely with what they experience in the world. In other words, in most cases their interviews demonstrate a gap between their ideals and their experiences.[10] For example, Marissa experienced an incongruity between her understanding of how people should come together and affirm one another and her experience of teacher bias and reticence to connect with students of color. Also looking specifically at her religious life, Marissa was uncertain about identifying herself as a Christian or not as a Christian because she had different standards. Actually, she had higher standards than her church. For Marissa, being a Christian meant more than merely attending church. Similarly, Dana's experience of her community as a place where each person just individually worked on themselves did not mesh with her conviction that people should come together to make a difference about specific concerns. Like Marissa, Dana experiences a conflict in how she sees herself—based on her inner convictions and based on the expectations of her community members (which may also include expectations of her parents, teachers, and society to strive toward personal middle-class success).

Beyond the interview data, recent experiences of youth in the news also remind us of the continued significance of the tensions Du Bois and James described at the beginning of the twentieth century. For example, Du Bois opens the *Souls of Black Folks* with an oft-quoted question of "What does it feel like to be a problem?" Du Bois is reflecting on the tentativeness with which European Americans approached him as a Black person in mostly white spaces, and as they danced around the direct questions about his experiences of being of African descent in the United States. Over the last century, young African Americans are still confronted with the tentative exchanges of well-meaning friends and teachers of different cultures. They are also constantly struggling to make sense of popular narratives regarding who Black youth are and media depictions that do not allow Black youth to simply be *children* or even human. Later we explore more fully the spiritual struggles in responding to violence, but this tension (described by Du Bois) still resonates today, as Black youth not only must address multiple arenas, but also have to wear masks that never fully afford them opportunities to be, without addressing the questions of what it feels like to grow up in a society that views them immediately as problems, thugs, or criminals.

Fragmentation and Identity Development

While Du Bois's understanding of double consciousness demonstrates a historical precursor to fragmented spirituality, an exploration of double consciousness points to and undergirds the potential for fragmentation in terms of selfhood, identity, and even loyalties and actions among African American youth. Fragmentation also can be considered a characteristic feature of adolescent psychological and social development in general. Or, in more positive terms, adolescent development is characterized by the striving for integration and wholeness, related to one's identity, purpose, and relationships. Du Bois's concept of double consciousness points to the tension between the social forces in African American lives and the efforts of African Americans to hold together the different worlds in which they live. However, what Du Bois and James describe is somewhat limited in light of the experiences of contemporary adolescents. In particular, Du Bois's concept of double consciousness only explores two spheres of influence and critique for the *male* negro. Du Bois's discussion focuses on Cartesian binaries/dualisms, which are representative of modernity (or modernist perspectives). For Du Bois in particular, double consciousness is a result of a social pathology and institutional racism, which does not allow for wholeness. While acknowledging the reality of living in a racist society, Du Bois never affirms the positive function and developmental characteristics that allow African Americans to hold together these gazes and consciousness. He does not affirm the ways that most would benefit by learning to process or hold together multiple perspectives (instead of simply being one unified essence from the beginning).

Many Womanist scholars have expanded the idea of double consciousness to include the influences and expectations based on gender and class as well—pointing toward a complicated, multilayered consciousness that the concept of *double* only begins to elucidate. Similarly, developmental theorists recognize a tension between the multiple forces in individuals' lives and the efforts to hold together diverse influences. Both social and psychological theorists recognize a dynamic movement between the existential reality of multiple forces and the existential longing for integration. Their descriptions and explanations vary, but, taken together, they illuminate the nature of fragmentation and the potential of a more integrated spirituality.

According to Erik Erikson's seminal theories on identity, at the heart of human development in general and adolescence in particular is the crisis of identity versus role confusion. Erikson defines identity as the ideal, which can be undercut if multiple social forces produce role confusion. Drawing on the work of Erikson, faith developmental theorist James Fowler describes identity as

> an accrued awareness of oneself that maintains continuity with one's past meanings to others and to oneself [and] that integrates the images of oneself given by significant others with one's own inner feelings of who one is and of what one can do, all in such a way as to enable one to anticipate the future without undue anxiety about "losing" oneself. Identity, thought of in this way, is by no means a fully conscious matter. But when it is present it gives rise to a feeling of inner firmness or of "being together" as a self. It communicates to others a sense of personal unity or integration.[11]

Accordingly, the catalyst for this crisis of identity versus role confusion is the adolescent's newfound capacity for mutual interpersonal perspective taking.[12] Adolescents recognize and incorporate into their being and identity the perspectives of others (be they true or imagined perspectives); in turn adolescents become susceptible to the "tyranny of they."[13] In this tyranny of "they," adolescents can become so caught up in the expectations of their significant others that they feel trapped, become incapable of choosing which voices will influence them, or struggle to filter out the unreasonable expectations of others. James W. Fowler summarizes this new capacity for perspective taking in the couplet, "I see you seeing me, I see the me I think you see."[14]

From the perspective of African American adolescents, this "tyranny of they" takes on another dimension; in addition to being cognizant of the opinions of one's peers, teachers or parents, African American teens also become cognizant of the communal and societal stereotypes and expectations associated with being a Black person. At this point, Black teens struggle to come to terms with what they see others believing and thinking about them—not personally but as a part of a group. Further emphasizing this point, educator Janie Ward expands the notion of the crisis of identity versus role confusion to include a crisis of both identity and ideology. Ward points to the fact that identity development involves more than just coming to know one's self: it is intricately interwoven with learning to know what one believes about one's self in an effort to reject what others believe about one:

> Identity (knowing who you are) and ideology (knowing what you believe) are critical to developmental processes in adolescence. Teenagers are consumed with these issues. For Black youth, moving beyond an internalization of racial subservience to racial pride begins first with a conscious confrontation with one's racial identity. Resolution of this so-called identity crisis of youth requires that all teenagers proclaim "I am not" as the first step to defining what "I am." At the threshold stage of the identity process, black teenagers . . ., who are all too familiar with the demeaning stereotypes held about [them] and [their] racial group, must add, "I am not what you believe black people to be, *and I am black.*"[15]

Fowler's recapitulation of Erikson's identity development theory and Janie Ward's discussion of the added dimensions of the identity crisis of African American youth point to the ways that identity development is connected with one's ability to *integrate*, and not fragment, one's myriad life experiences, the opinions of others, and one's self-understanding. This focus on integration as the goal of identity development has lead many theorists to misinterpret Erikson's work—arguing that he is calling for a much "firmer" or fixed sense of self than is possible. However, Fowler notes that the process of identity development and integration is not a conscious process, for the most part, rather it empowers adolescents to anticipate and plan for future events, as well as communicate to others a sense of integration. In this way, the process of identity formation, particularly as connected with one's spirituality and faith, is a process of integration, or at least attempting to hold multiple and often-competing pieces and voices together. Thus at many points in the process, if the youth "fails" to integrate or make sense of various pieces and experiences unresolved anxiety around the myriad opinions or experiences of their lives, then fragmentation is possible.

Although there remains much discussion of identity formation and how one defines *identity*, let alone achieves a sense of identity, one aspect that most theorists can agree on is that the resolution of this crisis in adolescence does *not* result in a coherent and unchanging identity for all time. Instead it requires ongoing integration and processing:

Contrary to popular misinterpretations of [Erikson's] identity development theory, identity is not the culmination of a key event or a
series of events, although key events can play an important role in
the larger process. In fact, it is not the culmination of anything. It is
rather, the lived experience of ongoing process—the process of *inte-*
grating successes, failures, routines, habits, rituals, novelties, thrills,
threats, violations, gratifications, and frustrations into a coherent
and evolving interpretation of who we are. *Identity is the embodiment*
of self-understanding. We are who we understand ourselves to be, as
that understanding is shaped and lived out in everyday experience.[16]

In the quote above, educational theorist Michael Nakkula attempts to
summarize the ambiguous and process-oriented nature of identity and
identity formation. He reiterates that identity formation is not something
that adolescents work out once and for all. Nakkula points us back to some
of Erikson's earliest articulations of the psychological and social dimensions of identity formation, where he writes,

The process [of identity formation] is always changing and developing: at its best it is a process of increasing individuation and it
becomes ever more inclusive as the individual grows aware of a wid-
ening circle of others significant to him . . . identity is never "established" as an "achievement" in the form of a personality armor, or
of anything static and unchangeable.[17]

Therefore, in looking at Fowler, Nakkula, and Erikson, we see that adolescent identity formation entails an ongoing, never-static process of integration and moving toward an inner sense of "firmness."

However, in noting that the process is never "established" or never
fully realized, what then does fragmentation of identity look like, or is it
problematic? And what are the implications for spirituality and formation?
Fragmentation of identity or an inability to integrate one's identity can
result in undue anxiety about one's future, but in most cases it results in
a limitation to draw upon the wealth of resources available. For example,
in the above interviews, as well as in the earlier data from Evelyn Parker,
fragmentation or fractured spirituality can be highly functional; yet it
is not fully adequate. More specifically, fragmentation can result in students who are unable to see within themselves and their communities the
resources to address the issues of concern to them and by extension to

fully develop as they work through those concerns. Therefore the move to more integrated identities and spiritualities does not arise simply out of an idealist understanding of congruence and integrity or from a naïve belief that knowing and doing always align. Rather, the problematic side of fragmented spirituality and identities is a functional one—in which fragmentation impedes the abilities of young people (and adults) from confidently navigating the world around them or seeing their understandings of self, God, and others as working together to help them address their concerns.

There are several additional dimensions to the questions regarding fragmentation within youth identity. For example, psychologist and priest David Gortner's work on the *Varieties of Personal Theology* among American young adults helps expand the conversation, by looking beyond the perennial question of "who am I?" to explore questions of "where am I?" or "what is this place that I find myself in?" Just as *who am I?* is the essential question in identity development, questions about place and the ground of our being are the orienting questions for constructing personal theologies.[18] Gortner's understanding of *personal theology* as "the beliefs and values contributing to how [people] made sense of the world, humanity, and life"[19] becomes a helpful framework in exploring the ways that young people hold together (or struggle to hold together) their beliefs and actions across the diverse arenas that they are called to operate in. In particular, Gortner's framework is helpful in considering how African American youth make sense of the world they are forced to inhabit, which does not fully embrace their humanity or see them as fully capable of working for change in it.

My discussion of fragmented spirituality is also challenged by Gortner's discussion of personal theologies, in part because unlike many modernist theorists, he refuses to place value on the diverse ways that youth approach and understand the world around them. Instead, he outlines the array of responses that youth and young adults hold regarding

- the overall quality and nature of the world as a place of existence (worldview);
- a human being's place and purpose vis-à-vis the world (life purpose);
- causes and meanings behind traumatic and tragic life events (theodicy); and
- human qualities and values most constitutive of (or most contrary to) a good life (ultimate values).[20]

Gortner's work pushes beyond simple bipolar, either-or constructs to push toward multiple variations in the ways that young adults make sense of the world around them. For example, with regards to theodicy, he argues that youth and young adults hold at least three perspectives; these included a deterministic view of tragic events (such as God has a plan for all things), a humanistic view (such as people cause most tragedies), and a randomistic view (things happen for unknown reasons). This is significant to our discussion in chapter 4, regarding the many ways that African American youth are attempting to makes sense of violence and tragedy in their lives—pushing them beyond simply blaming or questioning God or divorcing God from any events. To be sure, I argue that African American youth evidence more diversity of theodicies than these three and are simply in need of spaces to share these perspectives.

Populated and Plural Selves

Several scholars have expanded Erikson's discussion of identity and the impact of multiple social forces on identity formation in recent decades. Of particular interest are the discussions of populated and plural selves, which recognize the possibility that people can hold diverse forces together without losing the complexity and multiplicity that these forces bear. People can hold together plural selves in an integrated fashion. Therefore, while the challenge arising in postmodernity results from attentiveness (even if not emergence) to multiple spheres of influence and authority, psychologists offer more optimism about one's ability to function in this kind of world.

Erikson had his own ways of embracing such complexity, largely by making connections between the individual's life and the communities and contexts in which the individual lives. Erikson argued, for example, that "in discussing identity . . . we cannot separate personal growth and communal change, nor can we separate . . . the identity crisis in individual life and contemporary crises in historical development because the two help to define each other and are truly relative to each other."[21] He thus alluded to the myriad ways that communal and societal changes throughout history also affect the ways that adolescents come to understand and form their identities. Much recent scholarship has attempted to add further complexity to these ideas. Both empirical and theoretical research have expanded Erikson's claims as people seek to address issues of postmodernity and the increased voices and spheres of influence that people now face.

Kenneth Gergen, for example, describes the interconnection of technological advancement and a culture of saturation. His work *The Saturated Self* outlines the evolution of the self from a romantic to modern, and then to a postmodern or saturated self.[22] Each of these understandings of the self reflects and attends to the paralleling changes in society at that historical point. Gergen's understanding of the romanticist view is that it saw the core of the human as "his" soul, as driven by passions and genius; this contrasted with the modernist view of the self that saw the essence of man as rationality.[23] In his description of these perspectives on the self in history, he notes that the idea of the autonomous self was an invention of the eighteenth century and further points to the idea that psychology has never been value free.[24] In reviewing the prevalence of modernist theories of the self, he notes that psychology created norms and pathologies based on the assumption that a person should be autonomous and coherent. In moving toward a postmodern understanding of the self, Gergen argues that humans are experiencing a "populating of the self." Being exposed to an enormous range or saturation of information, relationships, and even feelings leads humans to "the acquisition of multiple and disparate potentials for being."[25] However, this is not all bad news. Gergen argued that the loss of what was assumed to be the "true self" could set the stage for "moving beyond the individualist tradition" and that it would empower humans to realize the tremendous significance of relationships for their lives.[26] However, Gergen, while still holding out hope of relational selves, notes that he underestimated the alternative that included "the fusion of people not with one another, but with material."[27] Gergen was unprepared for the ways that the distinctions between humans and machines would become lessened and the ways that technology would become more fused with human functions.[28]

Gergen further argues that "as social saturation adds incrementally to the population of self, each impulse toward well-formed identity is cast into increasing doubt; each is found absurd, shallow, limited, or flawed by the onlooking audience of the interior."[29] The more extreme, or negative effect of social saturation is *multiphrenia*, or "the splitting of the individual into a multiplicity of self-investments," which has the potential to lead to a *Vertigo of the Valued*. This occurs because the more freedoms one has, the more responsibilities one has; and thus, we have to recognize that with each new relationship there are requirements to maintain that relationship and a larger sense of competing expectations. *Mulitphrenia* also has the potential to expand our sense of inadequacy—manifest in the "seeping of self-doubt into every day consciousness ... a subtle feeling of inadequacy that smothers one's activities with an uneasy sense of impending emptiness," in that each value stands in conflict with others (duty vs. spontaneity, justice vs. love, etc.)—making us question whether we are or can ever be on the side of right.[30] Increasingly, the norm becomes that "the relatively coherent and unified sense of self inherent in a traditional culture gives way to manifold and competing potentials."[31]

In addition to a primarily psychological discussion of identity in postmodern adolescent development, practical theologians such as Friedrich Schweitzer and Kenda Creasy Dean offer practical theological reflections on the intersection of adolescent identity formation, postmodern society, and Christian ministry. Similar to Gergen's "populated self," Schweitzer describes postmodern persons as "plural selves." Dean, summarizing Gergen and other understandings of the plural self, writes that "the plural self is the result of chameleon adaptations to the multiple roles demanded by post-modern culture. The plural self seeks infinite flexibility, not integration, and thereby sacrifices 'integrity' for a widened repertoire of potential selves, and the agility to shift between them."[32] While I agree that there is a potentially problematic side to the experiences of plural selves or identities in youth, I do not agree with Dean's understanding that the problem lies in the inability to "distinguish between 'selves' and 'social roles.'" She argues that there is a "God-given identity as *homo religiosus*" that goes beyond social roles and serves as a means of critiquing cultural scripts and expectations of youth.[33] However, I have difficulty with the notion of *homo religiosus* as the normative identity of all humanity or even Christians. Those who have not fully attended to the cultural and embodied realities of human experience often espouse this theological perspective. Often, this understanding of a "God-given identity" does not adequately attend to other parts of our "God-given identities," such as the communities and cultures we inhabit, and even one's race and gender. While each of these are arguably social constructions, they also speak to the particular ways that humans represent the diversity and complexity of the image of God, and how a call for our overarching identity as *homo religiosus* fails to attend to the bias that becomes part of any attempt to define who and what makes us religious or even "normal."

Dean, however, argues that notions of the plural self are not incompatible with Christianity, in that "the Christian view of the self is not unitary in any way; Christian identity is irreducibly relational, involving the persons of the Trinity as well as the individual and the individual's community identifications."[34]

In other words, while there is potential for vertigo, multiplicity and dis-ease as part of the contemporary influences on one's identity, *plurality does not necessarily equal fragmentation*. Improperly integrated diversity and multiplicity of roles, identities, and opinions can, however, lead to fragmentation. The youth in my interview sample did not demonstrate the extreme or drastic signs of plural identities. They were all still trying to figure out what they believed about themselves, about their communities of origins, and about the world around them. Examples from the interviews point to the way that youth are experiencing an incongruity between these competing visions. Some youth find it problematic, while others have developed an understanding that "this is just as it should be."[35] In particular, the youth demonstrated a relative level of normalcy and acceptance of the myriad social circles they were participating in.[36] One telling difference was that many youth were also still processing recent experiences of being exposed to a different community (as they were away at a summer program) and were attempting to integrate the expanded social and religious worldviews and expectations they were experiencing. The young people speak candidly of these events, such as Marissa questioning if she is Christian now, based on an encounter with how others define Christianity. Similarly, another young woman wondered if her new friends and mentors were saying that she was not a good Christian if she did not fight against racism or other injustices.

Their narratives, in conjunction with theories of plural selves, remind us that what is needed is not to re-create a world where youth are not exposed to multiple ideas and values, but to learn with youth how they can make sense of and hold onto these sometimes competing voices and values for themselves.

Embracing the Communal and Relational Selves

One way of helping youth counter the negativity and extremes of plurality lies in embracing another way of thinking about the self (and our identities and actions). One of the major challenges to the modernist theory of the individual and autonomous self was reconceiving the self as both communal and relational. Theologian Dwight Hopkins helpfully summarizes this challenge as he explored "what it means to be a human being, singularly and in community."[37] Hopkins draws upon African understandings of *self/selves* that give priority to collectivity. With Nigerian scholar Ifeanyi

A. Menkiti, Hopkins argues that one "African view of [the human being] denies that persons can be defined by focusing on this or that physical or psychological characteristic of the lone individual. Rather, [the human being] is defined by reference to the environing community."[38] This emphasis on the communal nature of human beings also expands upon works like Archie Smith's *Relational Self* to better articulate how humans are both self (individual) and selves (communal or collective selves). The tension between self and selves is one that Hopkins signals in the choice of "self/selves" as a linguistic tool that consistently reminds us that we cannot conceive of humans without considering both aspects as well as attending to a communal "common good" and individual agency within communities. In other words, the individual self does not disappear, but it is balanced with a communal emphasis. As Womanist and feminists theorists also remind us, this balance is essential so that attention to the communal does not override the care and wellbeing of any individuals (particularly the oppressed of a given community).

For Hopkins, no selves are viable independent of one another.[39] Instead, "selves" include three interacting factors, according to Hopkins:

- each human being is dependent on other people for life and death, sustenance and joy, and survival and liberation;
- "the ultimate worth of the individual derives from transcendent legacies already bequeathed ... prior to his/her arrival on earth"; and
- "the self's ontology evolves from a spiritual dimension."[40]

In other words, there is no self apart from pre-existing and conditional "we." Of course, individuals can push back against and critique the cultures and collective values and beliefs into which they are born, but it is not possible that any individual comes to exist apart from some inherited beliefs, values, and rituals in addition to the physiological matter required for an individual human to exist. Hopkins notes that even "the pioneering ideas of an individual self emerge from the material left by those who preceded or from the crises of communities." And it is only in communities that one's genius or value is affirmed.[41]

Gergen also expands on his earlier work, lamenting the potential ills of plural and multiple selves to offer a larger treatise on the *relational being*, which he argues goes far beyond notions of a discrete self and community. Instead, like Hopkins and African proverbs that predate his research, Gergen affirms that we learn about or move toward personal autonomy through relationships. In other words, we come to know ourselves in relationships; relationships do not subsume the self.[42]

Communal and relational selves, or relationships as constitutive of (and a common-sense part of) identity formation, is not a recent phenomena or theory. From early social-psychological works that focus on human interactions and perceptions in community to later studies on moral reasoning by Carol Gilligan and others, which found relationships to be essential to how some women made moral and ethical decisions, to an increased interest in African traditions and communities that counter Western philosophical and theological narratives about the self, there is a long discussion of the self being constituted by relationships.[43] However, a relational concept of the self still does not have strong traction in our understanding of the spiritual development of youth.[44]

To be certain, the ideal and even longed-for autonomous self still reigns supreme in much of our common discourse and language. Much of the language of human development and maturity still relies on creating autonomous selves. Many of the critiques of various generations of young people rely on their "failure to launch" or notions that they are not maturing or demonstrating their maturity in the ways that befit autonomous individuals, who only need one romantic relationship and job to define them after they become full-fledged individuals. The prospect of individuation in an insecure world is almost fantastical to many young people. When this is coupled with growing up in a world where basic life skills include "keep your hands where everyone can see them" because of the presumptions of Black criminality, then it becomes even less tenable that African American youth can embrace a notion of adulthood modeled on the mythologies of autonomous selves and American meritocracy.

So how does shifting from this assumption of an autonomous self toward a better emphasis on relational and communal selves help counter fragmented spirituality? The power of relational selves is in the reorientation of human development toward working for a *common good*. It also opens up a better understanding of connected selves—such that youth and adults can better see how not only each person is connected to another, but how different systems of persons and expectations are connected (either for good or ill). In terms of spirituality, as noted above, relational and communal selves give us a better understanding of the image of God, by helping us attend to the communal nature of God *and* God's people. Much of the Christian biblical witness recounts the call of God to communities of people, and most often individuals are called by God to support God's will for a particular community/people.[45]

In regards to human development, full maturity emerges as a relational being or in relationships. Individualism is the "pathology" or a sign of underdevelopment. The concept of relational selves also pushes us to embrace the work on positive youth development. Positive youth development theory not only asks what can we do to prevent youth from getting in trouble, instead it creates opportunities for youth to be full partners in the youth-community relationship and to contribute to these communities in meaningful ways now.

As we will discuss later, reconceptualizing the self as communal also connects with the counterapproaches and models youth can take to embrace a more integrated spirituality. For example, in discussing the role of youth as public theologians, we see that public theologians reflect the self/selves orientation by speaking with the voices of the community and working for a common, communal good.

Each of the theories of identity formation and the ever-evolving understanding of the self or selves in postmodernity outline some of the psychological and psychosocial contexts in which fragmented spirituality among African American youth emerges. Each of the theories illustrates the increasing potential for fragmentation of identity, ideology, and even action.[46] However, they also offer some insights for how to move forward. The increased theorizing about the self as relational and social also reminds us that in order to explore the context in which fragmented spirituality emerges, examples and changes in the "sociological" and religious contexts must also be explored.

Sociological Dimensions of Fragmentation and Fragmented Spirituality

The psychological dimensions of fragmentation only offer part of the context and influences on adolescent identity and spirituality. It is equally important to attend to the sociological dimensions of fragmentation and to look at fragmented spirituality through the lens of the sociology of religion.

Secularization and Privatization of Religion

Once religion is disestablished, it tends to become part of the "private sphere," and privatization is part of the story

> of American Religion. Yet religion, and certainly biblical
> religion, is concerned with the whole of life—with social,
> economic, and political matters as well as private and
> personal ones.
>
> —HABITS OF THE HEART[47]

Although the modernist prediction of secularization (or the decline of religion) throughout the world has been refuted, many sociologists of religion have noted that instead of complete secularization, a privatization of religion has taken place.[48] Such sociologists of religion argue that a privatization of religion has taken place in the ways that religious beliefs became subjective in the face of "alternative interpretations of life" and the way that institutional religion became largely de-politicized "as a result of a functional differentiation of society."[49] The idea of "differentiation" refers primarily to an understanding that in modernity sharp and rigid "segmentation of the various institutional domains" took place in such a way that each domain became functionally autonomous, self-defined, and governed by its internal norms.[50]

According to Jose Casanova, earlier sociologists argued that "traditional religious institutions were becoming increasingly irrelevant and marginal to the functioning of the modern world, and that modern religion itself was no longer to be found inside the churches."[51] In other words, religion in a modern and postmodern world arguably comes under the primary domain of the self. In *Invisible Religion*, Thomas Luckmann further argued that the most prevalent emerging "invisible religion" of modernity was self-expression and self-realization.[52]

Noting the connections between individual and institutional role differentiation and privatization, sociologist of religion Jose Casanova argues that "since the individual's social existence becomes a series of unrelated performances of anonymous specialized social roles, institutional segmentation reproduces itself as segmentation within the individual's consciousness."[53] This segmentation of the individual's consciousness and performances in turn become problematic in the face of any attempt at "meaningful integration of specifically religious and nonreligious performances and norms with their respective jurisdictional claims."[54] Among sociologists there is a parallel to the above discussion of the increasing plurality of the self. Sociologists are arguing that integration or holding together the competing norms and expectations across different spheres becomes increasingly difficult. However, in addition to the psychosocial understanding of this issue, sociologists demonstrate the ways that the structures of the modern world thrive off the fact that the struggle for integration has become a "strictly personal affair." Casanova, building on Luckmann and Durkheim, writes,

> The primary "public" institutions (state, economy) no longer need or are interested in maintaining a sacred cosmos or a public religious worldview.... Individuals are on their own in their private efforts to patch together the fragments into a subjectively meaningful whole. Whether the individuals themselves are able to integrate these segmented performances into "a system of subjective significance" is not a relevant question for the dominant economic and political institutions—so long as it does not affect their efficient functioning adversely.[55]

Theories of the privatization of religion, based on subjectivity and role differentiation, factor heavily in the discussion of fragmented spirituality. These theories point to ways that many segments of modern society expected and fostered religions, particularly institutions and communities, to remain separate from and not to affect political and systemic change. In other words, a close inspection of the theories of privatization of religion highlights, on a societal level, a "requirement" of fragmented spirituality. Under the rubric of privatization and differentiation, non-subjective or public religious understandings and convictions become suspect, particularly expectations that God might influence or inspire individuals to influence spheres beyond the private or explicitly religious realms.

However, Casanova's larger work, along with many others, demonstrates that even against the backdrop of theories of privatization, there are still many examples of "public religions" or ways that religion becomes public in modern and postmodern times. Offering case studies of five "public religions" around the globe, he concludes by articulating a theory of *deprivatization* of religion. In other words, his work attempts to debunk, or at least complicate, the secularization theory's emphasis on the privatization of religion as well. Casanova, although hesitant about the usage of the word *deprivatization*, asserts that the term is satisfactory.

> [*Deprivatization* is satisfactory] as long as the term maintains its polemical value, that is, as long as it is not widely recognized that religions in the modern world are free to enter or not enter the

public sphere, to maintain more privativistic or more communal and public identities. Privatization and deprivatization are, therefore, historical options for religions in the modern world. Some religions will be induced … to remain basically private religions of individual salvation. Certain cultural traditions, religious doctrinal principles, and historical circumstances, by contrast, will induce other religions to enter, at least occasionally, the public sphere.[56]

Here, Casanova reiterates that he is not pointing to a simple choice or decision of religious organizations or institutions to choose to be public or private, but in looking at the cultural, political, and traditional influences, we can see throughout history how some groups are induced to respond in particular ways. Casanova asserts that most of the moves to public or private religious involvement are temporary and only in response to larger questions. He further reminds us that the deprivatization of religion does not impose a return of religion or the church to its "state-related" model. But it pushes us to look at the ways that churches, as institutions, and sometimes as individuals begin to relate in a different type of modern/postmodern public sphere, where questions of the common good and universal human rights are discussed (and not simply where one religious institution imposes its beliefs on the society as a whole).

Casanova's descriptive project illustrates the ways that particular religious communities have become public, without making normative claims as to how or whether religion should be more public. However, historian George Toulouse asserts that there are four distinctive ways that American Christianity and public life relate. Toulouse's project moves beyond description and begins to advocate for the model of a public church.[57] Although Casanova offers illustrations that counter an idea that everything within the larger societal context promotes or perpetuates religious and spiritual fragmentation, his illustrations still leave questions about the possibility of integration. His work also demonstrates the need for a fuller analysis of agency in the process of communal or individual integration of competing expectations and ways of being in differentiated spheres.

American Religion: American Individualism

Connected with discussions of privatization of religion in modern (and postmodern) periods is the concept of individualism, particularly American individualism. American individualism helps us explore the larger sociological context in which fragmentation occurs, in that American individualism goes hand in hand with the tendencies of postmodern youth to practice and express religious convictions that are primarily concerned with individual and personal themes.

Many scholars argue that American individualism, which develops alongside the Enlightenment and Great Awakening, holds equal weight in shaping the contours of American religious life.[58] In other words, American Christianity is not simply a revivalist Christianity, but it is also determined by individualism (and as noted above, it is a love affair with the ideal of an autonomous, self-determining self). Robert Bellah, Richard Madsen, William Sullivan, Ann Swidler, and Steven Tipton in their now-classic exploration of individualism in America point to the ways that individualism interconnects not only with public life, but also with the religious experiences and practices of Americans. As they explore the interconnections between religion and individualism, *Habits of the Heart* describes the narrative of the now-infamous "Sheila," who named her religion after herself:

> I believe in God. I'm not a religious fanatic. I can't remember the last time I went to church. My faith has carried me a long way. It's Sheilaism. Just my own little voice.... It's just try to love yourself and be gentle with yourself. You know, I guess, take care of each other. I think He would want us to take care of each other.[59]

Sheilaism parallels some of the youth interviews, particularly Marissa and Jackie, who were uncertain about what they believed about church. But they were each certain that being good, kind, and themselves was essential.[60] Bellah et al. describe "Sheilaism" as a "perfectly natural expression of current American religious life."[61] However, they argue that "Sheilaism" does not emerge in a vacuum; it reflects an American history and legacy. In particular, this phenomenon builds upon the early colonial legacy of religious pluralism and religious freedom (though defined much differently than we conceive of it today). Bellah et al. argue that even by the mid-nineteenth century, religious life in America had become drastically more privatized (compared to colonial periods), but it maintained a concern for moral order:

> It operated with a new emphasis on the individual and the voluntary association. Moral teaching came to emphasize self-control rather

than deference. It prepared the individual to maintain self-respect and establish ethical commitments in a dangerous and competitive world.... Religion, like the family, was a place of love and acceptance in an otherwise harsh and competitive society.[62]

Essentially, by the mid-nineteenth century, religious life in America was emphasizing the significance of the individual and showing signs that it was securely placed "in a compartmentalized sphere that provided loving support but could no longer challenge the dominance of utilitarian values in the society at large."[63]

Bellah et al.'s contemporary data reiterate that "most Americans see religion as something individual, prior to any organizational involvement."[64] This connects with their description of religious individualism, and they argue that it harkens back to seventeenth-century practices that make personal experiences of salvation requirements for church membership.[65] Thus they describe specific examples of religious individualism as not being contained in churches (even with the denominational arrays), but as pushing for generic and ambiguously defined values such as self-realization. Religious individualism and the extraordinary examples of people like Sheila, when placed in conversation with the narratives of African American youth, raise questions concerning the implications of religious individualism. In particular, how does a society full of religious individuals encourage adolescents to see or reconnect with understandings of God as working beyond their individual lives? And if we take seriously the above need to reframe our understanding of the self (beyond an autonomous individual), how does society respond in ways that empower Black youth to see beyond the false dichotomies of the public and the private, or the personal and communal? Bellah et al. offer one response as they conclude with a suggestion by Parker Palmer, who reiterates that American individualism does not need to be completely eradicated but rather may simply need to be refocused:

> We have seen a conflict between withdrawal into purely private spirituality and the biblical impetus to see religion as involved with the whole life. Parker Palmer suggests that this apparent contradiction can be overcome: "Perhaps the most important ministry the church can have in the renewal of public life is a 'ministry of paradox': not to resist the inward turn of American spirituality on behalf of public action, *but to deepen and direct and discipline that inwardness in the*

light of faith until God leads us back to a vision of the public and to faithful action on the public's behalf."[66]

Similarly, in reflecting on individualism in the Black Church, Dale Andrews writes,

> The individualism endemic to the age of Enlightenment did not spare black religious life. Though black churches nurtured a communal form of care, American culture remained axiomatic to the often "unreconciled strivings" of African American "double-consciousness." Thus, black churches emphasized personal salvation and religious piety under the impact of American individualism.[67]

Andrews argues that under the influence of American individualism and revivalist Christianity, African American religious life (particularly in Black churches) continued to struggle with a dueling emphasis—which he characterizes as the dual strivings toward survival and liberation. Like Lincoln and Mamiya, Andrews notes that the characterization of the Black church (and of African American spirituality) during the post-reconstruction and later during the post-Civil Rights epochs as otherworldly only offers part of the narrative. Instead, Lincoln and Mamiya see a continued *political ambiguity* within the Black church (as an institution).[68]

In other words, within African American Christianity (as practiced in Black churches), there is not simply an otherworldly orientation nor simply a politically driven spirituality; however, there remains within African American Christianity both components. While it can be problematic to parse out how we empower African American adolescents to live within this ambiguity and to draw upon the resources of personal (survival) *and* communal (liberation) oriented dimensions of African American Christianity, it is important to affirm that not all aspects of the political ambiguity of the African American church are problematic. Many elements of African American spirituality point to and support a robust and integrated faith. For example, Lincoln and Mamiya argue,

> A deep religious faith can be the bedrock for sustaining a person in courageous political acts of liberation. Religious piety does not have to be an opiate; it can be an inspiration to civil rights militancy. Other-worldly religious transcendence can be related dialectically

to the motivation, discipline, and courage needed for this-worldly political action.[69]

Moralistic Therapeutic Deism: De facto Youth Religion

Closely related to Bellah's discussion of the prevalence of religious individualism, and particularly Sheilaism, is a religious phenomenon documented specifically among American teenagers. Christian Smith, in the National Survey of Youth and Religion, offers insights into the spiritual lives among American teens across religious affiliations. After wading through the propensity of American youth to be particularly "inarticulate about religion," Smith asked the question, "What does the bigger picture of the religious and spiritual lives of US teenagers look like when we stand back and try to put it all together?"[70] Smith found that the majority of American teens thought of religion as making them feel good, helping them make good choices, solve problems or troubles, and serve their "felt needs."[71] However, Smith's team found fewer teens describing religion as "transforming people into ... what they are supposed to be ... what God wants them to be."[72] He writes,

> What our interviews almost never uncovered among teens was a view that religion summons people to embrace an obedience to truth regardless of the personal consequences or rewards. Hardly any teens spoke directly about more difficult religious subjects like repentance, love of neighbor, social justice, unmerited grace, self-discipline, humility, costs of discipleship, dying to self, the sovereignty of God, personal holiness, the struggles of sanctification ... or any number of historically key ideas in America's main religious tradition, Christianity.[73]

Instead, Smith summarizes his findings by offering what he calls a "general thesis about teenage religion and spirituality in the US." He argues that American youth religiosity tends toward "moralistic therapeutic deism"—a simplistic religion that includes a belief in God and focuses mostly on "feeling good, happy, safe, at peace," but does not stretch to a more complex sense of faith that also calls for passionate commitments or engagement.[74] The major tenets of this religion include the following:

- A God exists who created and orders the world and watches over human life on earth.
- God wants people to be good, nice, and fair to each other, as taught in the Bible and by most world religions.
- The central goal of life is to be happy and to feel good about oneself.
- God does not need to be particularly involved in one's life except when God is needed to resolve a problem.
- Good people go to heaven when they die.[75]

Smith also generalizes about these trends, writing that the majority of American teens understood God as a cosmic butler and divine therapist, and religion as something that helped them become nice and happy people. Thus his findings indicate that the religion or spirituality of the majority of American teens does not tend toward engaged and intentional religious reflection and action.[76]

Smith's data also point to the ways that the religious lives and practices of youth reflect the religious lives and practices of the significant adults in their lives (especially their parents). Smith asserts that contrary to popular stereotypes about youth as rebellious and in crisis, "the vast majority of American teenagers are *exceedingly conventional* in their religious identity and practices." The youth often describe their religious identity as "just how I was raised." Smith argues, "To the vast majority of teenagers, it was obvious that a teenager would naturally follow and believe what his or her parents believe."[77]

In other words, while Smith develops his understanding of Moralistic Therapeutic Deism in response to the narratives of teens in the United States, Smith argues that Moralistic Therapeutic Deism is prevalent among adults and well as teens. He further argues that it operates not at the level of individual religion and not quite in the same way as an American Civil Religion; instead it operates as something beyond the level of denominations and organized churches and thus is present among youth across denominations. More precisely, Smith defines moralistic therapeutic deism as a "parasitic religion" in that it not only coexists well with other religious traditions, but it requires (or feeds off) other religious worldviews and traditions.[78] While Smith argued that this trend was most evident among mainline Catholic and Protestant youth, he also found significant resonance among African American, Conservative Protestants, Jewish youth, and other "types of religious teens, [and] even nonreligious teens."[79]

This research, while helpful in giving a general overview of the religious lives of American teens, is particularly useful in reflecting on the spiritual lives of African American youth, in that African American fragmented spirituality has significant parallels with Smith's discussion of moralistic therapeutic deism. As noted above, in looking at the content of youth spirituality by assessing the frequency of key theological terms, Smith found that "relatively few US teenagers made reference to a variety of historically central religious and theological ideas."[80] This in turn presents particular challenges and raises questions of not only how to help youth respond to dehumanizing experiences in their daily lives, but it poses the question of whether youth even have a religious system in place that can be expanded and "tapped into."[81] In many ways, Smith's data affirm that youth find God and religion significant in their lives, while also challenging our assumptions about what youth know and how successful we have been in sharing our faith traditions with youth.

Embracing Communal and Public Religion

While noting the many social conditions, such as theories of the privatization of religion, individualism, and new parasitic forms of faith, such as *moralistic therapeutic deism*, which may contribute to and (at best) are occurring alongside of fragmented spirituality among African American youth; there are also trends within American religious life that can help ameliorate these trends. Similar to our discussion of the psychological context of fragmented spirituality and the resultant call to embrace communal and relational selves, I argue that an embrace or rethinking of the role of religion in communal and public life is also essential and possible within contemporary US culture. Building on Casanova's description of the temporary forays of communities or individual religious groups into the American public square, I suggest that African American youth need both reminders of the ways that religion can do this and models of how communities of faith engage in issues and actions beyond the private or personal arena (as postmodernity has already helped us to see that this dichotomy does not fully hold).

Thus in the next chapters, I continue my exploration of the context in which African American youth spirituality emerges by exploring the historical legacy of African American Christianity. I also point to how

African American Christianity can offer youth both a historical legacy of Black Public Theology and Social Gospel, as well as create the space for youth who are living their faith in very communal and public ways. I explore this legacy asking specifically what elements of this tradition offer alternatives to fragmented spirituality and asking how we can empower youth to "tap into" and reclaim this legacy.

3

Tapping into the Legacy

AFRICAN AMERICAN SPIRITUALITY AND THEOLOGICAL
ALTERNATIVES TO FRAGMENTED SPIRITUALITY

THE YOUNG AFRICAN Americans interviewed in this research had mixed understandings of their churches. They had equally mixed perspectives on how their churches and spirituality influence how they make sense of things taking place in the world around them. Young people like Elliott fondly reflected on the ways that his church's decision to become more "welcoming and affirming" shaped his faith. Likewise, Jackie was happy that her church "wasn't all about God and the Bible" and that it created space for other young people to share their concerns. The variety of their narratives pushed me to further ponder how *these* young African American Christians were being shaped and influenced by and in their religious communities. Their experiences pushed me to not only explore their current contexts and the larger societal context, but to keep exploring whether *alternatives to fragmented spirituality exist* and whether they exist *within their context and history.*

In this chapter I begin to assess the larger, historical context and understandings of African American spirituality—as another context in which African American youth spirituality is developing. Instead of rehashing the negative trends noted in chapter 1 regarding the educational resources of contemporary African American churches, here I look at African American spirituality and Black Churches as *also* containing correctives or alternatives to fragmented spirituality. I am not attempting to romanticize the history or practices of Black Churches, and I have on numerous occasions pondered whether the church (as well as the Black religious academy) is capable of providing resources from which to confront the ills and dehumanization that Black youth face today. In part, I recognize the continued debate among scholars of Black religion and community members regarding both high expectations of the Black Church and historical and contemporary limitations (and at time failures) of Black churches. For example, on the one hand, history of religions scholar Charles H. Long writes,

> The fact that black churches have been the locus of the civil rights struggle is not incidental, for the civil rights struggle represented the black confrontation with an American myth that dehumanized the black person's being.... The location of this struggle in the church enabled the civil rights movement to take on the resources of black cultural life in the form of organization, music, and artistic expression, and in the gathering of limited economic resources.[1]

Long recounts the organizing power and legacy of the Black Church as an agent for social change during the Civil Rights movement. For Long, the role of the Black Church and African American religion was not incidental—instead, Black churches and religion were crucial in the freedom efforts of the twentieth century. Thus, Long names and underscores the need to explore the history and resources within this community that have been instrumental in resisting dehumanization and in fighting against legal and social injustices.

However, many during and since the Civil Rights struggles of the twentieth century have questioned whether the centrality and organizing power of the Black Church was as strong as claimed and whether it persists. Barbara Savage contrasts Long's framing of the Black Church, writing that "throughout the twentieth century there were spirited debates among varied groups of African Americans about whether religious doctrines, religious people, and religious organizations were a blessing or a curse in the struggle for black freedom and racial progress."[2] Savage notes her own experiences of surprise as she observed the televised images of Black churches during the late 1950s and '60s. Savage also cautions many who theorize and create expectations about the Black Church by re-reading the relationship between African American religion and politics through the Civil Rights movement successes. Savage emphasizes that central role of the church in the Southern civil rights movement

> was a powerful and startling departure from that story [of treating religion with disdain], rather than a natural progression.... The

movement is best thought of not as inevitable triumph or a moment
of religious revival, but simply as a miracle. It was brief, bold, and
breathtaking, difficult to replicate or sustain, and experienced first-
hand by only a small remnant of true believers.[3]

With this ongoing debate and warning in mind, as well with careful attention to changes in the ways that churches (in general) function
within American public life, in the remainder of the book I outline elements of African American spirituality, historical and contemporary,
that reflect possibilities for integration for African American youth.
This chapter begins a longer conversation that will take place over the
next three chapters which leads us to explore alternatives to fragmented
spirituality, theological quandaries at the center of fragmented spirituality, and a theological vision of life with young African Americans. In
this chapter, I explore the major theological correctives to fragmentation, which emerge out of Black churches and theology, even if they have
not been dominant within Black churches or history. I draw upon the
work of ethicists, sociologists, historians, and theologians and I point to
the interdisciplinary nature of the conversation about the spirituality of
African Americans and the contested legacy of the Black Church in the
United States.

Spirituality as an Animating and Integrating Power

Peter J. Paris's description of *The Spirituality of African Peoples* illuminates
our discussion of the fragmented spirituality of African American youth
by pointing to (and reminding us) that there are alternatives to fragmented
or limited spirituality in the historical legacy of African people and in the
current praxis of African American communities. Paris defines the " 'spirituality' of a people" as "the animating and *integrative* power that constitutes
the principal frame of meaning for individual and collective experiences.
Metaphorically, the spirituality of a people is synonymous with the soul of
a people: the integrating center of power and meaning."[4] Paris's understanding of the spirituality of people of African descent contrasts with a
fragmented spirituality. By definition (and as many have experienced it),
spirituality is or should be the "frame of meaning" that integrates individual and collective experiences. In other words, spirituality for Paris is that

which integrates our experiences. He further argues, "Unity in diversity is another metaphor for African spirituality."[5] What appears to be missing or underemphasized in adolescent, fragmented spirituality is the ability to create or maintain unity.

In addition to defining spirituality in a way that problematizes fragmentation or any type of disconnection within the meaning of experiences, Paris's discussion of African and African American spirituality is part of his effort to define a "common moral discourse" between Africans on the continent and in the diaspora. His search for a common moral discourse points to a rich legacy of communal concern and embodied spirituality that always contains the goal of survival.[6] His understanding of the common moral discourse centers on four "integrally related and overlapping dimensions of African cosmological and societal thought." Paris includes

- the realm of the spirit (inclusive of the Supreme Deity, the sub-divinities, the ancestral spirits), which is the source and preserver of all life;
- the realm of tribal or ethnic community, which, in equilibrium with the realm of the spirit, constitutes the paramount goal of human life;
- the realm of family, which, in equilibrium with the realms of tribe and spirit, constitutes the principal guiding force for personal development; and
- the individual person who strives to integrate the three realms in his or her soul.[7]

Paris's understanding of the African cosmos, as well as the way that it undergirds the moral vision of African and African American people, offers one understanding of an African spiritual legacy, which connects (or strives to connect) the realm of the spirit with the community, family, and individual. While I am glossing over many of the nuances of this cosmology, which Paris develops, I lift it up as an example of a framework from which African American adolescent spirituality emerges and one that it can also reconnect with. In other words, it is helpful to reflect on the disconnections young people are experiencing with a more integrated model of spirituality in mind. This is not to say that we should push youth to embrace a "neat" cosmological schema, but that we should start a conversation with the hope that part of their spiritual lives may include finding equilibrium in these overlapping "realms."

A Black Sacred Cosmos: Freedom as
the Superlative Value

Similarly, sociologists of religion C. Eric Lincoln and Lawrence Mamiya, despite their assertion that "a general theory for the social analysis of black religious phenomena and a sociology of the Black Church has not yet appeared," contribute to the conversation of alternatives to fragmented spirituality.[8] They offer a description of the religious worldview, or spirituality, of African Americans and a framework for understanding the complicated history and functions of the Black Church. First, Lincoln and Mamiya describe the religious worldview of African Americans, or the "Black Sacred Cosmos," as the "experiential dimension" that gives rise to the Black Church.[9] Like Paris, they describe the Black sacred cosmos as drawing upon both the African heritage and the conversion to Christianity during slavery and after. Lincoln and Mamiya reaffirm the work of African Americans in creating "their own unique and distinctive forms of culture and worldviews as parallels rather than replications of the culture in which they were involuntary guests."[10]

This Black sacred cosmos, while dependent upon culture and history, centers on a variety of sacred objects or figures. For example, Lincoln and Mamiya describe the central role of the Old Testament God who is "avenging, conquering, liberating" within the faith of most Black Churches. They argue that "the older the church or the more elderly its congregation, the more likely the demand for the exciting imagery and the personal involvement of God in history is likely to be."[11] Lincoln and Mamiya also note the importance of "Jesus as the Son of God made flesh" in African American Christianity. This centrality of Jesus emerges because of the resonance between the experiences of oppression and the "incarnational view of the suffering, humiliation, death and eventual triumph of Jesus."[12] However, beyond the central role of these figures, Lincoln and Mamiya describe the "superlative value of the black sacred cosmos" as freedom, or "the absence of any restraint which might compromise one's responsibility to God."[13] They also assert that this value of freedom is, and has always been, communal in nature. Lincoln and Mamiya lift up the communal nature of freedom in the African American cosmos in contrast to "white freedom," which they define as supporting "the value of American individualism: to be free to pursue one's destiny without political or bureaucratic interference or restraint."[14]

Their description of the Black sacred cosmos also includes two religious practices: worship and personal conversion. Lincoln and Mamiya argue that in worship there remains a particularly emotional or spirited form, which serves both as a catharsis and as a means of intimacy with God. They write that "the Black Church was in search of transcendence, not a mere emptying of the emotions, but an enduring fellowship with God."[15] Connected with the spirit-filled worship was the experience of personal conversion. Personal conversion or "rebirth" represented a "fundamental reorientation in the approach to life"—moving one from feelings of unworthiness to an emotional experience of salvation.[16]

Exploring this Black sacred cosmos clarifies the larger history in which the spiritual lives of African American adolescents emerges and is shaped. The narratives of the youth and the content of the educational resources indicate continuity and divergence from this historical legacy. In particular, the educational resources and youth narratives demonstrate a level of continuity in the central role of God and Jesus. However, the emphasis on God as "avenging, conquering, liberating" or even actively involved in history is not primary. Similarly, the understanding of the superlative value of Black religion as "freedom"—specifically a communal freedom to be responsible to God—is not evidenced in the youth narratives or educational resources. Simply noting the frequency with which youth even mention Jesus indicates an additional point of divergence between this sacred cosmos and the narratives of the youth interviewed. Jesus or Christ was only mentioned, not discussed in great detail, in two of the interviews. Moreover, in these two interviews Jesus is not explicitly described as a central figure. This is telling of the beliefs of young people, as well as the hesitancy of using exclusively Christian language. In other words, a point of divergence reflects the larger trends in modern American spirituality such that belief in God persists, but discussions of Christianity and Jesus may be relegated to private discourse.

Dialectical and Dialogical Models of the Black Church

Beyond their discussion of the "Black Sacred Cosmos," Lincoln and Mamiya both expand and counter decades of theorizing about the Black Church by introducing a dialectical typology that seeks to hold in tension the major features or characterizations of the African American church.[17] They write, "Black churches are institutions that are involved in a constant series of dialectical tensions. The dialectic holds polar opposites in tension, constantly shifting between polarities in historical time."[18] In their examination of the social conditions of Black churches, they enumerate six main pairs of polar opposites between the:

· priestly and private functions,
· other-worldly versus this-worldly,
· universalism and particularism,
· communal and the privativistic,
· charismatic versus the bureaucratic, and
· resistance versus accommodation.[19]

This dialectical model, with its pairs of opposites, addresses the functions of the Black Church, the orientation that believers have toward the world, the orientation the institution has toward the larger American society and toward the African American community, as well as the organizational structure of Black churches. In articulating the dialectical model, Lincoln and Mamiya saw this typology as a needed corrective to the historical trends in theorizing about the Black Church as either "compensatory" or "other-worldly," which Lincoln and Mamiya noted soon becomes outdated. Instead, the dialectical model offers a "more comprehensive view of the complexity of Black churches as social institutions." In truth, while the pairs and tensions may change, what is offered is a model of attending to the historical "dynamism" of Black churches and the interactions within and across the polarities.[20]

This model of the Black Church holds together the historical legacy of African American religion and institutions, which includes both the radical traditions of Black religion and its active engagement with cultural movements. The radical traditions include those espoused by historian Gayraud Wilmore in his seminal text, *Black Religion and Black Radicalism*; the active engagement with cultural movements includes events such as the Civil Rights and Black Power movements, which characterize much of the early Black Liberation Theology.[21] Lincoln and Mamiya's model also holds these traditions in tension with the legacy of Black churches as spiritual oases in the midst of a harsh and oppressive society. Hence, their model outlines the complex and interactive trends within the Black Church and African American Christianity.

However, in response to Lincoln and Mamiya's dialectical model of the Black Church and the resultant views of African American Christians, Evelyn Brooks Higginbotham suggests that this dialectical model does not go far enough, and she offers a *dialogical* model. Higginbotham, in the introduction to *Righteous Discontent*, characterizes the dialogical model of the Black Church as "a multiplicity of protean and concurrent meanings and intentions more so than in a series of discrete polarities."[22] In other words, Higginbotham stresses the fact that the tensions and features of the Black Church are not a set of separate continua that it negotiates according to a particular socio-historical movement. Instead, a better model for the Black Church recognizes and incorporates the interconnectivity of each of the polarities described by Lincoln and Mamiya and goes beyond the polarities to see that at any moment the features and meanings are constantly impinging upon one another. Higginbotham would stress that it is impossible to treat each of the polarities separately. For example, even as we look at the priestly versus prophetic functions of the Black Church, we see that this trait is intricately connected with whether the church chooses a more resistant or accommodating stance toward the larger society, and whether the work of the church is focused on individual needs or communal concerns. While Lincoln and Mamiya's model is theoretically neater and makes it easier to describe attributes of Black Churches and to do comparative work among particular Black Churches, it does not capture the "messiness" and myriad overlapping constellations of meanings that are the Black Church and African American Christianity.

Higginbotham argues for a dialogical model of the Black Church, contending that

> multiple discourses—sometimes conflicting, sometimes unifying— are articulated between black men and women, and within each of these two groups as well. The Black Church constitutes a complex body of shifting cultural, ideological, and political significations. It represents a "heteroglot" conception in the Bakhtinian sense of a multiplicity of meanings and intentions that interact and condition each other. Such multiplicity transcends polarity—thus tending to blur the spiritual and secular, the eschatological and political, and the private and public.[23]

Essentially, beyond seeing that each of Lincoln and Mamiya's discrete pairs of polarities interacts with the other pairs of polarities, Higginbotham states that the polarities themselves do not hold; for instead of seeing things along a continuum, she argues that the Black Church blurs any set of discrete conceptions and characterizations. She draws on the Russian linguist Mikhail Bakhtin's discussion of "dialogism" and "heteroglossia" in his theory of language, where he writes, "Everything means, is understood, as part of a greater whole—there is a constant interaction between meanings, all of which have the potential of conditioning others."[24] In making this parallel, Higginbotham describes the Black Church as dialogical and heteroglot—indicating that in describing the greater whole and legacy of the Black Church, there will always be a constant interaction between meanings, and it is artificial not to stress how each of these meanings in turn conditions the others. New meaning and complex forms are created out of these "tensions" within the Black Church. New meanings and understandings are not created by holding discrete things in tension (because there is often no tension); instead, in moments when two seemingly opposite ways of being are brought together, something new emerges.[25]

While Higginbotham, Lincoln, and Mamiya are offering sociological and historical frameworks for theorizing about the African American church, I also see their work as outlining the complex, dialogical nature of African American Christian spirituality. In other words, Higginbotham (as well as Lincoln and Mamiya, as noted above) is pointing to an understanding of African American spirituality and the Black Church as including the "radical" trends as well as the healing rituals and practices of Pentecostal preachers, such as Lucy Smith.[26] In other words, Higginbotham attempts to push us toward a model of thinking about the religious lives of African Americans that holds together in constant and constructive dialogue many beliefs, actions, and ways of being in the world. In this way, Higginbotham's understanding of the Black Church and African American spirituality as "heteroglot"—where the integration of seemingly disparate parts results in the emergence of a spirituality that is both different from and more than the "sum of its parts"—offers an alternative to fragmentation among African American youth. Her dialogical model emphasizes the complex legacy of African American Christianity and challenges me to build upon and reconnect youth with this complex, dialogical legacy.[27]

African American spirituality (not simply the institutions) is "heteroglot." Building on Paris, Lincoln and Mamiya, and Higginbotham, I assert that African American Christianity is messy and complicated, holding together and creating anew radical and cathartic elements. Binaries and dichotomies have long been debunked, therefore our theorizing about African American religion and spirituality must account for the messiness of lived realities. Therefore part of what I hope to help young African Americans see within the African American religious tradition is the consistent complexity and the ability to hold things together within and through spiritual meaning making.

Normative Theological Conceptions: Expanding the Nascent Theologies of Youth

Closely related to the historical legacy of the Black Church and African American spirituality are the explicit theological claims and norms that offer alternatives to fragmented spirituality. In chapter 1, as I described the spiritual lives and perspectives of the African American youth interviewed, I outlined many of their understandings about God, the church, and the community. Embedded in their discussions of God, church, and community was evidence of fragmented spirituality in

- an emphasis on God to bless youth individually and only a nascent understanding of how God is "calling" youth to respond;
- a limited treatment of any concept of change, conversion, or transformation; and
- an emphasis on the personal and limited engagement with the communal and political.[28]

However, in addition to this evidence of fragmentation, their narratives include their nascent, if not fully articulated or realized, theology. Even as I name the limitations of fragmented spirituality and some of their theological musings, I also explore how we can build on their theological convictions and push toward an integrated spirituality. Thus, in offering theological alternatives, I am careful to not discount where young African Americans are starting. Their starting point is important as an indicator of the larger society, but more importantly their current beliefs and practices are the building blocks of a more robust spirituality.

Above I note the ways that African American Christianity historically includes complexity and holds together many trajectories; here I build on that dialogical model of spirituality as vital for young African Americans and name some of the concrete characteristics, values, and normative beliefs that are essential to responding to fragmented spirituality. In particular, Womanist theology is an indispensable conversation partner and influence on my theological commitments; and it shapes the norms that I outline as essential for African American adolescents to reconnect with. This does not imply that my work is not influenced greatly by Black Liberation Theology or even European, European American, and more contemporary process theologies. However, the themes raised by Womanist theologians have persisted throughout my faith and academic journey, and I find particular resonance with the narratives of the African American youth interviewed. Womanist thought has often been one of the few theological spaces where the experiences and concerns of young people and families were included. Womanist theological thought also maintains its contested and complicated relationship with the Black Church and communities; therefore, I explore this part of the African American Christian legacy in greater detail here.

Womanist Spirituality and Theology

Womanist spirituality and religious thought centers on the religious and social world of African American women. It includes and connects with the experiences of biblical women, as described in Delores Williams's exposition of the narrative of Hagar; the historical lives of African and African American women religious leaders, such as those described in Higginbotham's *Righteous Discontent*; as well as the lived realities of contemporary and even ordinary Black women.[29] Womanist theology takes the lives and experiences of African American women (and by extension the range of experiences that affect African American communities) as primary in the process of critical and constructive theological reflection. Linda E. Thomas writes that

> Womanist theology engages the macro-structural and the micro-structural issues that affect black women's lives and, since it is a theology of complete inclusivity, the lives of all black people. The freedom of black women entails the liberation of all peoples, since Womanist theology concerns notions of gender, race, class, heterosexism, and ecology. . . . Thus the tasks of Womanist theology are to claim history, to declare authority for ourselves, our men, and our children, to learn from the experience of our forebears, to admit shortcomings and errors, and to improve our quality of life.[30]

Thomas's succinct articulation of the discipline and work of Womanist theology outlines the tasks and points of resonance for theological reflections of young African Americans. In particular, the ability (or even call) to attend to the macro- and micro-structural issues that affect the lives of Black people pushes against notions of fragmentation that would hinder Black youth from responding to the varied dimensions of their unique experiences, as well to attend to the concerns of their entire community. Thomas also broadly defines the personal and social issues Womanist theology attempts to address, issues with which many young African Americans both within and outside of Christian communities are also wrestling: sexism and heterosexism. These are also issues that have historically placed some young people in opposition to Christian churches.

Thomas's definition also connects with and builds upon the work of other Womanist theorists, such as Delores Williams's autobiographical framing in the preface of *Sisters in the Wilderness*. Although, Williams's intent was simply to do responsible theological reflection and name her social location, her description offers a paradigm for understanding Womanist thought and spirituality. Williams underscores the role of faith in her life and how she came to theorize about faith and spirituality in the lives of African American women. For Williams, faith is connected to the everyday struggles of life that do not always include easy success and solutions. She instead calls her faith "hard won." Williams writes,

> I find myself testifying. Faith, hard won, has taught me how to value the gains, losses, stand-offs and victories in my life. Many times the painful moments would not have been healed were it not for the road I traveled to faith—learning to trust the righteousness of God in spite of trouble and injustice; learning to trust women of many colors regardless of sexism, racism, classism, and homophobia in our society; learning to believe in the sanctuary-power of family defined in many ways in addition to nuclear; discovering love in a variety of forms that heal, but also believing serious political action is absolutely necessary for justice to prevail in the world.... Faith has taught me to see the miraculous in everyday life: the miracle of ordinary black women resisting and rising above.[31]

Williams points to essential elements of trusting God, trusting other women, the sanctuary-power of family, discovering love, and serious political action as part of her journey of faith and as part of her Womanist thought and theological process. By extension, I see in her "testimony" a rich tapestry of an integrated faith and spirituality, which models for young African Americans both the possibility of seeing "the miraculous in everyday life" and the reality that this type of faith is not something that develops easily or without struggle, questions, doubts, and healing love in communities.

In order to understand Womanist epistemology and spirituality, it is also essential to look at the powerful self-defining project of Alice Walker, whose literary definition inspired and captured the religious understandings of generations of African American women and communities. Walker's multipart definition of Womanist begins as follows:

> From *womanish*. (Opp. of "girlish," i.e., frivolous, irresponsible, not serious.) A black feminist or feminist of color. From the black folk expression of mothers to female children, "you acting womanish," i.e., like a woman. Usually referring to outrageous, audacious, courageous or *willful* behavior. Wanting to know more and in greater depth than is considered "good" for one. Interested in grown up doings. Acting grown up. Being grown up. Interchangeable with another black folk expression: "You trying to be grown." Responsible. In charge. *Serious.*[32]

Walker's definition affirms that Womanist entails being (1) active, (2) outrageous, (3) inquisitive (never satisfied with the information deemed acceptable for one to have), and (4) serious. Thus, we can argue that a Womanist spirituality is not passive spirituality, but is actively seeking knowledge and depth. Walker's definition also illumines the ways that Womanist spirituality includes transgression, in that a Womanist spirit does not easily "stay in one's place"; neither is it easily contained or defined. Similarly, ethicist Emilie Townes's work on Womanist spirituality reiterates that *resistance, transgression,* and *social witness* of oppressive structures are essential parts of the womanish spirit.[33]

Looking at Walker's full definition of "Womanist" and the appropriation of this definition by Womanist religious scholars, we see that Womanist thought takes seriously the lives of African American women and offers a model for the integral role of faith, love, community, creative expression, and acts of resistance (including political action).[34] Womanist spirituality is both spiritual and resistant, and thus offers an alternative to fragmented spirituality by exemplifying a model of holding together and balancing love of spirit, self, others, and the community. It is also a model of active, transgressive, outrageous, and responsible spirituality. A *womanish spirit* pushes youth to embrace or reclaim a spirit of resistance and social witness—to embrace an understanding that wherever there is wrong in the world, wherever young people see and name concerns, there is also a need for them to resist wrongs and to work with God to improve the world. It couples that spirit of resistance with a commitment to self-love and to their communities' wholeness and survival.

Building on these definitions and reflections on Womanist spirituality, I begin to articulate a few theological claims that are essential in helping African American youth address the trends of fragmented spirituality, and to live in such a way that they are able to resist the daily affronts to their humanity. I begin with four concepts (which are expanded in the remaining chapters) to respond to the trends in the youth interview data toward a fragmented spirituality.

Cooperation with God

Expanding Understandings of God—Beyond Beneficent Friend or Sovereign Lord

A personal and beneficent God remains central in the theological understandings of young people and the educational resources presented in African American churches. As noted in chapter 1, all of the youth surveyed and interviewed described a time when they "experienced the presence" of God in their lives. The majority of the youth experienced God's presence in moments when God "blessed them" or did something for them. Youth were very articulate about this understanding of God, and some youth explicitly named God as very powerful in propelling them toward personal success. Similarly, the educational resources offered a broad and complex array of metaphors and images of God; they introduced images of a powerful, creative, and sovereign God, in addition to the beneficent and ever-present God.

Youth did not consistently discuss God in connection with the places where they articulated hopelessness or even frustration. For example, one young woman did not see God as connecting with her experiences of racism in her school. Equally, there was a great deal of ambiguity and uncertainty related to their understandings of God's work in their communities, the world, and politics. This ambiguity was also evidenced in the educational resources, in that these also contained limited discussions of the ways that God can or is working beyond personal and spiritual arenas.

In spite of the limitations and ambiguities in their discussions of God, youth should *not* get rid of their understanding of God's goodness and presence in their lives. It is important for young people to continue to see God as powerful and concerned about their lives. In many ways this is the most operative element in each of the interviews; and this understanding of God is also the most prevalent in the religious lives of youth within the larger body of research on youth religion.[35] Responding to a fragmented spirituality—where God is present and powerful only in certain areas and not mentioned in others—pushes us to explore strategies for expanding upon this understanding of a blessing, loving, and sometimes powerful God.

The most obvious corrective includes pushing youth to embrace a vision of God who is wonderfully good and all power in *all areas* of the lives of young people, and to affirm the miracle-working, transformative power of a God who can do all things well. For many African American Christian youth, a naïve belief in a wonderfully good and all-powerful God is already operative. However, a blind embrace of the goodness and power of God conflicts with their lived realities, even if only on a subconscious level. And because of the conflicting images of an all-wonderful and powerful God with their ongoing dehumanization, God is not seen in or expected to transform all areas of their lives, particularly areas of societal injustice. In other words, youth often temper their expectations of God and where God will work before they limit what they say God is truly capable of. God is good, even if we do not expect God to be good everywhere or in all things. Consequently, I am not calling for youth to believe that God will do all things miraculously and change society instantaneously. Instead I affirm that a more complex understanding of God, beyond being good and powerful, must become operative in the lives of African American adolescents.

In many ways, an expansion of their understandings of what God does is required—and this involves recognizing that God may not always operate in miraculous or instantaneous ways. This is not an attempt to downplay or lessen the *power* of God. Instead, I argue that if the only understanding youth have of God is one in which God is all-powerful, all-good, and only operates miraculously and instantaneously, then youth will constantly have to apologize for their God or regroup when their lived realities and dehumanizing experiences call this image of God into question. (In chapter 4, we expand upon many of the tensions between their understanding of God and their experiences of dehumanization.) Instead, a closer reading of biblical texts, both in the narrative of Hagar, which is essential to Delores Williams's Womanist god-talk, and in the narrative of Jesus Christ, reveals images of a God who does not always (or even usually) step in and miraculously change societal structures of oppression. The biblical narratives, however, present tremendous models and examples of humans who are strengthened to survive, persist, and endure in the face of injustice.

For example, Williams argues, "God's response to Hagar's story in the Hebrew testament is not liberation. Rather, God participated in Hagar and her child's survival. . . . Liberation in the Hagar stories is not given by God; it finds its source in human initiative."[36] In other words, while arguing that God's response is not always one of liberation, she is not calling liberation and resistance in the face of injustice into question. Williams is however calling us to a reorientation in our understanding of how liberation and resistance come about. Williams presses us to expand our understandings of God and human work in struggles of liberation. Williams, as well as other Womanist scholars, are pushing us beyond passively waiting on the miraculous intervention or gift of God. Instead, she emphasizes the role of human agency and initiative in the struggles toward liberation. Essentially, she offers a model of active cooperation with God and pushes us to reconnect with "the [African American] community's belief in God's presence in the struggle," even if or when the struggle persists and requires great endurance.[37] Similarly, postmodern Womanist theologian Monica Coleman aptly writes,

> Not all evil can be overcome in this world, and yet . . . [she] maintains hope in the struggle to creatively and constructively respond to it. . . . All-encompassing health, wholeness, unity, and salvation are never fully attained in this world. . . . God may not always lead us in ways that feel liberating. Sometimes God . . . will feel like a judge. But creative transformation is leading us to a way that will improve quality of life.[38]

In other words, Coleman's postmodern and process Womanist theology outlines key elements that push beyond a mere expectancy of a good or sovereign God to "fix everything" to a place of affirming that "salvation is an activity."[39] For Coleman, salvation is an ongoing activity, and we are called not to passively wait on God, but to live in "cooperation with God for the social transformation of the world."[40] Williams and Coleman are careful to hold God's work and human agency in tension. The two go together—one does not exclude the other. Therefore, expanding upon the youth understanding of God also requires conceiving of a God who calls youth to participate, cooperate, and act with God. Here, I am intentionally describing this as an "expansion" and not an introduction of the idea of youth cooperation with God; many youth already discuss God calling them to work for change or to respond to things that concern them in their community. Thus, I am simply asserting that we need to make an understanding of God who calls and expects our active participation normative, alongside of an understanding of God that blesses us or rules over us.

Conversion and Transformation

Expanding our understanding of God to see our selves as called to participate in transforming the world also requires a stronger theological understanding of both conversion and transformation. Conversion and transformation are not the same, historically or in contemporary parlance; however, youth need to see an interconnection between what is often characterized as personal and spiritual conversion experiences and social-communal transformation.[41]

In general, discussions of change, spiritual or communal, were decidedly absent or at best limited in their representation in the youth interviews and educational resources. For example, the interviews did not offer any evidence that religious conversion was significant in their religious experiences. Even in interviews with youth from more conservative traditions, only one youth named salvation, a relationship with God or accepting Jesus as their personal savior, and deliverance from particular bad habits or struggles, as part of the essential teachings of her church. While recognizing general trends in youth to be "inarticulate" about their religious lives, I argue that the youth interviewed are not merely lacking the words to describe these experiences; rather, these concepts are not a vital part of their religious experiences. Essentially, the ideas of conversion and transformation are missing in youth theological vocabulary and worldviews.

Yet I argue that conversion and transformation can provide a powerful corrective to fragmented spirituality, particularly trends that disconnect their understanding of God's calling on their lives from the concerns that many youth name and experience in the world around them. For example, the low salience of the idea of change or transformation in youth world-views can account for (or reflect) the many ways that youth describe situations, such as violence or racism in their communities, as never changing. Instead, by reclaiming or tapping into the spiritual practice of conversion and efforts to work for social and communal transformation, youth can begin to understand the power of God working in them in ways that catalyze their work for change and renew their spirits in the struggles.

Conversion as Reorientation and Re-Visioning

For example, in discussing dimensions of the "black experience," Delores Williams describes the strong emphasis placed on the "encounter between God and humans." Cecil Cone also describes this encounter and the resultant conversion experience:

> Recognition of one's sinfulness was merely the first step in the dynamics of the black religious experience. It was followed by what has commonly been known ... as saving conversion. The character of conversion was marked by the suddenness with which the slave's heart was changed. It was an abrupt change in his orientation toward reality; it affected every aspect of the slave's attitude and beliefs.... The new level of reality ... caused the slave to experience a sense of freedom in the midst of human bondage.[42]

Cone's description of the historical experience of conversion points to the way that conversion served as a reorientation in worldview and consciousness. And while I am not asserting a return to Great Awakening theologies of sin and damnation, which were often precursors for a personal conversion experience, I affirm that an understanding of one's self in relationship with God and even an experience of God should have the power to alter one's beliefs and attitudes, and to inform one's consciousness. Similarly, Delores Williams writes that

> the encounter between God and women in the wilderness experience does more than strengthen women's faith and empower them to persevere in spite of trouble.... [It] also provides these women with new vision to see survival resources where they saw none before.... Transformation of consciousness and epistemological process come together in the new great faith-consciousness this

meeting [between God and women] bestows upon black women. This faith-consciousness guides black women's ways of being and acting in the wide, wide world. Their stories tell of their absolute dependence on God generated by a faith-consciousness incorporating survival intelligence and visionary capacity.[43]

Essentially, Williams is asserting that an encounter between God and women and the resultant conversion experience empowers women to go beyond perseverance. Conversion encounters and the resultant "faith-consciousness" offer women new ways of seeing and acting in the world. Williams credits this type of encounter with God for many of the creative and visionary responses of women that shaped Black political history in the United States.[44]

In the twenty-first century, descriptions of this type of faith in God and conversion are missing at best. Often, in my observations, this language and experiences have been co-opted by religious conservatives, such that the joy, clarity, and empowerment of women and youth who would have this experience are used only to further a normalizing, dehumanizing, status-quo-maintaining world. However, I find that there is a similar type of consciousness-raising and conversion taking place among youth and young adults as they experience the "spirit" of activism and social change movements. Parallel to the fervor and excitement experienced during revivals and rousing religious services, I contend that protest, die-ins, marches, rallies, and sociopolitical campaigns (even if just for a moment or from the sidelines via social media) have the potential to produce within youth a reorientation that empowers them to see a different set of resources than they saw before and to feel that there is something that they can do to create a better world.

Conversion as Creative Transformation

Therefore, beyond the historical practices of conversion, postmodern Womanist thought also underscores the significant role of transformation and the understanding of salvation—often defined by Black women as survival and "making a way out of no way." In particular, Monica Coleman's articulation of *creative transformation* connects with my understanding of the role of conversion-transformation in responding to the fragmented spirituality of African American youth. Drawing upon the resources of process and Womanist theologies, Coleman describes the interconnected concepts of "creative transformation" and "making a way out of no way" as "a type of change that transforms humanity and the wider world." More specifically, Coleman argues that

> "Making a way out of no way" involves God's presentation of unforeseen possibilities; human agency; the goal of justice, survival, and quality of life; and a challenge to the existing order.... This constructive Womanist concept of salvation comes from the new vision that God provides to black women, who then have significant agency in moving the future toward a just and participatory society.... [Creative transformation,] to use Cobb's language, "struggle[s] against death-dealing powers that threaten us."[45]

Coleman's articulation of creative transformation thus pushes us to not only value the encounter between God and humanity, but reminds us (as did Williams) of the ways that God presents new possibilities in these encounters and calls on human agency in acting upon the new visions presented by God. Creative transformation, or "making a way out of no way" can offer youth a framework for responding to the myriad dehumanizing experiences, even when they do not see possibilities of change or of things getting better.

Conversion to the Neighbor: Spirituality of Liberation

In addition to naming the power of conversion and transformation in the reorientation of one's worldviews and actions, Latin American liberation theologian Gustavo Gutierrez discusses the significance of the direction of one's conversion. Gutierrez counters the traditional Christian understanding of converting to Christ by confessing Jesus Christ, and underscores the interconnection of Christ with our neighbors:

> A spirituality of liberation will center on a *conversion* to the neighbor, the oppressed person, the exploited social class, the despised race, the dominated country.... Conversion to the Lord implied conversion to the neighbor.... Conversion means radical transformation of ourselves; it means thinking, feeling, and living as Christ.[46]

In his understanding of conversion, Gutierrez argues that conversion is not simply changing one's beliefs or religious convictions; it includes a commitment to the process of liberation of the poor and oppressed. This understanding of conversion to one's neighbor and to the poor and oppressed is significant for young African Americans, because it offers another layer of interconnection between spirituality and the concerns they see and name in the world around them. If they take seriously Gutierrez's discussion of conversion to the neighbor, then their faith in God cannot focus simply on their personal success; rather it pushes them to wrestle with how they might concretely participate in the process of liberation: "To be converted means to commit oneself to the process of the liberation of the poor and oppressed, to commit oneself lucidly, real-istically, and concretely . . . with an analysis of the situation and a strategy for action."[47]

Gutierrez's understanding of conversion to the neighbor, in conjunc-tion with the definitions of Williams and Coleman, illustrates an explicit connection between a conversion experience and concern with and for the oppressed in the world. Therefore, in order to respond to fragmented spir-ituality among contemporary youth, who at times do not include them-selves among the oppressed and struggling, there is a need to underscore the ways that we are called to connect conversion to Christ with a commit-ment to strategically respond to the oppression of others.

Hope

Beyond Wishful Thinking—To Desire and Expectation

This is hope, to desire and to expect. To desire but not expect is not hope, for though you desire the moon, you hardly hope for it. To expect but not to desire is not hope, for who that expects his or her loved one to die could be said to hope for it? But to desire, and to expect the desire's fulfillment, that is hope. And we are saved by hope.[48]

Looking across the youth interviews and survey responses, the tone and content of the youth interviews are not overtly lacking in hope. The youth interviewed are upbeat in their conversations and tend to have a positive outlook on their individual lives and aspirations. However, when youth describe concerns in their communities, their hopeful tone turns to uncer-tainty and what Evelyn Parker came to describe as *wishful thinking*. Many of the young people discussed what they *wish* would happen in their com-munities, without a genuine expectation that it could happen. Likewise, in reviewing the educational resources, I was surprised to find that none of the sermons or Sunday school lessons emphasized hope as a theological or practical theme.

According to Mary Townes, hope is essential to Christianity and salvation. She describes hope as the combination of desire and expectation—and suggests that these two elements together are powerful. Similarly, Evelyn Parker, in her earliest responses to the fragmented spirituality she observed among African American youth in Chicago, develops the principle of "emancipatory hope." She defines it as the "expectation that dominant powers of racism, classism, sexism, and heterosexism will be toppled and that African American adolescents have agency in God's vision for dismantling these powers of domination."[49] She further defines this type of hope as part of "that intricately woven life of divine and human self-understanding that expects God's transformative power and acts in God's transformative power against economic, political, and social domination."[50] In line with the concepts outlined above (such as cooperation with God and conversion as God introducing new visions and resources with which humans are called to act to respond to injustice), this understanding of hope both expects God's transformative power and is manifest in our work or actions. Hope is actively expecting and anticipating God's movement in the world. In this way, fragmented spirituality and "emancipatory hope" are incompatible.

Expanding upon the work of Elisabeth Schüssler Fiorenza, Parker also calls for "oppositional imagination" in helping youth to "[envision] alternative ways of thinking" and begin to live out this type of emancipatory hope.[51] Coupled with the expectation and hope of God's transformative power in the world, an oppositional imagination invites youth into the practice of imagining the world "as it could be"—seeing an alternative to racism, sexism, violence, and other dehumanizing experiences.

However, in countering fragmented spirituality, hope cannot be limited to what happens immediately. Instead, Fernando Arzola Jr. outlines a vision of *eschatological hope* within "prophetic youth ministry." In outlining the distinctions between four types of ministry with urban youth, Arzola argues that

a prophetic youth ministry promotes eschatological hope.... [It] succeeds when the prophetic message has been spoken and enacted, not just when it sees results in terms of actual liberation or change of social conditions. Yet this prophetic hope must be held without giving in to defeatism or inactivity.[52]

Like Coleman above, Arzola emphasizes that in spite of the fact that not all systemic ills or oppressive structures will be overturned immediately (or in our lifetime), there remains a need for hope that transcends temporal successes or change. Here Arzola points to another dialogical tension that must be promoted in order to respond to fragmented spirituality in African American youth. Namely, we must invite young people to live within the tension of expecting and proclaiming God's prophetic word, "pointing to the kingdom of God which will only be fully realized in the future," while actively working toward change.[53]

In his work, Arzola juxtaposes his vision of prophetic youth ministry with radical or activist youth ministry, which simply strives to work for change and tends to only understand success in terms of the actualization or realization of change in the current or immediate community. However, Arzola reminds us that much of the prophetic ministry of the Hebrew Bible prophets and of Jesus is steeped not only in the actualized change, but in their persistence in speaking truth to power *and* pointing persons to a hope-filled vision of the world that goes beyond their current realities.

Both Parker's and Arzola's understandings of hope are helpful in responding to fragmented spirituality in youth, because it pushes youth to move beyond the ambiguity with which they describe racism or violence ending and even the ambiguity with which they describe God's activity in the world. Embracing an emancipatory and eschatological hope empowers youth to actively expect God's transformation and begin to see themselves as part of that transformative thrust.

Communal Care and Social Witness: Reorientation toward a Public Theology

In the previous sections of this chapter, I emphasize the communal orientation of African and African American spirituality; Paris, Lincoln and Mamiya, as well as Womanist thinkers point to community or communalism as undergirding the historical experiences of African Americans and as essential for their spirituality. Amazingly however, a communal orientation or emphasis is drastically underrepresented in the educational resources examined in this research. While all of the youth participants are active in their communities (engaged in some type of volunteer service), their motivations were not explicitly or clearly connected to their faith. Therefore, in order to help youth reconnect with and reclaim the communal legacy of African Americans, I argue that a stronger theological understanding of community must also be put in place, as well as a reorientation toward a "public theology."[54]

In other words, while it is important to reiterate that spirituality entails more than individual prayers, concerns, and relationships with the divine, the question remains, What can the non-individualistic, non-private dimensions of spirituality look like? In response, I argue that a reorientation toward public theology helps us when thinking about spirituality that empowers youth to connect their understanding of God, as personally concerned and significant, with an understanding of God who is relevant to their concerns for the world and requires their agency and cooperation in responding to the communal concerns around them.

While I do not wish to conflate understandings of community with that of the public sphere, I argue that reconnecting with an understanding of community as central to our survival, liberation, and freedom includes a call to theologically reflect on and address issues of public (societal and political) concern.

What is Public Theology?

Admittedly, the term public theology or public theologian is not without issues or problems; in some arenas it is highly contested.[55] Also, it is difficult to succinctly define public theology.[56] However, ethicist Robert M. Franklin's discussion of public theology is very helpful.[57] Franklin, in a sermon admonishing incoming students at Emory University to offer a new type of leadership for the church and world, states,

> Since the time of Reinhold Niebuhr, we have called them public theologians. [Public theologians] are women and men who take their faith out of the comfort of the sanctuary into the public square, of the nation and the globe. In times of stress and uncertainty, they "go public" not to impose their faith upon other people, but to give voice and to give body, yes to embody, a radical idea. The idea that love is the greatest force available to humanity for solving its ills. Not the weak and superficial sentimentality that passes for love in our time. But, love as a force of the soul. Love as a movement of the Spirit. . . . Public theologians show before they tell the world the meanings of faith, hope, love, justice, and reconciliation.[58]

From Franklin's definition, I argue that first and foremost, public theology is theology, and theological reflection, that is not confined to individual lives or religious intuitions. Instead, public theology risks vulnerability and scrutiny of one's deeply held convictions, as it offers a response (from those convictions) to the needs of the community at large. Similarly, public theology also seeks the good of the community ahead of church needs or religious agendas. Public theology and a communal reorientation do not eliminate autonomy and self-concern. However, public theology pushes us to take seriously questions of a common good and the survival and liberation of the entire community.

Similarly, public theology, while emerging in and being grounded in particular religious convictions and institutions, is not designed to protect the rights and privileges of the institution at the cost of a larger goal or common cause.[59] Instead, a reorientation toward a public theology pushes youth to draw on the resources of their religious traditions to offer distinctive and constructive responses to the crisis of the community and world. Historian Mark Toulouse, reflecting on James Gustafson's understanding of public theology, writes, "The church's task is to convey publicly the best that Christian tradition has to offer. Theology joins the conversation without apology . . . [and] must offer an interpretation of people and communities that take seriously their activities as moral agents."[60]

In other words, public theology and a communal reorientation of adolescent spirituality is not an attempt to reduce spirituality to purely political action. However, participating in public theological reflection and action attempts to push youth to draw upon their religious convictions and ideals to work for a communal good. Reflecting on the legacy of Rauschenbusch, Joan Chittister reiterates the need to hold our public and social work in balance with the personal piety and spiritual disciplines of Christian faith. She writes,

> Prophetic presence and personal piety, however, were of a piece in Christian life for Walter Rauschenbusch. One was not distinct from the other. The function of religion was not simply to believe what we were told we must. The function of religion, he taught, was to prod us to do what had to be done in this world because of what we believed. It was to save lives as well as souls.[61]

Chittister reminds us that religion should serve as a catalyst for action in the larger community. Along similar lines, Franklin maintains the idea that public theologians are called to embody the radical idea that "love is the greatest force available to humanity for solving its ills." Thus, a reorientation to a communal and public theology also reminds us of the significance of embodied theology; in that, public theology is primarily the way we "live out our faith." In other words, public theology corresponds with particular and specific action in and on behalf of the wider public.[62] Gustafson, in an attempt to define the essential elements of his understanding of public theology, paraphrases Romans 12:1–2:

> Individually and collectively offer yourselves, your minds, your hearts, your capacities and powers in piety, in devoted faithful service to God. Do not be conformed to the immediate and apparent possibilities or requirements of either your desires or the circumstances in which you live and act. But be enlarged in your vision and affections, so that you might better discern what the divine governance enables and requires you to be and to do, what are your appropriate relations to God, indeed, what are the appropriate relations of all things to God. Then you might discern the will of God.[63]

IN THIS CHAPTER, I have built upon the complex legacy of African American Christianity, affirming that alternatives to fragmented spirituality exist; and within African American communities of faith there are both the theological resources and practical strategies that can help youth embrace an integrated spirituality. Particularly, the dialogical model of the Black Church undergirds a way of theorizing about the role of the church and African American spirituality, which counters simplistic characterizations and fragmentation. Grounded in the framework of Womanist theologians and ethicists, I began to explore four alternatives to the theological dimensions of fragmentation in the youth interviews and surveys. The concepts of cooperation with God, conversion, hope, and public theology emerge primarily from mining the African American Christian theological tradition for responses to the limitations of the nascent theology of the young people. In the next three chapters, we switch gears to wrestle with what Black youth are teaching churches to reclaim and do. I have argued here and in other works that young people are equal partners in the youth-community relationship.[64] If we take this seriously, then we must ask both what churches and Christianity have to offer Black youth *and* what Black youth have to offer the church. What remains in the following chapters is an expansion and analysis of these concepts explored here, and others. From the examples of some young African American poets, activists, and the interviewees, we explore more than limitations in their spirituality; we instead go deeper into the seeds for renewal of African American Christianity and communities. The most promising alternatives to fragmented spirituality emerge by holding together what young people teach the church and reclaiming the best of African American Christianity.

4

Does God Care?

I wonder how could God know that diabetes peels twenty-seven years
off life like dead skin.
Yet he still allows my brother to have his fingers pricked every day.
. . .

Sometimes five shots a day isn't enough to fight juvenile diabetes.
I think how could God bless him with seizures and autism.
Why every time we rush him to the hospital it could be my last day

—Nova, Louder than a Bomb poet

We pray to whatever God is up there
that my lost light would be enough to dull the destruction
I only hope that there's a life after death.

—Alexis, Louder than a Bomb poet

THERE IS AN often unspoken issue at the center of African American youth's fragmented spirituality—in that for some youth it is easier to have "no expectation" that God should work in particular areas of their lives than to wrestle with questions of how a good God could not respond to the concerns of Black youth. African American youth experience evil and suffering in ways that are often incomprehensible to the wider society. Even after years of researching and walking with Black youth, I am often surprised and overwhelmed by their narratives and raw creative pieces about death and violence. Their words cut through the positive joys or masks that they present to reveal deeper concerns and questions about the world they have inherited and in which they attempt to survive (and thrive). These raw reflections also reveal deeper theological quandaries that hint at the varied ways that African American youth are connecting (or not connecting) their questions about God with their experiences of evil and suffering.

When I first began exploring the fragmented spirituality of African American youth, religious educator Carol Lakey Hess questioned whether the need to separate one's religious beliefs from what one could expect to happen or change in the world was primarily an issue of theodicy, of not being able to fully reconcile the notion of a loving, powerful, all-knowing God with their experiences of suffering. I pushed Hess's question to the periphery for years, but it returned often. This in part had to do with my going further into the contours of fragmented spirituality to explore not simply what it looked like but why it occurs, particularly among young African Americans. Theodicy is not a word that African American youth are using to frame their religious experiences (most people do not use this term), but they are exploring dimensions of many of the historical trajectories classified as theodicy. In particular, they are wrestling with questions of why some people or groups of people have it easier than others (regardless of how hard they work). They are wrestling with how anyone could blame Black youth for *all* of the violence going on in US communities, and not see it as a pandemic requiring national attention and outrage. And as the quotes at the beginning of this chapter suggest, young people are wrestling with trying to figure out who God is and why God "allows" particular forms of suffering to take place.

Theodicy, as I conceive it, is not a defense of God, but it is wrestling with whether it is possible for God to exist, to be all-good, all-powerful, all-knowing, and for evil and suffering to exist as well. Historically, some theologians have wrestled with the philosophical distinctions between moral and natural evil. More contemporary theologians have also attempted to make sense of suffering and pain, which all experience. Emilie Townes, for example, makes a distinction between pain and suffering as she argues how one conceives of these can affect how one interacts and lives in the face of the existence of evil in the world.[1]

My approach to questions of theodicy differs from other treatments in African American religious thought and in general within Christendom, in that I start with the reflections and experiences of young people. Young people have often been the recipients of theodicies, but not the creators of them; yet their experiences of evil and suffering are just as profound and often more tragic than the adults around them. I start with the voices of African American youth in order to both learn more about their experiences of evil and suffering and to listen carefully for what *they can teach* the African American Christian community and society in general. Additionally, I wrestle with how and where young people learn and express these truths and paradoxes about God and their lives. Thus, I focus both on the content of their reflections on evil and suffering around them, as well as on how and where they articulate and discuss these ideas.

Most of the young people interviewed in this text and who were involved in my research believe in God. However, that does not exclude them from wrestling with questions about God and the world around them. In some ways, a strong belief in God opened the youth up to more questions and more concerns about what God was and should be doing in their lives.

In particular, my discussion of the understandings of the nature of God within young people's interviews and Black and Womanist scholarship (in chapter 3) begins to attend to this issue, for at the core of most theodicy (and theological challenges) is the assertion of both an all-powerful and an all-good God. However, does that understanding of God work in the lives of African American youth? And is a different understanding of God sufficient to attend to the realities of evil and suffering that are part of the daily experiences of Black youth and young adults?[2] Given the violent realities that many Black youth continue to live with and the challenges this death and violence present to theological claims of the goodness and power of God, I felt that these questions warranted a longer discussion (than simply pointing to the need to rethink our theological assumptions about God). This chapter is not a quest to *redeem God*—no theodicy or text can or should do that—but it is an honest attempt to walk with young people, learning from their reflections and helping create new models with them for how they can engage these ongoing questions at the heart of a life of faith and living in a very corrupt, evil, and violent world.

Talking Fragments: Spoken Word Poetry of African American Youth

The interviews and surveys with African American youth served as a preliminary discussion of fragmented spirituality among Black youth; however, in order to address more fully the perspectives of Black youth on violence and suffering, I turn to spoken word poetry. While poetry does not summarize the thoughts of youth, I look at this genre because it offers a larger sample of perspectives on youth voices as well as a literary genre that creates space for youth to reflect upon and speak out about their thoughts and questions of God. The poems are powerful, not because they give us details about the lives of these individual young people, but because they reflect an important genre and a creative expression of the experiences of young people. Their poetry is similar to the collective creativity in much of early Hip-Hop and even in the Blues. Thus, as we read and interpret the poems, I am careful to note that their works are not "pages from their diaries" or even interview data. Instead, they offer us another, but different window into the reflections of young African Americans that we cannot glimpse in the other genres.

Unlike prayers or spirituals, poetry is not primarily a religious genre. In some ways it may appear outside of the expected norms that I am examining sources that are not explicitly or primarily religious for information regarding the internal musings and public critiques of African American youth. However, it is necessary to look beyond traditional religious literature and communities to see what youth are thinking about and to go beyond the confines or strictures of Christian religious life. I also look at spoken word poetry as an additional source of youth thought, particularly regarding questions about God and God's work in the world, because young people often do not feel comfortable or encouraged in asking these types of questions within religious communities. For example, during a recent presentation by the Young Chicago Authors at the Faith Forward conference,[3] several of the students poets seemed surprised that Christian communities welcomed their voices and would encourage deep reflection on the community and the changes they called for in their poems.[4] While the form of fragmented spirituality focused on most in this work pertains to Black Christian youth who do not connect their spirituality with the injustices around them, the young poets reiterate the other side of the ongoing challenges of fragmented spirituality in which youth who are actively reflecting on the world around them do not think that these reflections are welcomed or included in African American Christianity and churches. However, the voices of young people, through poetry and spoken word, in the heart of urban communities (like, but also beyond Chicago) that are in the throws of a pandemic of youth violence and systemic negligence offer us a vivid snapshot of the reflections of young people who are aching to see real change within their communities but who do not see political or religious leaders (even God) as part of this change.[5]

Poem Selection Criteria

The poems included do not come from religious communities or self-identified religious young people. Instead, the poems represent two national poetry slam contests that recruit college- and high-school-aged youth to participate in spoken word contests. College Union Poetry Slam Invitational (CUPSI) is an annual event sponsored by the Association of College Unions International.[6] Louder than a Bomb (LTAB) focuses primarily on high-school-aged youth. LTAB is also an annual event, which began in 2001; additionally LTAB staff host writing workshops for students in the Chicago area year round.[7] Both competitions are open to all students. LTAB, however, represents a primarily African American and lower-income group of poets.[8]

I selected poems based on several criteria, including the perceived demographic data of the poet (e.g., race/ethnicity, gender, age) and the content of their poems.[9] I selected both poems that had explicitly religious references to God or biblical figures, as well as poems focused on particularly poignant and pressing concerns to African American youth. For example, included are poems that outline the idea of "Black privilege"—countering a long narrative of *privileging* of minorities in recent years, as well as poems that discuss interpersonal issues such as molestation and bipolar disorders in family members.

Form and Function of Spoken Word among Black Youth

The genre of spoken word poetry sets up a transgression of rigid boundaries of the public and private, as well as the personal and communal. Even in individual poems, the young people speak in the first person, but from the audience's response, one clearly observes that the events described are not simply the experiences of one poet or one young person. Instead, the poet expresses the collective anxieties and experiences of young people and gives voices to experiences that the author may have not experienced directly or may never have dared to voice (apart from this genre). The audience receives his or her reflections, not in a voyeuristic way of looking into someone's private life, but as a way of echoing his or her narrative and holding it as true and representative of the community's experience.

The act of sharing a poem offers many parallels to other forms of communal sharing, such as testifying and testimony sharing within religious communities. Elsewhere, I describe the function of testimony sharing within African American religion, and in youth ministry.[10] Testimony becomes a means of transforming individual situations into communal situations and speaking the truth of one's experiences to God and to the community. It is through the *sharing* of testimonies that individuals and communities begin to experience the possibility of solutions and transformation for their lives. Even as I hesitate to draw the lines of comparison too closely between *spitting* a poem and sharing a testimony, I make note of the call-and-response nature of poetry sharing, as well as the ability of the personal to become the communal in the simple act of sharing a poem. Both genres are typically short (three minutes or less for most poems and even shorter for testimonies in churches) and structured (e.g., there are standards and parameters that one works within to create a poem or to share a testimony), and the role of the audience or receiver is crucial to the exchange of the poem or testimony. The hearer both authenticates what was shared as well as holds what was shared in order to form a collective community that can strategize responses.

Art historians also note the significant connection of "slam poetry" to larger traditions of spoken word within African American culture. For example, Smithsonian curators describe the ways that spoken word art forms have generated many of the most well-known American art forms. The spoken word art form connects and builds upon earlier forms,

> Just as Langston Hughes and writers of the Harlem Renaissance were inspired by the feelings of the blues and the African American spiritual, contemporary hip-hop and slam poetry artists are inspired by poets like Hughes in their use of metaphor, alliteration, rhythm, and wordplay. Similarly, the experimental and often radical statements of the Black Arts Movement ... provide space for increasingly alternative political ideologies to be raised, discussed, and acknowledged.... These oral traditions serve not merely as pieces of history; rather they have provided a way of remembering, a way of enduring, a way of mourning, a way of celebrating, a way of protesting and subverting, and, ultimately, a way of triumphing.[11]

The ability of these communally spoken (and written) words to provide African Americans modes of remembering, enduring, mourning, celebrating, protesting, subverting, and even triumphing speak to the powerful role that slam poetry plays in the lives of many young African Americans.

Part of the success of LTAB has been in the year-long programming where young people come together in high schools and community forums to write and share and create the space for their concerns to be heard and held. Many young people reflecting on their experiences affirmed that without LTAB they would not have made it through high school or would not have had any sense of who they were or could be. If one looks at LTAB or other poetry groups as simply extracurricular activities, this seems like an extreme claim. However, when understood in light of the history of oral traditions within African American culture and protest, we see that young people are reminding us of an untapped resource and tradition for thinking through and responding to the violence and injustices around us. It reminds us to think carefully about what we learn from this art form and about creating communities and channels of expression from African American youth. Therefore, this chapter invites us into the spaces where youth are empowered to express their questions and experiences of suffering; it also calls us to engage with the content of these reflections— on the nuanced, messy, and complex reflections and descriptions of their environment.

Racism is Real!

The narratives and reflections of ethnic minority youth foreground the systemic and overarching experiences of suffering. They attend to their experiences of racism and their experiences of having to fight even for these experiences to be acknowledged or validated. Jalen Kobayashi, a fourteen-year-old poet, describes the "force" that must be countered every day in a world where racism is still so prevalent. He performs a poem decrying the attempts of some to say that "racism does not exist" anymore or to point fingers back at Black youth for all of the destruction in their own lives. Jalen poignantly declares that

> *Racism is as prominent today as it was in the '50s.*
> *Segregation negates all the patience.*
> *It is necessary to keep things going at the same pace.*
> *They are strapping our legs behind our backs,*
> *Gagging us and force-feeding us sedatives so we can't see what's going on.*
> *That force has been blowing strong*
> *And we see who's going along with it.*
> *. . .*
> *But let's not forget where the finger of blame is being pointed here.*

So don't you ever try to simplify and say that racism isn't alive,
Because you are only adding to the propane that makes it erupt in
*   flames,*
Only adding to the Rogaine that makes it grow back every time,
Adding to the fact that this force can never truly be killed.[12]

His poem is neither particularly nihilistic nor angry. He counters the claims that racism does not exist and makes references to police brutality and outcries and protest in Ferguson. He indicts those who deny racism a part of the system, which prevents us from ever ending racism. Another young woman, a college student, creatively counters ongoing narratives that not only deny the suffering and experiences of Black youth, but that also attempt to argue that there is "reverse racism" or "black privilege." Crystal Valentine, in her widely popular poem entitled "On Evaluating Black Privilege" offers commentary on experiences of being Black (and the "privilege" it holds), which includes trying to forget the legacy of slavery, while at the same time having already memorized the eulogies of all the men in one's family. Crystal also reflects on the erroneous beliefs that one's sisters are safe in this schema of "Black privilege."[13]

Crystal's work expresses the anguish that goes along with this reality through the experiences of hearing about the death of other young Black people and feeling it so closely and personally. Her poetry is somewhat self-critical as she reflects on the ways that many young African Americans feel like (or pretend that) they knew Trayvon Martin "on a first-name basis" and for the ways that she has won poetry slams using "a dead boy's name."[14]

In other words, she expresses the ways that African American youth deal with their individual struggles and are forced to confront the reality that Black youth are murdered and harassed simply for being Black and that their story could be "Trayvon's" story.

Racism is Real; Religion is Racist

Crystal's poem also includes direct religious and Christian references, which give us a glimpse of the complicated connections (and disconnections) young people have with religion in light of their experiences of being Black in the United States. Crystal offers one of the most profound theological reflections when she writes,

Black privilege is being so unique that not even God will look like you.
Black privilege is still being the first person in line to meet him.[15]

Here, her poem underscores the ways that mainstream religion, and more precisely Western Christianity, has portrayed the divine as White. There are scores of paintings both in European American and African American Christian communities where Jesus is depicted as white.[16] And while we can challenge the collapsing of Jesus with God, her statement remains just as profound. She underscores that most often, even the *Imago Dei* does not include Black people. However, within this alienation or exclusion from the image of God, Crystal is quick to note that it does not fully exclude one from the "privilege" of seeing God. Here, Crystal's poem can be interpreted in multiple ways. It critiques the ongoing relationship that Black people have with mainstream Christianity (such that, in spite of the ongoing oppression related to the image of God and in churches, African Americans still remain religious and Christian). This line also reflects another dimension of systemic racism, in that as an African American, one's life expectancy is not as long. Therefore the Black experience includes narratives of "having to see God" or dying sooner than other groups inspite of not being considered like this God.

As Crystal continues, her language turns more explicitly Christian, indicating a familiarity with the details of Jesus's life and experiences on the cross. She echoes the voices of Black liberation and Womanist theologians, but offers a perspective that is uniquely hers. She describes how "Black privilege" includes having to face death in similar ways as Jesus. She ironically discusses Jesus' "sense of humor" and his smiling on the cross.[17]

Her words cut through the generations of Black experiences and makes a connection to the crucifixion of Jesus and the ongoing calls (by Black and white Christians) for Black people to "suffer" like Jesus, or at best to live like Jesus. She notes that it is really not a privilege and that Jesus really did not smile on a cross, as she connects it to a more recent historical and religious leader, Malcolm X, who also had to face death with a "sense of humor." Her connecting humor with death and murder pushes hearers to experience the absurdity of "Black privilege" and the ongoing death of Black people.[18]

Crystal Valentine's religious and theological language flows seamlessly into her discussion and representation of the experiences and suffering of Black people, and her poem does not employ any sense that religion is the elixir that fixes the suffering or even one that empowers youth to continue in their struggles against oppression. Instead, it represents another example of the ways that Black people are alienated and the ways that their leaders, even the religious leaders, are expected to stay strong, smile, or laugh even in the face of death. Earlier in the same poem, she describes how tiring Black privilege is, in that it requires one to always be strong.[19]

Black privilege requires youth to be strong even in death.

While Crystal's poem contains some of the most explicitly theological language, other young poets also write about death as an ongoing reality in of the lives of young African Americans—just like the youth in my interviews. Alexis Pettis, a high-school poet from Chicago, shared reflections of Black youth suffering framed as a discussion of her first suicidal thoughts. Alexis's poem presents yet another dimension of Black youth suffering in terms of the effects of racism and perpetual fear on the mental health of young African Americans.

Alexis begins singing a familiar lullaby, with words so haunting that when overlaid on a melody meant to soothe babies, it adds multiple layers of meaning to both the experiences of death she portrays, and also to the possibility of death in her life and in the lives of those like her:

> *Hush little baby, don't you cry,*
> *Your tears won't make you stay alive.*
> *If you scream no one will hear.*
> *You'll be gone in an early year.*[20]

As I listened to her poem, I could sense the audience's inhaled breath, as they too were not sure what to do with her words. Assuredly, she was not the only youth to write about suicide (much less the only poet to ever do so). It some ways, there is an entire literary genre of reflections on death (which may or may not reflect their own experiences). However, Alexis's creative framing of how thoughts of ending life entered her existence cuts deep and could not be easily dismissed or understood as that of "depressed teen":

> *Was, I want to be a was.*
> *They say those who commit suicide are depressed.*
> *. . .*
> *I'm not depressed,*
> *But I want out.*
> *A dead person is worth more than a live,*
> *And I want to be someone's inspiration.*[21]

Her work offers a counter-narrative to popular understandings of suicide or death. She also points to the irony that young Black people are worth more dead than alive. (This theme is echoed by so many of the other young Black poets that I struggled initially to recount all the places where this ideology appeared.) For example, Crystal also wrote about the irony of knowing that if Black youth die, at least figures like Al Sharpton will come to their funerals and remind them that the only thing they are "worthy of is our death."[22]

It is a gross understatement to say that it should break one's heart to imagine that there is an entire generation of young people who believe that the "only thing they are worthy of is death"—and yet this sentiment is echoed in their reflections repeatedly. Returning to Alexis's poem on suicide, she writes that death is more inviting than the oppression of her current reality and the racism so entrenched in it. Alexis plays on popular literary tropes of equating death with blackness and writes,

> *Death seems more inviting than people's smiles.*
> *Death is black like you call me.*
> *So it can't be that harmful if it's just me.*[23]

In discussing suicide, she also includes various popular dogmas of what happens to Christians or people if they commit suicide. She responds with another indictment of the ways that religion and religious ideas are implicated in racist systems. In her poem, religion becomes another indicator of why living in an unjust world is not worth it:

> *They say those who commit suicide don't get to see heaven,*
> *Heaven, which is white and gold, dreams made of clouds and jasmine,*
> *If that is heaven, why would I want to go any place that's white,*
> *When I couldn't go any place that was white for a very long time, see*
> *I feel comfortable in the dark.*
> *If death is just darker days infinite,*
> *Then I'll be infinitely black,*
> *Cause that's the system anyway*
> *Defined by race and colors, languages and borders.*
> *Being on planet earth is not all it's cracked up to be.*[24]

Again, Alexis (like Crystal) calls her audience to reject any of the "easy" tropes or fixes, and to confront head-on the ways that the experiences of Black youth in this life are not at all what that they expected or "what it's cracked up to be." Alexis's poem expresses rage at the idea of heaven; it also reflects more critically on the systemic oppression of a world based on racism and oppression. She underscores the ways that "this world" treats African American youth as commodities and not as persons to be valued. Her reflections also do not hold out genuine hope that there is a God who wants anything better for their lives or who wants her to do something in light of her experiences. Absent from her poem (or any of their pieces) is an idea that God would affirm their rage or fight with them against oppression.[25]

Alexis's final stanza reveals anger and concern at how God operates, and she concludes with the assertion that death is God:

> We pray to whatever God is up there that my lost light would be
>   enough to dull the destruction.
> I only hope that there's a life after death.
> I only hope that my bloody plea will be enough to make the gods
>   reconsider earth.
> Let me be known as the girl who committed suicide so that others
>   could live life as they were meant to.
> . . .
> Death is as powerful as God.
> Death is God.
> And what way is there to be more closer to God than death?[26]

Will Suffering Appease the Gods?

Somewhat ironically, both Crystal and Alexis's poems contain dimensions of the rhetoric of a *suffering servant*, or sacrificing one's life for others. They each challenge this idea, but Alexis's poem ends with an aspiration that maybe the sacrifice of life could help others live, could appease the *gods* and make them reconsider all that is happening on earth. The religious background and upbringing of the youth poets is not explicitly named in their poems—neither is there an expectation that creative pieces are direct articulations of their personal religious beliefs or practices. Instead, there are only allusions to their religious upbringing and belief systems. (As with the interviewees, I only have basic demographic data and cannot presume that they know or hold to the theological positions of their traditions or denominations, as there is always diversity among belief and practice within groups.) However, there is a clear indication of familiarity with religious worldviews and ideas that gods have to be appeased and that the concept of God is somehow implicated in the destruction or wellbeing of the world. However, Alexis's work in particular does not stay here, holding out hope for "whatever God is up there" to do anything. Instead, she shifts her poem and describes death as the most powerful thing, as powerful as God.[27]

The youth poems force us to wrestle with the prevalence of the ideal of suffering to make a situation better. It does not appear that these young people are seeking to place blame on themselves (or other young people). Likewise, there does not seem to be a sense that they affirm the need for young people to die in order to fix the world around them. However, their poems are trying to make sense of dying and to hold out hope that these deaths can make sense. This is coupled with the notion that they are worth more dead—thus it seems that there is a strong undercurrent in both their creative expressions and the religious resources available to them, which pushes Black youth to say that death is better than anything that life has to offer. The young people are affirming simply that death *is*, and the best that they can hope for is death for a cause, or their death to inspire. Again, as a literary genre, poems about death are not taken as direct statements of the beliefs of young African Americans. However, in all art forms there is a level of creative expression that pushes the artist and hearers to wrestle with and even critique the dominant narratives surrounding their lives.

Respectable or Not: No Hope, No Outs

However, other poets do not demonstrate agency or voice hope that they can respond to the violence or racism around them (even through death). Some do not attempt to make sense of death or the prevalence of gun violence in their communities. They simply describe what young African Americans are experiencing. For example, one male teen, Antwon Funches, describes the insidious gun violence on the streets of Chicago. He notes that things are so bad that young people cannot venture far, and he recognizes that even walking to school is a risky event:

> *All it takes is block boys to ask*
> *"What's in your pockets, b?"*
> *My next walk to school may very well be my last,*
> *Because alphabet boys shooting boys who trying to learn*
> * their alphabets.*[28]

Antwon challenges the ideas that "respectability" or even doing exactly what one is "supposed" to do will help Black youth in his community:

> That's the Chi-rite militia, don't be in opposition,
> Just play your position.
> Stay focused on your mission.
> . . .
> These brothers didn't pass math.
> They never learned trajectory,
> Aiming for Ray Ray, but oops you done shot Dae Dae.[29]

He notes that regardless of what one attempts to do, the current reality for so many youth in the United States is gun violence and death. Regardless of the choices, behaviors, or strategies that he takes, the overwhelming reality of his life is that he lives in world where the randomness of the violence almost nullifies any personal choice, agency, and responsibility that young people could attempt to take for their own future. He calls this violence a cancer and asks "who can afford the chemo therapy?" His poem makes allusions to the lynching of Black people in previous generations as he calls the boys on his block "strange fruit," and he notes that other youth, too, are strange fruit, ready to be consumed by the systems of corruption:

> Strange fruit,
> These block boys are strange fruit.
> And they want you to hang too.
> . . .
> To these hitters, you're edible,
> With that black skin and that book bag,
> Police find you delectable.
> With that heart beat and that strong pulse
> They can't wait to take breath from you
>
> . . .
> these streets are so obsessed with you.[30]

It is powerful that his poetry does not completely vilify the "block boys" but includes the block boys as well as their targets, as *strange fruit* within a larger system of corruption. However, the recurring theme throughout his poem (and so many of the words of the other youth) is the reality of living in constant fear:

> *I know what it's like to have to fear for your life.*
> *You may get caught lacking.*
> *You may be on the right path, but*
> *You may get caught in traffic.*
> *I know hitters are out for my life.*[31]

What does it mean to be a high-school student whose most pressing concern is that someone could kill him at any given moment, for no reason? Antwon notes that there is no real expectation that young Black men will live to see twenty-one, so he should just drink now.

> *So pass the drinks,*
> *Not like I'll live to see twenty-one.*
> *Pass the vodka and rum.*
> *Beyonce tour, I'm on the run.*[32]

It is striking that the only thing Antwon thinks there is to do in light of this culture of death and suffering is to live and do all the things that one would typically put off until later in life. But it is important to note that he does not suggest doing things that are hopeful or connected to building a future. He closes the poem, entitled "OUCH," with a dream where he thinks he is safe, but gets shot anyway:

> *Last night I had a dream,*
> *It was me and another team*
> *In an alley way, clear as day*
> *I saw them point that gun,*
> *Gave my phone up as he asked,*
> *Thought that I was safe at last,*
> *still he pulled out the gat.*
> *I tried to dash.*
> *I saw it flash*
> *And screamed OUCH.*[33]

The last scream of "ouch" feels severely inadequate as a response to the ending of a young person's life and to the systemic oppression that creates a culture where Black youth can feel powerless and hopeless, and have to constantly fear for their lives. However, I wonder at the message of this word—is it an attempt to convey the inadequate responses of those around them and the absurdity of this culture and existence, such that the only responses can be those that are also absurd? Questions of the absurdity of African American experiences in the United States persist and have to be taken seriously. Antwon alludes to this larger history and to the fact that in the midst of these experiences and fears, all of the typical responses of *go to school; don't hang on the streets; don't resist the "block boys"; mind your own business; be a church kid; or dress well* are inadequate in a culture of disposability, youth violence, and suffering. They are all *absurd* in the face of a society that is structured to produce fear and squash all of the hopes and dreams of young people.

Why Would God?

Other young people focus less directly on death and dying, but they also offer a somewhat different perspective of the suffering of Black and minority youth. For example, Novana Venerable, a high-school poet featured in the LTAB documentary, wrote about her brother who was suffering from juvenile diabetes and autism.[34] Nova describes her experiences of fearing for Cody's survival and having to play a more grown-up role in her brother's life, because her mother had left them.[35] Nova's soft-spoken but powerful discussion of her brother's experiences reveals her personal experiences of suffering, all while alluding to the myriad systemic issues at play that allow this to be her experience as a teenager. Nova is one of the few youth who directly questions God regarding the suffering of her brother:

> And when I see him [Cody],
> I wonder how could God know that diabetes peels twenty-seven years
>   off life like dead skin.
> Yet he still allows my brother to have his fingers pricked every day.
> . . .
> Sometimes five shots a day isn't enough to fight juvenile diabetes.
> I think how could God bless him with seizures and autism.
> Why every time we rush him to the hospital it could be my last day.[36]

She questions both God's knowledge and actions. The irony of her word choice is striking. It is ironic to call autism and seizures blessings. This could speak to and critique an understanding of the nature of God as totally good—which implies that if God gives it, then it must be good or a blessing. Calling autism and seizures blessings could also reflect the layers of sarcasm in her reflections. For Nova is not content to accept these ideas; she wants answers from God. However, she does not offer an alternative nor completely dismiss the existence of God in her narrative; instead, she turns to her questions and concerns about what her brother will remember and whether he will forget how to say her name when she goes off to college:

> *Will he miss me when I am not there to run my fingers*
> *through his hair like Pink Oil when he wakes up from ear*
> *tube surgeries or seizures?*
> *Will he remember how he slept in my bed every night after*
> *mama left, . . .*
> *Or when my arms were his restraints when daddy said put*
> *him in middle without seatbelt so he would be the first to*
> *die in car accident.*
> *Can he know how he found a mother in big sister?*
> *For now, I will pray for him every night that his kidneys will*
> *stop trying to fail on us, that his blood sugar won't send*
> *him into a coma.*
> *I hope that he won't grow accustomed to not pronouncing my*
> *name when I go away to college,*
> *and I pray I pray that his seizures won't kill him before his*
> *diabetes does.*[37]

Nova's poem reminds us that violence is only part of the overarching contours of suffering that young people deal with. Her experience reminds us of the physical effects of centuries of oppression and the limited resources available in poor and minority communities to help families address the myriad health disparities. Often, scholars and medical professionals overlook the effects of these health disparities on the lives of young people. In reality, the complexities of systemic oppression make young people primary targets and victims in failing health care systems.

In reflecting on Nova's statements about God, I am struck by the directness of her questions, even in poetic form, and the certainty in her demand that God should have been able to do something for her brother and should not have *blessed* him like this. At first, I assumed that Nova simply had a different starting place than some of the other youth, such that she felt empowered to question God and voice her concerns directly. However, upon deeper reflection, I see that she addressed God with concerns about the personal, and her indictment does not implicate God or religion in any systemic concerns, in contrast to the indictments of Crystal and Alexis. However, her direct questions most closely parallel philosophical accounts of theodicy, but do not question God outside the realm of the personal. In other words, Nova's starting point reminds us of the ways that young people (even in creative formats) have been taught to engage God in and for personal and interpersonal concerns. Thus, I wonder if Nova was reflecting on a less personal experience; if she was writing about systemic violence, racism, government, and so on, would she feel as comfortable in her questioning and expectations of God?[38]

Resist! You are Moses!

Another college student also helps us to look at youth understandings of suffering that go beyond experiences of violence and death.[39] Tonya Ingram also puts her experiences of being Black in conversation with her experiences as a woman. She offers a poem in the form of advice, "Unsolicited Advice to Skinny Girls," and the beginning line haunts the audience with questions regarding what happened and how many young women did not have, heed, or know to heed this advice. Tonya starts, "When your best friend's father invites you over, say no."[40] Without warning or explanation, Tonya alludes to the inappropriateness of this request and the prevalence of lewd requests and suggestions from adults who should know better and should be in a position to respect and treat youth correctly. However, she points to the reality that Black young women and girls have to fight and counter advances in a variety of inappropriate ways.

Ingram intersperses her more serious advice with humor, but touches on a range of issues concerning Black youth and micro-aggressions directed toward them. For example, she writes,

> When the boy with the intrusive shadow calls you a white girl,
> Do not cower your head, do not question your black.
> . . .
> When the next NYU student asks to touch your hair, laugh,
> Then ask if you can touch theirs.
> When your best friend's father invites you over, say no.
> When your mother asks why you take so long in the shower,

Tell her you hate this cancer, this dark skin that raids you like the
    plague.

. . .

When you discover that your grandmother is bipolar and schizophrenic,
Hug her, then Google each illness.
When you question if you are anything like her,
Hug yourself, then Google each illness.[41]

Tonya's words speak of the personal struggles of young Black women, as well as struggles to address self-understanding or how to make sense of family dynamics. Stepping back from the telling lines and personal advice, I can also see the connections between Tonya's words and generations of family-systems dynamics that plague Black women and families. In particular, she gives advice on how to deal with having to buy a pregnancy test for one's own mother, of having to deal with catching a brother with porn, of how to respond when visiting your brother at Riker's, of having to fight one's own fears in order to hold and love your little sister (who your mom just had). Tonya's poem is hauntingly silent regarding the protagonist's own father. She does not offer any advice for how to deal with one's father and does not offer any indication of where he is or why he does not feature prominently in her narrative. Instead, the recurring line focuses on "her best friend's father." Underneath this seemingly humorous poem is a wealth of pain, of words unspoken, which do not have the ability to address or resolve these experiences.

Unlike some of the other poems, Tonya's does not implicate God or even address God as an active agent or potentially one who could be responsible or connected to anything. However, she employs explicitly religious language four times, and each time she does so in ways that point back to her agency and what young people can do:

> *When you visit your brother at Riker's Island, do not blink to*
>   *hold back the tears,*
> *You are Moses. He is the miracle. This is the Red Sea.*[42]

Her allusion to Moses, and seeing one's self as Moses, has many potential layers of meaning. First of all, it is telling that she equates young people (the poem's presumed audience) with the leader, the messenger, the one sent (by God) to lead the people. In this religious allusion, Tonya alludes to a larger cultural history of connecting with Moses figures as liberators of oppressed people and to religious and cultural narratives of having to speak truth to power, in efforts to stop the oppression of those one loves. Along these lines, it is also powerful that she holds onto the idea that, even in prison, one's brother is a miracle and that the system that they are struggling with is the Red Sea.

Tonya's second usage of directly religious language is also from a place of power as she responds to the insults of an older lady.

> When the older woman with silver hair and loose teeth calls you a
>   nigger.
> [Pause]
> Give her the finger.
> Give her Jay-Z's The Blueprint.
> Give her the word of God.[43]

Again, there is no clarity regarding her understanding of the *word of God* here. She could be referring to Jay-Z's lyrics as the word of God and/or this could reference any range of religious texts. In either case, she employs this imagery as a response to someone calling her out of her name. In many ways (regardless of the direct reference), she implies that the word of God is the thing that one can and should use in order to respond to a personal attack and the affront of being called a nigger. Perhaps the response *becomes* the word of God as it offers a corrective to insults and dehumanizing attempts. This is not simply a call to passively smile or laugh (as she advised to other micro-aggressions). Here she is advising the young person to do something bolder—to actively and directly address her anger toward this older woman and to do it under the rubric of "giving her the word of God."[44]

Her comment of offering the offensive woman the word of God builds to her poem to its climax, where she advises "skinny girls" of how they must respond when they witness the abuse of their loved ones:

> When your mother's ex-boyfriend puts his hands on your brother grab a
>   chair.
> When your mother's ex-boyfriend puts his hands on your sister grab a
>   frying pan.
> When your mother's ex-boyfriend puts his hands on your mother,
> Grab a phone, grab a knife, grab your voice.
> This is Armageddon!

. . .

Do not fear, do not cower, do not question.
When your best friend's father invites you over, say no.
You are resurrection,
You are silence turned shot gun, and
Death has no place here.[45]

There is powerful agency called for and affirmed in this poem. In each reference to religious symbols, there is a call to embody the religious ideal. The agency is not delegated, and the references are not to some detached or distant deity (as alluded to in other poems) or to some corrupt system of beliefs, which have not benefited Black youth. Tonya's use of religious symbols and metaphors could also demonstrate a humanist turn in her understanding of religion. Yet it also models the possibility of a young woman seeing herself as actively involved in the life choices and outcomes around her—such that she represents the "resurrection" and the power to oust death in the face of domestic violence against her family and the potential disempowerment of herself.

There is a striking difference in the tone and purpose of Tonya's poem, in relationship to the poems of other youth who are directly addressing systemic injustices (versus interpersonal or individual issues—which youth across the board feel more empowered to address). And while her starting place is individual and personal, I do not want to undermine the courage inherent in her call to action and the call to embody the religious ideas instead of simply believing in them. Instead, Tonya reminds both youth and adults of their ability to embody the power and agency of the religious symbols they often reference. Tonya pushes us beyond a questioning of where is God to the possibility that God is in us and working through us.

Dreams Are Powerful!

One final high-school poet, Eric Simpson, offers another direct call to confront and think differently about the world and the experiences of Black youth in a violent society. In his poem entitled "Hopes and Dreams," he uses the refrain of "young people like me don't last here" to illumine the ways that the world is structured in opposition to young people who would dare to hope for a different type of world or even a society in which the status quo is *not* maintained. At first glance, he appears to simply offer a limited critique of the harsh realities of urban life, as he describes walking through streets that are blind to hope and passion; but Eric's larger criticism is that there are so many people (young and old) who no longer dream or envision a better world. He even argues that dreaming and writing are what makes them so powerful, dangerous, and endangered.[46]

Like Tonya (and Alexis), he connects agency with embodying the religious ideal, with being *a god*.[47] He also continues the theme of seeing power in the death of a young person, as he argues that even if he is gunned down, he will "resurrect." However, Eric also reminds us of a different type of agency and pushes the discussion of youth suffering to the question of how youth understand themselves in relationship to it. Eric pushes the audience to embrace the idea that dreams and hopes are also active and dangerous. I was initially struck by the rhetoric of "young teens like me don't survive here." I wondered if he was pointing to distinctions between groups of young people in his community, to continue a narrative of "bad seed" verse good youth. And while there are layers of this trope of bad versus good youth, his words also open up a discussion of seeing that any young person who dares to dream, to imagine a different world, does not survive in the conditions created for them by the larger culture of disposability. Eric, with the other poets, ends by offering a reminder that when young people begin to speak and write, they can transform their current realities.

Speaking a True Word

Paulo Freire writes that to "speak a true word is to transform the world."[48] I argue that African American youth poets are engaging in dialogue and attempting to speak a true word. Freire asserts that a true word includes both reflection and action—and in the creation and sharing of their poems, these young people are offering "true words." Freire also notes that speaking a true word cannot be done alone or for someone else. Therefore, the young people have to speak with their communities and for themselves in order for their words to be truly transformational. The youth poets are both reminding us of the power of speaking a true word in transforming evil and suffering in their lives, but they are offering fierce correctives to many of our (African American religious and scholarly) attempts at making sense of evil and suffering and the presence of God. In particular, throughout Christian history, there have been attempts to reconcile the theological challenges and quandaries of suffering and evil with the existence of a good God. These debates have been particularly pressing in light of the history of injustice to and oppression of African Americans. And many Black and Womanist theologians have wrestled with this question. Most notably Anthony Pinn, Emilie Townes, William R. Jones, and Delores Williams have offered insights to help with these challenges. While exploring and valuing their contributions to this work, I find that the youth poets actually push beyond these scholarly reflections and offer insights that cannot be ignored by African American scholars and churches.

For example, Anthony Pinn's earliest works on evil and suffering, *Why, Lord?: Suffering and Evil in Black Theology* invites us into his personal narrative as a young man growing up in the AME church, being called to preach at fourteen and subsequently raising questions about the tension between his lived reality and Christian truths.[49] Pinn also wrestled with the ability of the Christian message to say anything liberating to suffering humanity and with whether theological conversations serve to make a positive difference in the way the oppressed respond to their existential plight. Pinn's initial response was to call for a rethinking of the nature of God to transfer "responsibility" for moral evil from God to humanity. His later works also push the African American religious community to fully engage Black humanism, instead of holding onto an idea of redemptive suffering. I appreciate Pinn's work because he takes to task the easy move toward "redemptive suffering"—which attempts to make sense of oppression by saying either that some good emerges from suffering or, in the more extreme case, that God requires suffering in order to fulfill God's plan for humanity.[50]

However, the move toward humanism raises further questions for my work with young people, in that it suggests that the primary means of empowering young people to make sense of their experiences of violence, evil, and suffering is to fragment more. It suggests that the best or primary solution is to shift perspectives such that there is a genuine sense that there is nothing wrong with *not* seeing God as involved in certain areas of their lives. In Pinn's discussion, this belief could be justified because God is not responsible, or *there is no God*. However, Pinn's responses are helpful in addressing a secondary effect of fragmented spirituality, in that many youth interviewed also did not feel empowered to act for change in their communities. Shifting responsibility from God to humans could serve as a powerful catalyst for action, if utilized properly. Similarly, humanism is steeped in a strong faith in the efficacy of humans in effecting change among themselves. However, these responses are not as helpful to the questions of African American youth who strongly hold to a belief in God and therefore would push back at Pinn's solutions, simply as the cynicism of a non-believer.

Pinn's call to move beyond traditional categories and theodicy to see the variety of religious articulations and reflections available to Black people is helpful. However, in this move, he seems to have failed to fully account for the material reality of the lives and struggles of Black folks. In other words, his shift is a strong and necessary theoretical and ideological shift that could be helpful in empowering Black young people, but he does not seem to have accounted for what actual, effective change and the ending of suffering looks like. Therefore, instead of addressing the massiveness of Black suffering, Pinn's work appears to just challenge or blame the category of God (and/or the community's reliance upon the idea of God). In other words, if God is seen as causing or allowing suffering, and our love affair with this kind of God is unhelpful, then just get rid of God. However, does this move address suffering? Is it a necessary step in addressing suffering? Does it blame those who suffer for having "bad beliefs" that contribute to their suffering? Does it empower others to work to eradicate suffering? Or is it a peripheral move afforded to those whose daily reality is not/no longer the constant struggle to survive—such that it becomes the navel-gazing that early Black theologians rallied against and which does not sit well with the young people who have to walk in a world where erudite theorizing does not protect one from bullets? Neither do the categorical shifts made by Pinn change the systems sufficiently to push for a complete overhaul of the respectability politics that purports to afford opportunities to those who simply play by the rules. Antwon and other youth poets remind us that it is not because scholars have theorized incorrectly that young people are suffering. Instead, scholars and concerned adults have failed to fully understand their narratives and work with young people to respond to these situations, and we have failed to dismantle systems of evil and oppression, and as a result, we are currently experiencing a pandemic of violence and suffering.

While Pinn, following in the tradition of the William R. Jones, represents one way of wrestling with theodicy and theological challenges (which I name as insufficient in the face of Black youth suffering), other scholars, like James Melvin Washington, also contribute some helpful reflections. For example, Washington, in the introduction to *Conversations with God: Two Centuries of Prayers by African Americans*, also offers a helpful discussion of issues at the heart of both the lived reality and study of African American religion.[51] Washington recounts his personal experiences with

Christianity and his observations of people of other religions at worship. He reflects on how his observations, along with his own emergence as a pastor and a scholar during the Black Power Movement, pushes him to continue to wrestle with questions of faith (and of theodicy), such as, "why do people who suffer continue to believe in a God who supposedly has the power to prevent and alleviate suffering?"[52] Washington, like Pinn, notes that one way of dealing with these questions is to no longer believe in the existence of God, and in many ways he *wishes* that he could take that posture. But this was not the path he chose (or could choose), and thus he offers a different perspective on the questions of Black suffering for young people who still want or feel compelled to believe in God. Washington rather recounts his experience of learning to pray from his mother. His mother and faith community also taught him the necessity of prayer as a way of life. He writes, "The reigning assumption of the African American Christian community that nurtured me [was] God is a living, personal presence that is insinuated at all times and in all circumstance."[53] This statement and structure is the flip-side of the theodicean conundrum for African American youth. First, it pushes us to wrestle with whether African American youth still experience this overarching assurance of God's presence. Second, it pushes us to wrestle with how an assurance of God's presence squares with their experiences of injustice and oppression all around them.

The primary religious practice of Washington's reflections is prayer—but what he writes about prayer illuminates many questions about the continuing role of religion and spirituality in the lives of African American youth. He writes the following about the power of prayer: "Prayer in the midst of the abortion of one's human, political, and social rights is an act of justice education insofar as it reminds the one who prays, and the one who overhears it, that the one praying is a child of God."[54] Washington, like the young poets, again pushes us to remember the power of both the speaker and the hearer—he points to the communal nature of prayer as well. He further notes the educational nature of prayers as they were prayed in corporate worship and as they are read generations later. Even prayer was not a one-sided individual exchange with God; rather, there was something communal about praying to God.

Washington's reflections, however, are not without challenges. This is in part because he has not set out to offer a nuanced treatment of the faith and theology of African Americans and thus to make some broad statements regarding the character of God. Washington's reflections travel close to a narrative of redemptive suffering, as he discusses the role of prayer in the history of African American social-change movements. He writes,

> African American prayers as a literary genre, and a religious social practice, assume that God is just and loving, and that the human dilemma is that we cannot always experience and see God's justice and love. We pray for faith to trust God's ultimate disclosure.[55]

Again, the overall sentiment is strong and conveys the tensions of believing in a just and loving God, while not being able to experience the justice of God on earth. However, this statement also has another layer that does not acknowledge any room for understandings of God beyond just and loving. As a result, the "failure" to see or experience the justice or love of God is on humanity (indicating a pretty ineffective Godhead). Likewise, the inability of humanity to experience the justice of God can easily be read as an individual failing or experience, and not one in which there are persistent and *evil* systems in place that actively thwart the abilities of all humans to experience the love and justice of God. Washington also argues that prayer teaches African American believers to exercise "revolutionary patience"—a concept that raises many questions regarding the ability or need for urgent and impatient action in the face of injustices. The promise of prayer and faith is realizing the "spiritual legacy" of the ancestors.

> But the literary history of African American prayers suggests that, besides anticipating God's ultimate self-disclosure in the history of the oppressed, we are the trustees of a spiritual legacy paid for with the blood, sweat, tears, and dreams of a noble, even if not triumphant, people. The culture, grammar, and promise of the African American prayer tradition is in our hands. Only time will tell whether or not their faith in us was worth the price they paid.[56]

The sentiments of this hope that "time will tell" emerges from a popular desire for the hopes of the ancestors to be fulfilled in the generations to come, particularly if flourishing was not possible in their lifetime. It is important to note that this sentiment still borders on redemptive suffering or meaningful suffering. It can easily be read as, "If the blood, sweat, and tears of previous generation produces better faith in us, then it was worth something." The tension within redemptive suffering is that we want our lives to mean something, and if a great deal of life has been suffering, then we want that to mean something too. I fear however, that this move toward meaning is disempowering when it too easily leads people to just endure suffering instead of seeking to transform the world and structures that create suffering. Therefore, I cannot hope with Washington that the suffering of our ancestors and their faith in us is worthwhile. However, I can hope that young people learn from their actions, their faith, and their failures to act—so that they too can figure out how to resist and survive in a world where the suffering of Black people is not seen as absurd, but taken for granted as part of our lived reality.

In contrast to Pinn and Washington (who begin their reflections with their personal religious experiences and reflections on the historical oppression of African Americans), Emilie Townes in the introduction to her edited volume on evil and suffering recounts how the volume came together during the aftermath of the "Rodney King Verdict."[57] And the resounding question of the volume was, "Where is the Black church (and its women, men, and children) as we face evil and suffering in the United States and in our world?"[58] Townes rejects the idea of suffering as God's will. She writes that Womanist thought rejects suffering as God's will; instead, suffering is an outrage.[59] But this Womanist idea has not permeated society at large. For example, one can look at President Obama's eulogy for the victims in Charleston and see that there is a narrative of God using suffering for a greater good.[60] Townes writes, "Many Black folk in the church grew up with the stories of Moses, Abraham, Ishmael, Ruth and Esther." The effect of growing up with these stories was an overarching narrative where *suffering* was "the entry key to the kingdom." She affirms that "the inevitability and desirability of suffering needs to be challenged."[61] Within the framework of Christianity, Townes argues that the experiences and conditions of suffering are antithetical to the experiences of a resurrected people. She writes,

> To live and work through pain acknowledges our human ability to effect change in individual lives and in the lives of others. We must learn to move from the reactive position of suffering to that of the transforming power of pain, to use it as a critical standing and refuse to accept the "facts" handed to us.
>
> The roots of this stance are grounded in the liberating message of the empty cross and the resurrection. God has taken suffering

out of the world through the resurrection of Jesus. Because God loves humanity, God gives all people the opportunity to embrace the victory of the resurrection. The resurrection moves the oppressed past suffering to pain and struggle and from pain and struggle to new life and wholeness.[62]

Townes categorically rejects any understanding of suffering as good. She grounds this in a practical ethic that asserts, "Suffering and any discussion that accepts suffering is good is susceptible to being shaped into a tool of oppression."[63] Townes further uses a distinction between pain and suffering employed by Audre Lorde, where Lorde argues, "suffering is the inescapable cycle of reliving pain over and over again when it is triggered by events or people."[64] Therefore, Townes acknowledges that all experience pain, but she argues that we must resist the inescapable cycles of suffering and the people and systems that seek to normalize and capitalize on the suffering of others.

While Townes offers one of the most helpful discussions of suffering and evil, which holds in tension the Christian narrative and the lived realities of current young people, I fear that her analysis in this earlier volume does not complicate or challenge the ways in which even the language of "an empty cross" and God taking suffering out of the world through the resurrection of Jesus is another side of redemptive suffering. It takes the necessity and value of suffering away from humankind, but it still holds onto an image of God who uses the suffering of Jesus to take away the suffering of other oppressed persons. Townes's work here rests on an ongoing tension within the Christian narrative even as she critiques the valorizing of suffering in our current situations. In some ways, the young people parallel these tensions in their poems that hold out hope that if they are going to die then at least their death can have value for others, in that they died trying to resist.

Townes draws upon the work of Ida B. Wells-Barnett and her admonition to pray and trust in a God who is capable of assisting in our current struggles, versus praying for acceptance when or after we die. Wells-Barnett is quoted, saying,

You have talked and sung and prayed about dying, and forgiving your enemies, and of feeling sure you are going to be received in the new Jerusalem.... But why don't you pray to live and ask to be freed? ... Let all of your songs and prayers hereafter be songs of faith and hope that God will set you free.... Quit talking about dying; if you believe your God is all powerful, believe [God] is powerful enough to open these prison doors, and say so.... Pray to live and believe you are going to get out.[65]

Wells-Barnett serves as a powerful reminder of the ethic of "choosing life," of choosing to live and not simply being prepared to die. This is an essential corrective to questions of evil and suffering. Part of the challenge of these types of questions rests in the type of actions youth feel empowered to take and the types of outcomes that youth hope for in the face of the overwhelming and absurd realities of evil and suffering.

For example, Alexis writes about death in juxtaposition to heaven, and she names suicide as a positive action and viable response. Her words push against the presumed wisdom of most of society and even most of the African American community, that suicide or choosing death could *never* be preferable to life or to even the hope of heaven.[66] However, this sentiment is not completely foreign to African Americans, for whom the realities of life are often absurd at best. There are also echoes of the spiritual calling for freedom, with the refrain of "before I be a slave, I'll be buried in my grave, and go home to my Lord and be free."[67] This type of response to evil and suffering has often been criticized as "escapism" or other-worldly. But there is something powerfully resistant about proclaiming to fight so hard for what is right in this world, but to also never take death off the table as the corrective to life in a world that does not value your life. These questions of death and the place of death in the lives of Black youth come up for several of the poets.

Similarly, in the interviews, most youth also discuss death. Kira talks about being concerned about what will happen to her friends who are constantly in dangerous situations and who have become numb to hearing about the death of young people. Jackie talks about shooting deaths and events. Charles talks about the death of one of his close friends. Marissa talks about the shooting deaths of Black youth that have made national news. Even in the years before a "full-fledged" Black Lives Matters campaign, death, specifically the death of young people, has been on the minds of young African Americans. They are living it and experiencing so many different aspects of it. The previous groundswell of attention regarding racism and police brutality converged around Rodney King and the inability to be treated fairly by police. Yet this generation of young African Americans receive daily reminders that police and vigilantes can kill youth, just because.

Conclusion

The poetry and reflections of African American and minority adolescents offer a rich, creative, and heart-wrenching account of experiences of systemic and personal suffering. Racism is real and still defines much of their experiences. Violence (often intricately connected with racism) is also normal for most of these youth. Living in fear and wondering about death (their own or their loved ones) are daily occurrences. And in the face of their lived realities and reflections, I have wrestled with the questions of where God is and where these young people see God or even expect God to operate.

Their reflections further undergird my assessment that African American youth are experiencing fragmented spirituality, in that there is a limitation to the places that God shows up, even in their complaints and laments about the evil and suffering that they are experiencing. However, their narratives nuance our understandings of fragmented spirituality by helping us to explore both the "justifications" of/for God and Christianity, but also the indictments of the ways that God and Western Christianity have been implicated in the suffering and oppression of Black people, including young people.

So What Now?

Reviewing these poems has both confirmed my understandings of youth experiences and pushed me to question more fully the role of Christianity in young persons' lives and formation. To be honest, I clearly want to affirm that Christianity and the Black churches and communities have tremendous resources for young people to tap into (some of which I name in chapter 3), but in terms of evil and suffering, the traditional resources have not been sufficient. As noted in the writing of Black Liberationist, Humanist, and Womanist religious scholars, Black people have been reflecting on and wrestling with these issues for generations. They have also expanded upon and countered attempts to discuss suffering and evil within European Christian contexts. However, at each turn and each reflection I have asked, How do the current realities of African American youth fit in this narrative? (And how do the reflections of African American youth expand these conversations?)

Can we explain their current experiences of suffering away with the call to "persist in the face of evil" or to pray that they will live up to the faith and courage of their ancestors (as Washington suggests)? Can we hope that they become liberated from belief in God, such that they can be more self-actualized and act in response to evil (instead of expecting God to or getting frustrated if/when God does not, as Pinn suggests)? To be certain, the scholarly reflections on evil, suffering, and even their theodicies are more complicated that these one-line summaries. However, the summaries remind us that none of these are sufficient individually (or collectively) to help youth, who are already fragmenting their spiritual lives to make sense of their experiences of evil and/or suffering.

There is ongoing hesitation in most communities (and particularly among mainline denominations) to even discuss evil. Often people cannot or do not want to think of evil (either its manifestations or even the idea that in order for their to be evil, there has to be an explanation of where it came from). However, these discussions do not help us with the suffering of Black youth. My work is not to question or articulate whether evil and suffering exist. This snapshot of the youth reflections offers numerous examples and evidence that evil does exist. Evil is real. Suffering is taking place. And the lives of Black children and youth are being impacted because of the inabilities of systems to reduce their suffering. And yet, I wonder about what prescriptive role I could espouse for youth in light of this kind of suffering. Honestly, I still hold onto a belief in an involved and a sovereign God. And I do not want youth for whom this image of God and understanding of God functions to give this up in favor of, say, a humanist or atheistic turn, which philosophically makes more sense and is easier to explain, but is not functioning or present in the lives of many young people. I want to honor the reality that many Black youth still believe in some type of God and expect *that God to act* in their lives. However, what African American Christian communities are offering youth in terms of theology and processes is sorely insufficient.

In particular, it would be rare to find any large group of Black Christian youth who have read or reflected on the ideas presented above regarding Christian understanding of suffering and other reflections on evil. It would be rare to find a group that both lifts up the power of God or prayer in the resistance of Black Christians or that has allowed Black youth to actively question God beyond their personal experiences (or who demand action from God).

Alexis's suicide poem and the ensuing ideas that Black youth are worth more dead than alive (or that death is better than being alive) gave me pause. It challenged both my understanding of Black youth's daily struggles, as well as the mental suffering and anguish they experience. However, I also paused, wondering where the community was that could challenge the growing consensus that Black youth are worth more dead than alive, or that death is more appealing than life. I wondered about whether in the reflections of Emilie Townes, these young people had ever been challenged to resist the inevitability of death in light of a bold affirmation of life. I wondered if they knew of the call of Ida Wells-Barnett, quoted above to pray to live.

Nova, too, gives us hope that young people would question God's role in the suffering of a sibling. But Nova also left so much unsaid (as is expected in a three-minute poem) in how she really expected God to act or whether she understood God both in the giving of life and illnesses, as well as in the blessing of her little brother to have an older sibling like her to look out for him. In other words, Nova's reflections push us to consider if she could see God in herself and understand God empowering her as a counter-narrative to one of a God who gives diabetes and seizures as blessings. In other words, where was a Christian community's challenge of this way of thinking? Did anyone ever suggest to her that diabetes and autism were not blessings from God and that the lack of resources to cure or respond to these issues was vastly interconnected with systems of oppression and profits? Did anyone suggest that her brother could have a better quality of life with different types of resources and that she could work to get these resources?

Tonya also gives hope that she can see herself (and other young women) in the religious symbols that permeate US culture. However, I too wonder at the communities that influence even this type of creative theological connection (or that influence Crystal and Alexis, Antwon, and all the others). I reflect on the types of communities that can affirm youth agency and religious reflections, while also pushing and helping them to see and create strategies for longer and more sustainable responses to the injustices around them. In particular, Tonya makes me reflect on the types of communities that can help youth see that they, individually, are not the only hope or agents in their communities.

Each young poet and interviewee pushes us to question not only the content of his or her theological reflections and questions (of God or others), but also to ask what it would look like to walk with African American youth as they balance attending to their experiences of suffering and learning to persist, resist, and transform their experiences and the world. African American youth do not need another theology of suffering (even if I felt equipped to write one in light of their experiences). What I see as most needful is a full-fledged embracing of the questions and reflections of young people toward God and the world around them.

So instead of a theology of suffering, a theology that says that Black youth should not suffer, or even that they should resist systems that support suffering, the primary need is offering youth a better process and space in which to reflect and ask these questions of God, themselves, and their lives. One of the major gifts in the practice of sharing youth poems (because often they are written together in communities and shared locally and nationally) is that their experiences are held together. Looking specifically at questions of theodicy, I am aware and wary of any attempts to offer youth a rigid set of beliefs for them to hold onto regarding who and what God is to them or how God connects to their experiences of suffering. But it is imperative to invite youth into a community of reflection and accountability, as well as a community of pushing and holding. These communities are necessary so youth are allowed to move beyond parroting societal themes or dominant Christianity to wrestling with what hope, liberation, and life could look like in light of their experiences.

5

Being Young, Active, and Faithful

BLACK YOUTH ACTIVISM RESHAPING
BLACK CHRISTIAN SOCIAL WITNESS

Youth Speaking Out!

Sixteen shots! Sixteen shots! Sixteen shots! became the rallying cry when the mayor of Chicago visited an esteemed high school, where he usually gets a warm reception and where the students represent the "success" stories of urban youth with a 100 percent graduation rate and college acceptance rate.[1] Why would these "good" kids decide to chant against the mayor instead of standing to recite the school's creed? They were protesting the fatal police shooting of seventeen-year-old LaQuan McDonald and calling for the mayor's resignation for his delaying the release and possible cover-up of the information that led to the indictment of Officer Jason Van Dyke. But more than this specific chant and protest, these "well-behaved and respectable" students made a conscious choice to participate in a larger and longer legacy of civil disobedience in order to bring attention to injustices around them.[2] In truth, the frustrations and outright rage at systems and structures that continue to oppress minorities and youth in the United States are forcing us to rethink attempts to label youth as apathetic or rebellious without a cause (as adolescents have been labeled and dismissed in the past).

As noted in chapter 1, youth engagement in community issues and service was prevalent in my sample of youth attending YTI in the past decade, in that all youth participated in some type of community service. However, the youth I interviewed did not often participate in direct action, corresponding to the things that were of most concern to them. But this chapter focuses on more than community service or activities. It looks specifically at youth involvement in political activism and civil disobedience. And while my interview sample did not offer a large percentage of youth who were engaged in political change (or even registering to vote or writing to politicians) during the heart of my study (2007–2009), the last seven years demonstrate an uptick in youth activism and political engagement.[3] Many credit this increase in activism and civic engagement (particularly among African American youth and young adults) to the presence of a president of African descent. Others, however, are noting the resurgence of a type of activism across socio-economic classes and pointing to an increased interest in community organizing and to the unique role of social media. Protests such as Occupy Wall St. and #BlackLivesMatter are becoming key historical markers and movements within this generation of young people. Regardless of how we theorize it, Black youth are organizing and living in a world where apathy, fear, and even respectability are not the only options. Instead, young people are responding in ways that are both uniquely reflective of the current struggle for freedom and connected with historical strategies and efforts to effect mass social change. I am intentional in naming both the uniqueness of this generation of youth activism and the similarities to activism and movements of prior generations. This dual attention is important in order to better theorize about what young people are up to. It is also essential to helping concerned adults walk with youth in ways that empower youth to draw upon resources and strategies that have worked in the past and to navigate the potential pitfalls of working in a different era (with new rules and new technologies).

Black Youth Activism, Unchurched?

The overall dissatisfaction with the status quo and institutions, and the unwillingness to just *take it* echo the voices of the young poets who creatively expressed their concerns and convictions about what is wrong in our current society and what is wrong with God and religion (see the previous chapter).[4] In fact, the youth poets are offering a type of protest and activism of their own. However, in addition to the reflection of youth poets and these student protestors, student unrest and outcries are more the "norm" than the exception, and far too often young people who are Christian do not see or feel space for their outcries within Christian contexts. Likewise, most do not have frameworks for reflecting on their faith and values in light of the protest and unrest that they want to participate in.

Contemporary youth protests can be read as another indicator of the fragmented spirituality of young African Americans, in that their social and political protests do not have a theological or religious lens/space. However, instead of arguing, as some recent scholars have done, that these protests are "replacing the church" in the lives of youth and in the efforts for social change, I affirm that this kind of activism and protest creates opportunities for youth and adults to re-envision their faith in news ways and to re-integrate their faith with efforts to work for change now.

Many scholars and commentators have also asked, "Is this the first generation [of African Americans] for whom God or the Church is irrelevant to their activism?"[5] And while this is an interesting question, it is one that disregards the complex and nuanced ways that Black churches and religion have functioned throughout the course of African American history. Truthfully, referring to the theoretical construct of the *Black church* overemphasizes a unity and cohesion of thought and practice. As Barbara Savage affirms, Black churches "are among the most local, the most decentralized, and the most idiosyncratic of all social organizations. Despite common usage, there is no such thing as the 'Black church.'"[6] There is no single narrative or way of theorizing the connection of social activism and the Black church, because of the diversity underlying this concept and institutions. As a result, most who would argue that the church is *dead* or irrelevant are in fact arguing that dominant ways of theorizing about it have been debunked or relativized in the wake of having to tell a more complete story of this connection. In particular, the comparison between contemporary activism and the Civil Rights Movement demonstrates a redacted narrative and romanticized connection between the institutional church and *that* movement as well. For example, a recent interview with Pastor Jeremiah Wright helpfully summarizes and reminds us of the re-narrating of the connections between the Black church and the Civil Rights Movement of the 1950s–1960s. Wright boldly states,

> The church up North and out West were not involved in the civil rights. In fact, the church up North was anti-King. I live in Chicago. In Chicago, J. H. Jackson, president of the then-National Baptist Convention, was rabidly opposed to Dr. King. And so was the whole National Baptist Convention, the largest Black convention at the time of Baptists. Church of God in Christ weren't involved at all. Pentecostal ... not at all. And up North? Not at all. It was not a church movement. And neither is Black Lives Matter.

There are a lot of similarities I see in terms of where the church is, where the church was, where the church is not today. Some of our activists in the Black Lives Matter movement are put out with the Black church because it's so silent, or so laid back, or so uninvolved. So was the Black church in the Civil Rights Movement. The Black church became mobilized by King after he was dead.[7]

In Wright's assessment, much of the Church was silent during the Civil Rights era as well. Even before this critique, we see countless accusations and assertions that the Black church (and the larger Christian church) has so often been found silent or even on the "wrong" side of history. In other words, this is not a contemporary issue—and we would do well to not overstate the role that churches have played within movements for social change at any point in history.

Du Bois, writing over a hundred years ago, echoes (and predicts) the reactionary stances of churches in the face of injustices and in light of pressing questions about what the church should be doing. He writes,

> This paper is a frank attempt to express my belief that the Christian Church will do nothing conclusive or effective; that it will not settle these problems [of the color line in the U.S.]; that, on the contrary, it will as long as possible and wherever possible avoid them; that in this, as in nearly every great modern moral controversy, it will be found consistently on the wrong side and that when, by the blood and tears of radicals and fanatics of the despised and rejected largely outside the church, some settlement of these problems is found, the church will be among the first to claim full and original credit for this result.[8]

Du Bois's critique is much harsher than Wright's. Du Bois further pushes current questions (or even frustrations) about the connection between Black churches and justice-seeking into a larger, somewhat nihilistic framing. Du Bois asserts that the Church has never been at the forefront of these types of movements, and in his assessment they never would be. And counter to the oft-touted and positive understanding of the church and religion within African American life, Du Bois represents an earlier strand of theorizing about the Black church. Historian Barbara Savage summarizes this earlier strand noting that earlier "Black religion and Black churches figured first and foremost as innately a 'problem' for the race."[9] Therefore, in reflecting on questions of this generation's connections to Black religion and churches, the narrative is more complex than a rise of unaffiliated or un-churched activism.

Furthermore, in part, this work and the work of Black youth activism, both within and apart from Black churches, offer hope that Du Bois's critique will not always be true (that while his assessment of the past may be correct, that his prediction of what role churches can play in the future will not persist). Scholars and practitioners are forced to attend to the reality that the spirituality and activism of young African Americans are shaped and expressed in complex ways (often outside of the control or purview of established institutions).[10] Attention to this reality must become more important than narrowly focused attempts to reinvigorate the Black Christian church. It also forces us to attend to the reality that the activism of young African Americans may serve as the "conclusive and effective" action needed to settle the problems and concerns facing this generation.[11]

Therefore, in reflecting on the contemporary activism of young African Americans, this is not the first generation to have a less-than-stellar connection with the Black church or Christian religious traditions. This tension persists throughout the struggles for freedom in the United States with often high but unfulfilled expectations of the role that churches will play. The history also reflects the ways that major turns in the struggle for freedom often resulted in the emergence of strong civic organizations or other religious organizations, such as Marcus Garvey's Universal Negro Improvement Association and the Nation of Islam. However, in addition to the history of complex relations between the church and social change, many young African Americans are still intricately connected with and reflecting on the Black Christian tradition. And part of the work of this chapter is to provide snapshots of Black Christian youth activists. This is not to say that integrating Christianity and activism is the predominant way that young people are understanding their social and political agency, but it is part of the conversation. Inclusion of these narratives is required, so that we do not too easily or uncritically embrace narratives that proclaim "*nones* to be on the rise" and contemporary Black activism to have more of an agnostic or atheist bent. Furthermore, as a practical theologian, it is still important to offer youth models of an interconnection and integration between their faith and activism—such that their faith empowers them and does not simply pull them further toward anarchy or nihilism in the face of change, which is often slow (or without lasting results).

Thus far in the book, I have attended to different parts of the Black Christian tradition that I suggest are beneficial for youth to better connect with. Responses and correctives to fragmented spirituality among African American youth abound within the complexity and richness of African American Christianity and the historical moves to connect faith and action, witness and work. Within this framework, there are also significant spaces where young people are already expanding upon the historical legacy of Black Christian traditions and activism and moving toward a way of being in the world that models for other adults, Christians, and youth what a robust and integrated spirituality looks like.

Young, Black, Christian, and Activist
Snapshots of Black Youth Activism

In this chapter I reflect on the current protests and Christian public witness of young African Americans. As I looked at the array of youth activism, the landscape is full of young African Americans such as Makayla Gilliam Price, a seventeen-year-old activist in Baltimore, Maryland, who has spoken out against police brutality as well as economic issues facing the residents of Baltimore.[12] This generation of young activist includes the three young queer African American women, Alicia Garza, Patrisse Cullors, and Opal Tometi, who created #Blacklivesmatter.[13] It includes others who later took up this mantle and began to protest, write, and reflect on the current injustices facing people of color in the United States and globally.[14] Within this group, there are also myriad African American Christians who have vocally participated in and reflected upon the ways that activism (and the model of other young African Americans) is strengthening and often challenging their faith and practices. These include scholars, such Brittney Cooper and Eddie Glaude (to name only a few), and pastors around the country who led their congregations in "hoodie Sunday" worship as a protest to the shooting death of Trayvon Martin.[15] It also includes persons of faith, like Jonathan Butler, a graduate student who participated in a hunger strike at the University of Missouri (Mizzou), in order to demand change on that campus. Jonathan took seriously what he was embarking upon and recounts how he had to draw up his faith, pray, and call his mentors and pastors, because he knew that he could die fighting for what he believed in.[16]

This landscape also includes other groups and communities, like the Inner Harbor Project, a teen-led community organization that has developed training for the Baltimore Police Department to improve relations between police officers and Black youth. It also includes the young seminarians and students on campuses across the country (sponsoring die-ins and marching to protest the names of buildings, which reflect parts of their schools' histories that are both offensive and unacknowledged). These groups also coalesced around issues such as racial profiling and harassment by campus police and cultures of sexual abuse on campus. In other words, there are a wealth of examples of Black youth activism and protest from just the past few years.

However, beyond noting the array of Black youth activism, here I attend to the intersections of the Black youth and young adult activism and faith (specifically Christian spirituality). I lift up the narratives of four young African Americans, some I have known since they were early adolescents and others who have made national attention for their activism. These are not a representative sample of the array of youth activism, but they reflect the diversity of models of interconnecting faith and activism: some in explicit Christian framing, motivations, and reflections; others as activists who seek to transform the world and the Christian church; as well as others who reflect older models of Black Christian and civic leadership; and yet another who struggles with what role faith in God should have in her activism.

I also demonstrate how these current practices are both connecting with and expanding the historical categories and practices of Black public theologians, proponents of Black Social Gospels, and other calls for Christian-based social change. As a result of this critical expansion and reflection, I theorize the ways that Black youth activism extends progressive Christian efforts to change and models correctives to fragmented spirituality for youth and adults.

Bree Newsome: Spirit-Led, Direct Action

Bree Newsome came to national attention after climbing the flag pole to remove the Confederate flag from the South Carolina capital building days after the violent shooting of nine African Americans, including a pastor in an African Methodist Episcopal church in Charleston, South Carolina. In a time of national mourning, where most felt overwhelmed by the ongoing tragedies and violence, such that logging on to social media often came with a subconscious prayer of "please Lord, not again," Newsome flooded social media and news outlets. Instead of a story of another tragedy or even the typical march or protest requesting action, she was taking direct action—embodying strength and freedom that many young African Americans longed to see and experience.

Newsome was both impressive for her athleticism and her strong convictions to do something that heretofore others had only talked about. Newsome quoted Psalm 27 and the Lord's Prayer as she scaled the flagpole and brought the flag down. She also boldly stated, "You come against me with hatred and oppression and violence. I come against you in the name of God. This flag comes down today!"[17] For some, the rhetoric was less significant than the fact that she boldly transgressed state property and removed a symbol of racial hatred and discord. However, her explicitly religious language was not lost on me or on many young adults who observed and rallied around Newsome for her courageous actions.

Scholar and public intellectual Brittney Cooper wrote of the ways that Newsome offered a different model of public religion in the wake of tragedy and violence against Black bodies.[18] Most often, the only "religious" responses are calls to pray for peace or family members offering forgiveness to the perpetrators (out of or because of their religious convictions). However, Cooper argues that Newsome embodied a *theology of resistance*, writing,

> Bree Newsome offered the holiest of "fuck thats" to such foolery and went up the pole and took that shit down. My heart still swells for her courage. But I also think we would do well to see all the ways in which her act of resistance opens up space and possibility for us in the realms of faith and feminism.[19]

Cooper commends Newsome for the reminder that Black faith, and public faith in general, can be much more than "forgiveness"—as most recently demonstrated in the words of grieving family members who stated that they forgave the murderer of their loved ones, or even in the calls of some Black clergy for peace, civility, and obedience instead of anger and unrest in the wake of innumerable verdicts and non-indictments. Cooper's analysis resonates with my response to seeing Bree Newsome scale the flag pole and framing it within religious language.

Initially, I was unsure of the direct forethought or intentionality of Newsome's actions as Christian social witness. But in a later interview, Newsome affirmed,

I was in an intense state of peace during the action. My activism is indeed informed by my faith in Jesus Christ who was "sent to set the oppressed free."

I firmly believe that we are all children of God created equally. I consider myself to be following not only in the footsteps of freedom fighters, but also in the footsteps of the first Christians who often faced imprisonment in the course of spreading the gospel and acting upon prophetic faith.[20]

Here she offers her self-definition of her actions and her understanding of her Christian faith. While many assume that social action today is completely disconnected from the historical public theologies of the social gospel movement or those articulated in the Civil Rights Movement, there is ongoing evidence of the presence of both Christian intentionality and inspiration for social action among contemporary activists, like Newsome. This should not be surprising, even if it is not the most dominant part of the narrative or depiction of Christianity or social change movements.

Newsome further describes her participation in this act of civil disobedience as being "spirit-lead."[21] For some, her religious language is off-putting, hard to decipher, or connect with. For others, she is connecting Christian language to struggles for social change in ways that they have never experienced in their faith communities. Newsome frames her understanding of justice in the commandment of Jesus to love God and neighbor. This framework of loving God, self, and neighbor translates well into the public sphere, but Newsome also employs more specifically conservative Christian language and categories. For example, Newsome also uses language of fighting oppressive political and social systems as "spiritual warfare." Newsome also describes calling her sister, who is a "prayer warrior," to pray for her after she heard about the shooting in South Carolina.[22] In some ways, Newsome's discussion of faith and the work of the Holy Spirit in her activism parallel the narrative of one of the youth interviewed in this work, Kira. Newsome and Kira employ explicitly religious practices in response to civic, political, and communal transformation. It is important to note that this interconnection between standing up for what is right and feeling "led" or "called" to do so is not unprecedented; however, it seems to be less prevalent in contemporary movements and persons. Newsome notes the "soul searching" and praying she had to do in order to commit to participating in the direct action of taking down the Confederate flag.

Preparing for Direct Action: More Than Passion

Newsome also highlights much of what is glossed over in the media coverage of community organizing and direct action. She notes that she was the one in the spotlight, but it took the direct efforts of nine to ten people and countless others doing reconnaissance work in order for the action to take place and for the message to be effective. Her colleague Jimmy Tyson also speaks candidly of knowing what it would symbolize for a woman of African descent to take the lead in this action and for him to stand with her, as a White ally.[23] Newsome also situates her actions and self-understanding into a larger historical narrative, as a way reminding others of the intentional, collective, and sustained efforts to effect change that were taking place in the Civil Right movements of the past and in the preparation for the direct action in South Carolina. Newsome and others note in a panel interview the ways that "white supremacy" attempts to re-narrate history such that moments of transformation, such as Rosa Parks sitting on the bus, looks like a singular instance of a "tired" seamstress instead of the culmination of years of training at the Highlander School and work in her local NAACP chapter. Essentially, Newsome is careful to frame the work of youth and young adult activists and organizers within a larger framework that requires training, planning, being prepared to go to jail, developing a strategy that will have the greatest impact, as well as being spiritually and mentally prepared for the action as well.

Newsome's later reflections remind us of the practices of Christian social witness, where leaders and some martyrs had to intentionally count the cost of their actions and to make peace with the fact that they indeed could be persecuted, arrested, and killed for their actions. It is hard to imagine the parallels to possible physical harm and death for peacefully protesting and participating in direction social action in 2015, but Newsome was threatened with a Taser gun by police officers, and she could have been electrocuted and killed. In that moment she had to reassure the police officers she was no threat and that she was connecting with a long line of protesters who took direct action to stand up for and carefully demarcate the lines between just and unjust laws in the United States. Newsome demonstrated years of training in organizing in preparation for this direct action, reminding us that when we see youth and young adults participating in protests and organizing for change, it is not just extemporaneous youthful zeal or passion; rather, it is a commitment. They have worked and been taught by others to feel empowered to make a difference.

Watershed Events

In addition to situating her activism within a larger historical context, Newsome carefully attends to the reality that there have been watershed events in recent years that have paralleled events of the 1950s. These events have called young African Americans to respond in particular and direct ways. For many young African Americans, the watershed moment was the shooting death of Trayvon Martin. (Other activists and leaders who formed Black Lives Matter also name Martin's death as the turning point.) Stepping back from this event, we also see other events prior to this, which have faded into obscurity, such as Jena 6 and the murders of Sean Bell and Amadou Dialoo,[24] which occurred in the decades before the murder of Trayvon Martin and which also served as reminders of injustices and calls to act. Martin's death also was not just one event that rallied supporters and mobilized another generation of young people, but it was just the beginning of several months of highly publicized and mishandled incidents of police and vigilante violence against Black people. Likewise, Newsome names the repeal of many components of the Voting Rights Act that also occurred in 2013 as a catalyst for her involvement in organizing and movements for change.

In many ways, her direct action of "unhooking a flag" capitalized on a moment and set of strategies of organizing which pushes the "envelope" or creates just enough tension that people and systems have to respond. Newsome reflects that she was somewhat disturbed by the idea that taking down the flag would be the thing that "rocked people's consciousness" and would make people upset in ways that the years and months of violence toward Black and Brown people had not. Newsome echoes the reality that in choosing to act or create change, one does not often connect with the governments' understanding of what is morally good and right to do; rather, one has to determine where enough tension can be created so that there is no longer space for them to not respond.[25]

Newsome's actions and reflections serve as one case and reminder of the intricate preparation that one undergoes as one discerns a call to act for change or to live in such a way that when one sees the world around him or her, one is no longer able to turn a blind eye to the work and struggles of others (particularly other Black youth). Newsome offers not only a push beyond "forgiveness" as the highest public theological value, but her work is a reminder that there are many practices that Black Christians have internalized and personalized that have public and communal impact and significance. The communal significance of these religious practices becomes clearer if we better understand the ways that God can and does push humanity to engage in the world and with one another. For example, Newsome's framing of civil disobedience in religious language is not a brand-new concept, but it pushes us to imagine not simply how youth can mimic the practices of their predecessors, but what type of creative imagination and exchange will emerge in this generation, which does not often connect well with what we hope or expect of young people.

Her Legacy? Dying to Self

When asked about her vision for her work and what legacy she wanted to leave, Newsome also responded in richly theological language. She spoke of both living in the spirit and dying to the self. In a somewhat self-deprecating way, she mentions that she does not actually think about what legacy she will leave. At a certain point, she prayed and asked God to really take all the things that she has prayed for and dreamed of, and just allow her to be. In this, she asserts that she trusts that God will attend to all the dreams that she has for herself and for her community. Of course, there are many layers to unpack in this response and myriad critiques that one might offer in terms of where this type of relinquishing of control can go wrong. However, it is important to note how much of her life and actions reflect her understanding of trusting God and her trust of God does not lead her to passivity in the face of injustice (as one might assume). Instead, her trust in God leads her to being at peace as she works for justice, because she is not worrying about how getting arrested or standing up for justice is going to negatively or positively effect her life. And this type of freedom and confidence in the spirit is helpful. Newsome recites the writings of the Apostle Paul, saying, to "live is Christ, but to die is gain."[26] She echoes many early Christians and previous Black Christian social witnesses, who had to contend with the reality that what they were feeling called to do could lead to death, could be ineffective or inconsequential, or it could help reshape the course of history. However, none of these could be the motivating or inhibiting factors. Instead, they needed to focus on the greater calling of following God in the midst of this.

Nyle Fort: Liturgy as Christian Social Witness

Almost at the opposite end of the spectrum of contemporary Black Christian social witness is a young theologically trained activist in the New

Jersey area. Nyle Fort has not garnered the same type of national attention, nor has he been arrested in such a public manner as Newsome, but he is making a name for himself in his community organizing and scholarship. Like Newsome, I first learned of Fort through social media—through the live video streaming of one of his sermons and the numerous "tweets and re-tweets" of his message.

Seminary, a Place of Political and Theological Awakening

Fort identifies as an activist now, but he notes that he did not become "political" until he was in seminary. It was in listening to a teleconference with Mumia Abu Jamal in a theology class that Fort began to wrestle with questions about the intersection of faith and justice, and in that same year he attended his first rally for Mumia. However, Fort is clear that as a much younger teen he began to observe injustices and inequities around him, but he did not have the language or a theological framework for what he observed. As a young preacher (preaching since age sixteen), he started in ministry trying to be like his mentor and pastor. Since then, Fort has struggled both with whether he could even call himself Christian, as that title had been taken over by the "religious right" and he struggled regarding the types of actions he wanted to take in the face of so much ongoing oppression. He notes that almost his entire seminary experience was him wrestling with how he would fuse together his theological convictions and his political commitments.[27] Fort speaks candidly about the impact of the death of Michael Brown on the evolution of his work. Like Newsome, Fort experienced Ferguson as a watershed event. He notes that he was just angry: "he was full of rage and he did not know what to do with his body," so he just got on the bus with other seminarians and students and went to Ferguson. And Ferguson became the crash course in organizing for him.

Later, as he was reflecting on his involvement in grassroots organizing both in New Jersey and in Ferguson, MO, he acknowledges that it was his faith, his family, and his race (the color of his skin) that drew him to activism. He states that the color of his skin "scares him, and it shouldn't"—and it was the desire to overcome this fear and overcome the stigmas attached to being Black in the United States that were part of the catalyst for him getting involved.[28] Fort underscores what I have heard many young people of color say over the years, that often there is not an option to remain unaffected by what is happening in the world around them. As people of color, they see and recognize that the shooting deaths of Black youth and young adults are not isolated events happening to one stranger across the country; rather, there are systems of oppression that are in place that effect myriad young African Americans. Simply by being Black, one is affected, and thus being Black can become part of the catalyst to work for change.

Unlike the other young activists in this chapter, Nyle Fort represents a call to address injustices in *specifically religious* ways. One of his modes and locations of social witness and activism is within the religious community. On the way back from Ferguson, he came up with the idea of doing a worship service, a seven last words service in honor of the many victims of police and vigilante violence in the United States. Fort notes that he was heartbroken, both over the injustice, but also because he felt like he could not go to a church and express his rage there. He wanted to "sit in a sanctuary and just cry, and cuss if [he] needed to," and to just be himself. But he could not think of any church that would allow him that space. So he wanted to create it for himself and others.

The Seven Last Words: Strange Fruit Speaks worship service was modeled after some of the most holy and sacred of religious traditions within Black Christianity. He combines preaching and the celebration of Good Friday (central to the Black Church liturgical year) with the conversations and words of Black people who have been murdered by vigilantes or police officers. Fort places the life and death of Black and Brown people at the center of core elements of Black Christianity, preaching, and worship. As a result, he creates sacred space for lament and remembrance and creates a call to action for the churches to respond to the death of so many.

Again, Fort is participating in a longer legacy of people who connect with the suffering of Jesus on the cross. He is continuing in a Black Liberation theological tradition of interconnecting the suffering of Jesus with Black people's suffering and the Roman Empire with White supremacy in the United States.[29] However, Fort makes a move to not only connect Jesus's life with that of Black and Brown people, but to use the words of Black and Brown victims as *sacred texts* for personal and public theological reflection.

Fort is not doing the same thing as his mid-twentieth century Civil Rights clergy predecessors, in that he is not attempting to use the "White man's Christianity" and government documents to hold White Americans accountable for living up to their highest values. Instead, the juxtaposition of the words of the Black people with the suffering Christ offers a way of seeing in one's religious traditions a narrative of a God who understands and has experienced the truth of their suffering. It is also a way of saying to young people and society at large that the deaths of Black people (as well as their lives) are just as sacred as the life (and death) of Christ.

While larger dominant institutions co-sponsored or hosted the services,[30] there persisted a sense that the call for action was to Black Christians and less to the wider US society. These platforms allowed for some of the best of the Black religious public intellectual traditions to emerge, but I wonder if these narratives could have taken place in smaller, religious bodies. In other words, could these services happen in a less "academic" space? Are these services or this type of preaching taking place in more traditional African American churches? And if so, to what end/results? And if not, is this a predictor of the disconnect many name between the church and the concerns of young African Americans? And is this the work that Fort is pushing for, to model theological reflection on the issues facing young African Americans, and to do so in religious spaces and modes?

In fact, Fort speaks of the struggles of the planning committee both in determining the locations and in the content. In particular, Jordan Davis's last words were "F*ck that! Turn it back up!"[31] but questions were raised over whether one could curse vocally or in print in a church, from a pulpit, and as a clergy person. Fort and the planning team decided that honoring the words of Jordan was a non-negotiable, but it raised questions of whether the service, which they wanted to take place in a church, could happen in a church. In many ways this chapter attempts to respond to these tensions and to every young African American who asks, "Really, is there a church like that? I mean are there Black churches that affirm women, gay people, transgender persons, and are pushing people to work for justice?"[32]

Married to the Movement

Both in these special worship services (with political, local, and national leaders) and in his everyday preaching, Fort offers theological reflections that foreground interconnections between historical oppression and overcoming with the recent events and murders of Black people in the United States. For example, as the seventh and final sacred saying at a Strange Fruit Speaks worship service at the historical Riverside Church, Fort reflects on the shooting of Sean Bell, whose last words were "I love you, too." Fort offers a treatise on love among African Americans—noting first that marriage and love among enslaved and free Africans was "policed." Their love was not sanctioned, legitimated, as they were often not legally permitted to marry. However, in spite of the legal systems, which limited the rights of Black people to marry, this did not squelch the expressions of love among African Americans. Fort asserts, "The miracle of Black love is that it has never been predicated on the logic or laws or recognition of white American society."[33] In the course of the sermon he juxtaposes this historical reality with the current reality that even as the laws and experiences of Black love have changed over time, there are still systems in place that make it impossible for some young Africans Americans to live, let alone love and marry. Fort raises the question to the audience of what does it mean for the same authority to have the power to marry you as the one that has the power to murder you? Fort employs the style of much Black preaching of positing a quandary for the congregation to wrestle with and which the text will hopefully help illuminate—however, in utilizing this familiar form, he offers something less familiar in response. He uses the context of Sean Bell being murdered on his wedding day to push the hearers to wrestle with what hopes and dreams of their own and others are being thwarted because of unjust laws, and he invites them to take vows of their own. Fort uses a rhetorical strategy of not simply asking how people are going to respond, but he carries this theme of Black love and marriage to create an invitation for people to marry the movement. Fort closes with a creative set of wedding vows to the movement:

> *I vow to love Black people unapologetically.*
> *I vow to love myself. . . .*
> *I vow to fight as I unlearn systems. . . .*
> *I vow to stand alongside my transgender brothers and sisters. . . .*
> *I vow to speak truth to power. . . .*
> *I vow to never be silent . . . because silence in the face of suffering is sin.*
> *I vow to mentor the next Aiyana Stanley Jones. . . .*
> *I vow to organize within my community, to take care of my elders and*
> *   to inspire a generation that has been marked as disposable to marry*
> *   a new movement.*
> *I vow to never give up. . . .*
> *I vow to not simply preach love with my lips, but to practice love with*
> *   my life. . . .*
> *I vow to always remember.*[34]

Again Fort imbues elements of Christian worship and sacred liturgy with new meaning as he infuses the familiar genre with reflections of the tragedy and invitations to commit fully to a movement for social transformation.

Nothing Redemptive about Suffering

In addition to the creativity of the sermon's call to action, and explicit critique of forms of Black Christianity and life that do not actively respond to injustices, Fort demonstrates years of wrestling with some of the problematic dimensions of Christianity, and he tries to address some of the erroneous moves that have been made in the name of religion, moves that may not be helpful as he calls people to reflect and act. For example, he states that there is nothing redemptive about suffering. Fort here anticipates the question that is often raised when looking at and addressing the suffering of Jesus, as well as in making parallels between the suffering of Black people and the suffering of Jesus. He states firmly that there is nothing redemptive about what happened to Sean Bell (and countless others), but there is a call to wrestle with how the church and world respond to his suffering. In other words, he is attempting to hold the line between using theological and Christian resources to reflect on the suffering of Black people without sanctifying, sanctioning, or deeming this suffering necessary. Again he is incorporating years of theological reflections and writings by some Black liberationist and Womanist scholars (such as Delores Williams, who challenges the narrative of redemptive suffering, so often articulated in atonement theories).

Wrestling with Scripture, Preaching as Social Witness

In other sermons and writings, Fort also reflects on traditional Christian sacred text and biblical passages—reading them in light of the current realities of oppressed people. In other words, he does not just use the *genre* of Christian liturgy and Black preaching; he also wrestles with the sacred texts, reading them beyond the traditional and at times status quo affirming interpretations. For example, in a sermon or ode to Renisha McBride, Fort, preaching in an African American Baptist church (where he was serving as youth pastor), begins his sermon recounting the ways that Luke 7:36–50 has been interpreted. He then pushes beyond readings that have focused on individualistic understandings of the passage and on sin/forgiveness to look more closely at "cultural perceptions and social profiling" that are part of the story and our current realities. Fort is noting the dominant narratives of individual sin that have helped foster fragmented spirituality and that must be countered in order for young African Americans to better connect their faith traditions and practices with the world around them. Fort models this pushing for a more culturally attentive and contextualized reading of the biblical passage—and for actions both grounded in biblical faith and the witness of Jesus to transform our society, but also for a transformation of the practices of Christian faith:

> As friends of God, we must be careful not to allow bigotry to cloak itself in a biblical vocabulary that seeks to justify our own prejudices instead of affirm God's principles. And we must be critical enough to challenge any form of misogyny that masquerades as "divine truth" or racism that reifies itself as "biblical revelation."[35]

What does it mean to use a Christian practice to critique Christian practice? In reality, this often is the case, rhetorically one makes a "straw man" argument where one pushes against the perceptions of how a text is typically or traditionally read in order to situate how the preacher wants the hearers to read the text (or at best, the claim that the preacher wants to make).[36] However, while this rhetorical strategy is often employed within Black preaching and in rhetoric of social change movements, it is important to note Fort's ability to employ these strategies as part of his activism, offering another example of the richness and complexity of African American Christian Social Witness even within this current generation.[37]

A People's Movement?

Fort notes too that his activism in and around Ferguson, Missouri connects him with a larger, historical movement for change among the people. He calls it a people's movement. While he acknowledges the historical connections, he notes the ways that new forms of media and social media are changing the ways the message is shared and how information is garnered. He is excited it is changing who is in charge and that it is creating space for people whose voices have been marginalized to be front and center in shaping actions and effecting change. In particular, Fort is attentive to the ways the voices of women, young people, LGBT, and gender nonconforming persons are able to lead in these spaces.[38] He even notes how this challenges the predominant model of a singular, male leader as the one who takes charge of the movement or who is esteemed as the leader of that day.

Of course, even as Fort reflects on the shift of who is in charge, as well as the multiple voices and sites of leadership within this *new* movement, his theological reflections do not fully call for or incorporate a rethinking of the centrality of one lone, revolutionary messiah/leader: Jesus. However, his activism and theological reflections open us to this shift. For example, a few Womanist and feminist scholars have offered a critique of the continued reliance, in our sacred texts and traditions, on the centrality of the *solo* Christ figure. Instead, it is helpful to add to our sacred canon the narratives of struggle and overcoming of everyday people of faith. We need to mine the Christian tradition for sources of communal liberation and communal efforts toward change. In truth, this corrective is not to call into question the significance of Jesus Christ, but to more effectively narrate his work of liberation and transformation and to affirm the communal models of leadership he employed. Re-emphasizing the communal forms of liberation counters the redaction of Jesus's revolutionary leadership and does not allow Jesus to be reduced to our comfortable and established models of the solitary, charismatic male leader. Historically, we have looked for and esteemed this type of male leadership, and even struggled (offering critiques of the Black community) when we have failed to rally around one solo leader. Instead, there is a need to acknowledge the complexity of issues that need combating and the myriad sources and leaders required to effect change within the United States and the global community. But I assert that the attractiveness of singular charismatic leadership is interconnected with the traditional Christian narrative, and they mutually reinforce the other. And in this current moment, both realities are being challenged, and as such we have to attend to what, if any, models and narratives we esteem from within the Christian tradition.[39]

Newsome and Fort challenge the traditional mores of conservative Black Christianity because they trample on the respectability that was often aspired to and affirmed as an outward reflection of the "rightness" of the Black Christian cause. But they are also expanding the traditions of Black liberal Christianity and young African American spirituality. They are pushing for a connection of Black Christian spirituality with contemporary efforts for social change, and they are doing so in ways that call youth to rethink who and what being Christian means in the face of current realities and cultures that do not love or affirm Black youth and the lives of Black people.

Stephen Green

The remaining young adult activists I met when they were rising high-school seniors attending the Youth Theological Initiative.[40] Beyond this summer experience, the ways that they are currently involved in activism and even what they would offer as their rationale for why they are engaged are quite distinct from one another. For example, I met Stephen when he was sixteen-years-old. He was what I considered "an overly churched kid." He was the son of an African Methodist Episcopal Church bishop and was being groomed in many ways for excellence in Christian ministry and leadership. He was like so many of the students attending YTI, some of the best and brightest of his generation of Christian youth. And yet, he was not immune to wrestling with questions about his faith and different issues (social justice and otherwise), which were raised for him at YTI. Often I found him engaged in vigorous debates or conversations with his friends and mentors at YTI. And while I could not predict how Stephen would grow up and what role his faith would have in his future endeavors, I was not surprised to see that Stephen has continued his journey of wrestling with questions about injustices, not taking easy answers, and boldly connecting this with actions in his community.

Stephen's activism as a seventeen-year-old included organizing a major rally at the state capitol building in Little Rock, Arkansas to raise awareness about homicides there. A speaker, Steve Nawojczyk, inspired Stephen's work while he was at Boys State. Nawojczyk worked as a coroner during a surge of gang violence in Arkansas in the 1990s, but spoke about seeing an uptick in the rates in the late 2000s.[41] Stephen became part of the steering committee for Arkansas's first statewide youth summit on violence and took charge of organizing the rally and speaking out against the ongoing violence in his city. Stephen's activism continued as he went to Morehouse College, where he participated in protests and marches after the shooting death of Trayvon Martin and others, and outside of college his involvement continues in his current position as the president of the Youth and College Division of the NAACP.

Of the activists described here, Stephen represents the strongest connection to traditional or older models of Black charismatic, male leadership. Like Fort, Stephen is a young preacher and seminarian, but he is also working within one of the oldest and more established civil rights organizations. The NAACP historically has a particular legal and political bent, which could make its organizational structure difficult for younger activists to engage with.[42] However, Stephen has found his niche here and is pushing the NAACP to take seriously the voices and leadership of young African Americans. While the official and broader focus of the Youth and College Division of NAACP includes education, economic development, health, juvenile justice, and voter empowerment,[43] most of the recent issues that Green advocates for, as well as the protests, are at the nexus of legal and civil rights violations, such as police and vigilante violence against people of color.

Likewise, his modes of protest are quite familiar, from demonstrations and the willingness to get arrested in protests, to writing letters to political leaders, and participating in summits or meetings with high-ranking officials.[44] For example, Stephen has planned or participated in several protests calling for an overhaul of the police department and other governmental structures in the city of Chicago. He was arrested alongside the president of the NAACP and other students and seminarians in a planned protest after the improper investigation of the shooting death of LaQuan McDonald.[45] In interviews on major media outlets, Stephen often goes head to head with pundits who support the police department, or who are attempting to lay the blame for the continued cycles of violence only at the feet of "thugs" and "bad guys" in the inner city.[46] Stephen asserts that he is part of a generation calling for overhaul, and despite criticism of it, this generation is one that "will mobilize and put people in office who represent [their] ideals."[47] While Stephen is part of a younger generation that is rightly dissatisfied with the corruption taking place in Chicago and around the globe, Stephen is advocating for navigating traditional channels of leadership and reform: primarily through the justice department and legal action. For many younger activists, these departments have also failed them, and thus they are calling for complete revolution, or they are supporting movements that shut down systems (instead of trying to work within them). However, Stephen's activism serves as a reminder of the need to not only participate in civil disobedience but to have a larger structure that sustains battles against an array of legal and political injustices. In other words, his activism reminds us of the intricate connection between policy, voting, and legal avenues to change.

Even as I argue that Stephen is the most traditional youth activist in this text, I also note that Stephen is not explicitly, or vocally, Christian in his activism. Some might note a paradox in this. However, I note that while Stephen is a Christian minister who preaches regularly, he most often maintains a separation between his preaching ministry and the public work activism that he offers. And while this line between public and private is often invisible, and dichotomies between one's religious self and public self are somewhat false and unhelpful, Stephen is still carefully navigating these tensions. For example, he is careful to advocate for change in ways that are inclusive of the plurality (religious and otherwise) of all. For example, few to none of his interviews to date include explicitly religious or Christian undertones. His media appearances are an extension of his role in the NAACP and the content is not tacitly religious. At most, we get an embodied Black religiosity in the cadence of his discourse and the richly metaphorical rhetoric that is often associated with Black preaching.[48] In a CNN interview, when asked if he supported the impeachment of an incumbent politician, Stephen offered the metaphor, "You may change the dancers, but you are still listening to the same tune. We are calling for a remix of the entire system."[49]

In other words, the policies and changes he is advocating for are not primarily or explicitly religious, but he is embodying a particular performance of Black male clergy leadership in this space. However, what is missing or not fully articulated is how he sees or frames his activism. One can assume that his activism is an extension of his faith, but he does not articulate this or make this part of his public or activist stand. This stands in direct contrast to the rich theological reflections and articulation of Bree Newsome, who names her process of praying before direct actions, and to Nyle Fort also, who offers nuanced liberationist critiques and theological reflections.

However, in Stephen's preaching, he offers social commentary and critique of US society, the church, and Christian ministers. For example, Stephen offers a strong analysis of more conservative religious (and even African Methodist Episcopal) scripts and calls the church out on its homophobia and oppressions of gay and lesbian people.[50] In a sermon at the Academy of Preachers, Stephen also calls out African American clergy for talking about the size of thier honoraria or how many revivals they are preaching instead of focusing on worship of God.[51]

Stephen's most explicit social commentary is made in his preaching to other Christians, which pushes us to ask how this message translates and how Stephen self-identifies. For example, is he simply a Christian minister who participates in social change, or does his understanding of his faith and ministry directly intersect with his understanding of social change? This is an important distinction for us to continue wrestling with, and perhaps one that Stephen is still forming as he continues his theological training and his civil rights work. In other words, there is a possibility of continued fragmented spirituality, even as one fully embraces a life of faith and a call to work for social transformation. The fragmentation remains when one's faith does not inform one's activism and one's transformative action in the world does not inform one's faith. To be certain, this lack of explicit or direct theological articulation of social change is not unprecedented. Historically, Black male clergy became civic leaders because of their charisma and ability to command the attention of significant portions of the African American community (because most African Americans were members of churches). However, this did not make preachers particularly self-reflective or nuanced in their understanding of the role of Christianity in working for good (or even in articulating a common vision for all). In other words, many clergy could move to the forefront of communal and political leadership without having a complex Christian public theology. And in translation, often being a preacher did not make one critically and theologically reflective on the conditions of Black people. Instead, it simply became part of the presumed pedigree of the more traditional Black male political and civic leadership.

However, a more generous reading of this tacitly Christian clergy posture (and one that I ascribe to in my description of Green, even as I note the cautions and potential pitfalls historically in this model of clergy civic leadership) is that of embodying his religious convictions, and as such feeling called to work for a common good. Too often, within academic and theological circles, we privilege articulation and direct rational connections. However, how one lives should offer another articulation of one's faith and life. Therefore, Stephen, like Bree, Nyle, and Quita, offers another snapshot of the multiple ways that Christian faith and activism interconnect among young African Americans. Each of the snapshots points to possibilities for ameliorating fragmentation and potential pitfalls as well.

Quita Tinsley

Within our discussion of Black youth activism, we must also attend to the peripherally or even "quietly religious" activism.[52] Even within my understanding of exemplars of activism among young African Americans Christians, I recognize the ways that religion is both central to some and a stumbling block to others. In truth, every young activist I researched and interviewed had stories of colleagues and friends for whom religion was not the animating force of their work, and even more who spoke of fellow activists who stated clearly that "religion was not for them" at all. So what do we make of this? Do we circle back to the questions of where religion or the Church is now, or to a simplistic narrative that affirms that Black youth activism is "no longer" connected to religion or the Black church? Or do we offer a more nuanced account of youth and young adults who have wrestled with religion (and many who still wrestle) and who feel a sense of *calling* to work for change, even as they have not fully reconciled their understanding of what religion and even God looks like for them? In fact, other youth interviewees, such as Marissa and even Nyle Fort, note wrestling with whether they were Christian, either for a season or as an ongoing struggle. And the ways that they resolve these strivings often depended on the models, narratives, and practices of Christianity around them.

In other words, discussions of youth activism, even Black Christian youth activism, require that we also look at young African Americans who are committed to working for justice, who at one point in their lives identified as Christians, and who for a variety of reasons no longer see Christianity as the unifying force in their lives. One particular form that this narrative takes emerges among youth who have struggled with their sexual or gender identity and who have seen Christianity as a source of pain and not a source of affirmation in their lives.[53] And as a result, many of these young people do not readily name Christianity as part of their work; instead it may be part of their narrative, often mentioned as part of their history, but not as fully integrated in their current work and realities. And rightly so. One youth activist helps offer more insights into what this tension looks like.

Quita Tinsely is a "self-described city femme with small town roots."[54] This opening line to her bio does not fully convey her work as a writer, organizer, and reproductive justice activist. Instead, the description is a reminder that much of her work is interconnected with her lived realities and experiences as a queer southern Black woman. It also is a reminder that her self-understanding includes a complex and beautiful interconnection with sexuality, gender, race, place, and spirituality. Like Stephen, I met Quita when she was a rising high-school senior. She too was studying at the Youth Theological Initiative over the summer, and I had the job of re-assuring her very religious and conservative parents that she would be safe and that she would come back intact and with her faith renewed (or at least not torn apart). I honestly cannot say that we achieved either of those (beyond keeping her physically safe), because part of what happens at places like YTI and other immersion experiences is that worldviews are stretched and hopefully transformed for the better. Over the past few years, I have stayed in touch with Quita primarily through social media, and to my initial surprise, she has moved far beyond the quiet young woman I interacted with when she was seventeen to become a youth activist in the state of Georgia, and further to become a national youth leader for reproductive justice and health. Through organizations like SPARK and articles on websites like *The Body Is Not an Apology*, Quita has helped organize youth and young adults for transformation in Georgia and the southern United States.[55]

In some ways Quita is an "unlikely" activist. She notes that as an introvert and as a person of color, she was often uncertain about participating in large-scale protests, marches, or other acts of civil disobedience.[56] The large crowds of people she did not know, as well as the real possibilities of getting arrested made this type of public protesting difficult for her. However, she participated in her first protest in 2014. It was rally for Michael Brown, and she marched with about five thousand people to the CNN center in Atlanta. Participating in a rally organized by another Black queer activist (organized primarily through social media), Quita began to face her fears and to feel at home in the world of public political protests and activism. Quita also notes seeing Congressman John Lewis at the rally, marching in the rain and knowing then that "this is the right time, the right moment for me to be doing this."[57]

Quita is also somewhat of an unlikely activist, because unlike many Black youth, she did not grow up in an urban area where protest and politics were all around. She notes that no one else in her family is involved in activism. Her working-class family was very much concerned with survival, and she gave examples of her mother working in the fields over the summers to help her family.[58] Instead, Quita became an activist through her experiences of being a queer Black woman in the South and through her attempts to make sense of her experiences and to improve the experiences of others. Quita has worked to empower young people. In her work as the youth organizer with the "Fierce Youth Reclaiming and Empowering" initiative of SPARK, she has worked with youth to help them realize that they have a voice and that, at any age, what they say matters.

Quita is also a writer, and while most of the activist discussed here write and maintain a web presence to help raise awareness of the causes they advocate, Quita writes as a mode of activism. For example, her writing is featured on websites such as *Echoing Ida*, which was created as a platform for Black women to both gain access to the field of journalism and to support and present issues related to the experiences of Black women in all of their complexity.[59] As the name suggests, these writers are connecting with the legacy of Ida B. Wells, using writing as a tool and expression of justice work. Quita writes often about the difficult experiences of embodying and navigating stereotypes and respectability politics that are so often imposed on her. In "Unapologetically Owning the

Stereotypes and Nuances of Me," Quita explores the stereotypes around her name, which throughout her life has been both a source of shame and, later, pride, and which has exposed her to unwarranted and unwelcomed stereotypes regarding who she is, simply because of her name. She recounts the often-painful struggles of having teachers choose to alter her name both out of being too lazy to learn to correctly pronounce it and out of abuses of power that allowed them to alter her name in ways they determined were more respectful. Quita also reflects on the pervasiveness of this practice among little Black girls, noting the example of journalists avoiding or attempting to alter the name of then-nine-year-old, Quvenzhanè Wallis.[60]

Most of Quita's writing draws on her deep well of personal experiences, but as one reads them (even without her making direct connections to contemporary figures or issues), one immediately feels the larger implications of her experiences, as they speak to experiences that many Black, queer, young people have had to struggle with. For example, further in "Unapologetically Owning the Stereotypes and Nuances of Me," she outlines the often-awkward and painful interactions with friends (not just strangers), who demand that she play into the stereotypes expected of her and her uniquely ethnic name—the expectation that she live up to stereotypes of being the loud, sassy, life-of-the-party Black woman, regardless of how she feels. These struggles to just be abound.

These personal writings, and the community of readers and social media followers, again push beyond many of the types of activism characterized above and what we often attend to in our discussions of faith-based activism. In part, what Quita offers is a reminder of the power of the individual narrative and particular experiences at the core of our work for justice. She also lays her life open to others as a way of offering a way forward as well as a model of critical self-reflection and acceptance as part of the struggle for freedom.

Another example of her writing is a letter to her younger self. In this personal and powerful essay, Quita notes the struggles of her own development and offers wisdom for other youth and young adults who are navigating the many questions of maturation and identity formation currently. Quita starts this essay with the reminder that *she is enough*—as in, she is beautiful and whole and worthy of love, already! It is in this essay that her most explicitly religious musings emerge. For example, she writes about experiencing depression, recounting the difficulty of even going about her day-to-day tasks, and she tells her younger self, "Prayer won't always be the answer or give you the solace you need, because you need other places of refuge."[61] In this simple reminder, there is a wealth of meaning and attempts to counter both external and internal narratives that prayer should be all that she needs in order to deal with her depressions and attempts to make sense of life, but as she learns later (and as those around her should have affirmed), she needed more than "just prayer."[62]

Quita also writes about the ways that religion was hell for her when she was growing up:

> And speaking of hell, religion is tough for you. You have a tough time reconciling your Black, Southern Baptist faith and your identities. That's understandable. You spend your Sundays and Tuesdays being told you're going to hell for being yourself. It's going to take some time to figure out your relationship with God. Years later, you will still be struggling with it, but know that it's okay to struggle.[63]

Without offering a great deal of detail, she underscores that religion has been difficult and that she is still struggling with her relationship with God, but she has finally made peace with this struggling. Even in a more recent conversation with Quita, I noted how reticent she was to talk about religion (in some ways I feared that she thought I still expected of her the same eagerness or worldviews of her seventeen-year-old self, or that I even represented established Black Christianity to her and the world), but she underscored that religion, faith, and values were still things that she and her fellow activists at SPARK discussed a lot. While she does not articulate any one way that religion or her understanding of God intersects with her work, it is not completely absent from her life either. It is in the wrestling and the ability to be okay wrestling that I am excited about the work that Quita does. Again, she is offering us both a reminder and a model of the ongoing critical reflection that should be part of a life of faith, as well as the long and arduous process of unlearning and undoing dominant forms of religiosity and Christian narratives, such as those criticizing one's sexual identity, gender, race, and other aspects of her personhood.

Questions of spirituality are important for her and her colleagues, but she would not identify as a faith-based organizer or as explicitly inspired by her religious convictions or upbringing. In some ways, activism has become the animating force in her life. While some scholars question the sustainability of activism that is not grounded in a larger framework or community, young activists like Quita are reminding us that religious groups are not the only (or often the primary) institutions that can offer this sustaining framework and community. As such, Quita offers us another expression and model of the activism of young African Americans that pushes the church and other youth to develop a more integrated spirituality, one of ongoing wrestling, reflection, and action.

In Quita's activism, I find resonance with Womanist theology and pedagogy, which enters conversations with the goal or "bottom line" of justice for African American women, and by extension for all.[64] This starting place of the lived experiences of Black women, or in Quita's case, the intersectional identities and communities of queer, Black, femme youth, pushes one to seek solutions and strategies that ameliorate the conditions and struggles of this community. Starting with the experiences of her multiple communities pushes Quita to embrace the richness and beauty of these experiences and bodies. In many ways, Quita's activism and writings push beyond some of the earliest articulations of Black and Womanist theology, which often looked only to ameliorating the problems and systemic struggles of Black people. The early Womanist articulations sometimes glossed over the struggles of LGBTQI persons, but they also overlooked the sources of joy and identity, which were more than "the struggle for liberation," and more than what could be defined in opposition to White oppression. Quita, like Nyle and many other young Black activists, is also fighting to re-center the experiences of Black people even within their own discourse and self-definition—such that the work of fighting for justice does not overwhelm the definitions of wholeness and sufficiency that are essential to flourishing (above and/or apart from the oppression by White supremacist, hetero-patriarchal structures). Quita embodies this, as she writes to her younger self,

> I want to reiterate to you that you are enough. I have to say that again because I know how hard it is for you to believe that. You feel like you always play the supporting role to the prettiest and smartest girls in school. But you are just in great company. Your fierceness and honesty inspire you to do all that you do. As you get older, you should always trust in yourself because you are your own guiding light. . . . Frankly speaking, you are a badass. You can't weigh yourself down with the negative thoughts and standards that tell you that you aren't. You are beautiful. You are fierce. And you are enough.[65]

Historical Context of Black Youth Activism

Black youth activism did not emerge in the past ten years. Young people of African descent have been protesting injustice, participating in civil disobedience, and working to enhance their quality of life in every moment in American history. Black youth activism has many historical antecedents. But another dimension of the ongoing struggles of fragmented spirituality and conversations of the irrelevance of religion in the twenty-first century intersects with a cultural amnesia (or ahistorical nature) in which young people, in particular, do not fully connect with or claim the precursors of particular traditions and events.[66] Therefore, in addition to exploring the examples of contemporary Black youth and Christian activism, here I place their contemporary activism into conversation with the larger history of movements for change and Black Christian social witness. The conversation helps us begin to answer questions of how contemporary young activists can benefit from and expand the larger and varied history of Black Christian social witness, as well as inspire young Black Christians for whom social action does not connect with their spirituality.

And a Little Child Shall Lead ...

Part of the narrative that often goes overlooked in the discussions of activism in general is the consistent presence of radical young leaders, activists, and organizers.[67] Children, teens, and college students were on the front lines of mid-twentieth-century Civil Rights work. Yet before the Civil Rights Movement, children and youth participated in and led the first mass African American march in 1917.[68] The march through the streets of New York City was organized to protest the mistreatment of Blacks during a race riot in East St. Louis, Illinois and to protest lynching and the "lawless treatment of Blacks nationwide."[69] According to newspaper reports, there were eight hundred children, some as young as six, participating in this silent protest.[70] This event speaks greatly to the significant and long history of youth activism in African American struggles for freedom and just treatment. The signs from the march capture the questions and hopes inspired by young people, as well as point to the intersecting of social issues of the day and their religious understandings. For example the banners and signs read,

"MOTHER, DO LYNCHERS GO TO HEAVEN?"
"GIVE ME A CHANCE TO LIVE."

"TREAT US SO THAT WE MAY LOVE OUR COUNTRY."

"MR. PRESIDENT, WHY NOT MAKE AMERICA SAFE FOR DEMOCRACY?" and

"YOUR HANDS ARE FULL OF BLOOD."[71]

The first sign resonates with many of the hard-hitting and direct questions of the youth poets discussed in the previous chapter. It also points to the traumatic nature of lynching, and how it makes one question if it resulted in losing one's salvation and not being able to go to heaven. While one cannot know if this was an actual question asked of a mother, the sign signifies the reality of little children having to wrestle with whether they will live or die, *and* whether those who commit these crimes get to experience the same promises of life in heaven, which has so often been used as the only consolation for the ridiculousness of this world.

In addition to the involvement of children and youth in this early mass protest, their participation continued in mass demonstrations and events, such as the Children's Crusade of 1963, which turned the tide of civil rights negotiations in Birmingham, Alabama and around the country. Thousands of viewers watched as police were ordered and allowed to turn water hoses and dogs on groups of children and youth peacefully protesting.[72] While many esteemed the charisma and leadership of persons like Martin L. King Jr., this crusade took place after he had already been arrested (where he wrote his "Letter from Birmingham City Jail" on April 16, 1963). Young African Americans volunteered and were trained in nonviolent social change strategies, and even when hundreds were arrested on May 2, young people continued to volunteer and protest, risking arrest and expulsion from school. Black children were among the many martyrs and heroes of the Civil Rights Movement—including four little girls who died later that summer at church in Birmingham, as well as the students being subjected to all manner of insults and evils as they simply tried to integrate schools.

The significance of telling the longer history of activism among young African Americans lies in part in the need speak to the broader society of the ongoing import and value of the critical reflection and practice of young people. However, it also reminds young African Americans of what others like them have accomplished and how they can expand upon the foundations and actions created by others. Combined with stories of contemporary activists and the larger history of Christian activism is an invitation to explore how youth will contribute to creating change in their historical moment.

God Is Black: History of Black Christian Social Witness

There is also a significant history of the intersection of Black Christianity and social change. While there is no monolithic or essential understanding of the ways that religion has influenced and been influenced by the social concerns and struggles around it, there are examples of these connections across the history of African American Christianity.[73] Often this interconnection is manifest in the writings and reflections of Black and Womanist theologians and ethicists. In particular, for many, James Cone's *A Black Theology of Liberation* and later works such as *The Cross and the Lynching Tree* become the introduction to the possibility that Christian faith could have something to say to the current struggles of Black people in America.[74] The Black Liberation theological tradition of the mid-twentieth century re-infused Christian theological categories with attentiveness to the realities of Black lives, struggles, and culture. Not only did Cone proclaim, like earlier preacher Henry McNeal Turner, that God was Black; he argued that God was on the side of the oppressed.[75] Young Black activists are reminding us of the significance of this tradition and the need to invite young people into this conversation and history, still. For example, Nyle Fort went as far as saying that "Black liberation theology saved his life" because it offered him a framework for wrestling with the injustices in the world around him and offered him hope of being able to hold together his political commitments and theological convictions. In truth, seminaries and theological classrooms are often places that spark social transformation (and deep theological wrestling). And yet the ongoing divide between theological education and African American churches reminds us that young people are hungry for this tradition, but the church and academy have failed to creatively invite young people (and often other laity) into these conversations.

However, in addition to the Black Liberation theological tradition (and even before the emergence of Cone's work in the late 1960s), there was a rich and ongoing Black social gospel tradition, a tradition of Black public theology (which I point to in chapter 3), a strong and continued history of Black Christian women organizing for social change and racial uplift, as well as a larger tradition of social teachings emerging from African American churches. Just as I affirm the diversity of activism, historically and currently among African American youth, I affirm the richness and nuanced history of Black Christian social witness. Again, it would be a gross oversimplification to assume that because there are historical antecedents, this tradition is the most prevalent among Black Christianity.

Ironically, the activism of young African Americans has opened up a host of questions and assumptions about Black churches and traditional locations of political and social influence. Most often, the dominant assumption is that Black churches and clergy have been consistently respected for their roles in leading social transformation. However, this narrative around the Black church is more recent and assumed than actual. For example, scholars like Peter Paris, in attempting to outline the social teachings of Black churches, had to begin by countering older forms of Black scholarship that simply sought to describe the impact of oppression and that never allowed Black people to be viewed as "agents of constructive social change."[76] But Paris also had to expand the view of the Black Church's relationship to American society, which had previously been viewed only as "compensatory"—focused on otherworldly matters as relief to the harsh experiences in the United States *or* as only "political"—indicating dynamic agency for social change. The history of Black churches was not afforded complexity and nuance, such that it could be much more than compensatory or purely political.[77] Thus, Paris outlined a tradition of social teaching related to the Black church as (by necessity) concerned with *both* "current reality and future goals" as well the turn to emphasize the power to act and the agency of Black people and churches at every point in history, in spite of social constraints.[78]

However, another dominant assumption (from an academic position at least—there are other dominant narratives among Black youth) is that those who advocate for the interconnection between social transformation and Black Christianity are in the majority or at least well received within Black churches. This assumption has also been disputed. Gary Dorrien, in his book-length treatment of the Black social gospel tradition, argues that the proponents of the Black social gospel

> belonged to *embattled minorities* in their denominations, because the social gospel was divisive and it threatened to get people in trouble. The founders and their successors fought hard for the right to advocate progressive theology and social justice politics.[79]

In other words, the tradition of interconnecting progressive Christianity with social change has been a struggle. And yet, young African Americans who attempt to hold onto an understanding of Christianity that speaks to and informs their social action are in positions to create anew a theological and biblical discourse that speaks to their strivings, and to follow in the traditions of these "embattled minorities" in their religious communities or among their non-religious peers. Also, they are in a position to push African American churches and scholars who have not persisted in a tradition of interconnecting the Christian faith with social witness to reconsider their work and actions moving forward.

Black Social Gospel

Within this embattled Black social gospel tradition, Dorrien argues that there persisted four strands, which were often in tension with each other regarding what political agendas they should support and what social forms their Christianity should take. Included were (1) the Accommodationist social religion of Booker T. Washington, who favored economic empowerment even if it came at the cost of "Black dignity and rights"; and (2) Nationalists who wanted their own nation or Black civilization. (3) "The third group espoused social justice politics and modernist theology, joining Du Bois in the Niagara Movement and the NAACP." And (4) a fourth group attempted to hold a middle ground between Washington and Du Bois, asserting that both were required.[80]

These four ideological strands persisted and shaped what would emerge as the dominant narrative and understanding of the interconnection of Christianity and social change for King and much of the 1950s Civil Rights era.

> This story shaped the succeeding generation of Black social gospel leaders, who taught that the struggle for racial justice would go nowhere lacking support from the churches. King was steeped in the defining Black social gospel claim that the church had to deal constructively with modern intellectual criticism, emphasize the social ethical teaching of Jesus and the Hebrew prophets, struggle for social justice, and defy white racism.[81]

However, just as within Du Bois's era, there were others who opposed his methods and shaped it, such as Washington and Ida B. Wells; alongside King were other clergy and theologians, such as James Lawson and Andrew Young, who pushed for an interconnection of a modern intellectual movement and a progressive Christianity. What is distinctive about this tradition of the Black social gospel is that it countered many of the attempts to render or expel Black Christianity and churches as "hopelessly self-centered, provincial, insular, anti-intellectual, and conservative."[82] Instead, according to Dorrien, those within the social gospel tradition throughout the early and later twentieth century civil rights struggles "countered that Christian faith, critical rationality, and civil rights advocacy went together, or at least it needed to do so."[83] In other words, they were attempting to offer more than an apologetic for Black churches—they sought to offer models for using the faith and activism that issued from generations of African Americans.

Black Public Moralists and Theology

Closely related to, but not quite the same as what Dorrien defines as the Black social gospel tradition, Black public theological tradition expanded the conversation of what and where theological discourse can and should take place, as well as how Christians have engaged pressing social interests over time. As noted in chapter 3, public theology and theological reflections offer another framework for understanding and shaping the intersection of one's faith and the community and world that one inhabits. Black public theology and the historical Black social gospel strands overlap in intricate ways. However, I argue that the Black social gospel tradition fits under the larger framework or umbrella of Black public theology, such that the Black social gospel tradition is one expression of Black public theology, but others persist. For example, one of the hallmarks of the Black social gospel is an adoption of modern intellectualism and progressive theology. However, there are examples of Black public theological reflection that do not include progressive theology. In fact, Bree Newsome's theological framing of her acts of civil disobedience place her within a tradition of followers of a radical Jesus, but who also employs decidedly conservative (or non-modernist and progressive) understandings of prayer and spiritual warfare. As such, some would not place her theological reflections or actions within either of the trajectories of the Black social gospel and Black public theology, but I assert that she fits squarely within the larger framework and history of Black public theology; she also connects with the organizing tradition of Black Christian women.

Black public theology in some ways is a more widely understood concept than the Black social gospel tradition; however, it has not received careful theorizing or scholarly attention in the creation of a history of Black public theologians. Instead, most often, key figures within the histories of particular denominations are remembered for their contributions to the growth of that body and not to an overall expansion of our under-standing of how Black religion or theology enters and reflects upon public life. Many key figures can be afforded the label of Black public theologian; for example, many of the same figures included in the social gospel tradi-tions, such as Howard Thurman, Benjamin E. Mays, Ida B. Wells, and later figures like King are included in this tradition of drawing upon the deep wellsprings of their Christian faith and beliefs to offer a response to the concerns and injustices taking place in the world.

As noted in chapter 3, public theology helps African American youth reconnect with an emphasis on communities and the communal dimen-sions of their spirituality (and not just the individual). However, as we shift to the question of what Black youth are teaching the Christian church and wider society, we see in Black youth activism (Christian and otherwise) a reminder to take action in response to the injustices and oppressions they encounter. For, as defined by Robert Franklin, public theology is primarily embodied theology, where one is called to "show before they tell the world the meanings of faith, hope, love, justice, and reconciliation."[84] While this does not offer a neat theoretical framework of Black public theology, it is helpful as yet another reminder of the diversity of expressions and histori-cal antecedents available to younger African Americans, to which they are now adding their voices. For example, Black public theology has significant historical precedents, not simply in social change movements and political agendas, but in the lives and visions of exemplary African Americans.

In addition to discussions of public theology in his work *Liberating Visions*, Franklin expands this idea to explore the visions of public moral-ists. Indeed, he explores similar figures as Dorrien: Washington, Du Bois, King, and Malcolm X, offering yet another hermeneutic and way of inter-preting the lives of these figures. Franklin's understanding of these figures differs in that he is attempting to counter what he calls the naïve romanti-cism of much Black liberation theology and even of the social gospel, in that these traditions have often failed to account for what the "authenti-cally free and liberated person" looks like. He notes that these theological treatments often overlook "a host of issues related to personal identity, wholeness, and fulfillment."[85] And they have failed to look carefully at the intersection of public theology and private practices of renewal.

This reflection on and even attentiveness to what wholeness and per-sonal wellbeing looks like within the larger narratives of activism and social change are the historical precursors for what Quita is offering us, and even what Nyle and many other young African Americans are striving for. They do not simply want to revive or enliven Black Christianity or even the Black political sphere, but they want to know what it looks like to live as communities of whole and fulfilled persons. Part of the activism of this generation is geared toward changing systems so that humans can thrive. As Franklin suggests, there is a need and a tradition of attending to this alongside struggles for liberation and freedom.

Black Christian Women's Organizing: Defying the Odds and Categorization

As I reflect on the activism and spirituality of young African Americans, I most immediately note the connections with the particular and unique organizing of African American women who also sought to hold in tension their faith and their belief in overcoming injustices. While Black women were intricately connected to the history and development of the Black social gospel tradition and are exemplars of public theology, these trajectories (and the writing about them) do not fully encapsulate the work of many African American Christian women, and I point to the ways that women's organizing offers another dimension of the history of Black Christian social witness. This history of Black Christian women's community and social organizing offers another helpful reference point for youth activism, as it offers a more nuanced interconnection of faith and activism (which does not always dismiss religion or religious leaders as useless or superstitious). As political historian Barbara Savage notes, even when early twentieth-century women leaders offered critiques of Black religion and ministers, they were more nuanced than male contemporaries, like Du Bois, "because they allowed for the possibility that emotional styles of worship could coexist with community engagement."[86]

Within the Black social gospel and Black public theology framework and in separate and unique ways, Black Christian women have also modeled holding together strong understandings of faith and advocacy for social change. At various points in history, Black women have been esteemed as the unfailing supports of African American life, particularly religious and social uplift programs. And historically, Black women have been written about and esteemed for their supportive roles, in fundraising and helping to advance the agendas of male leaders and organizations, but these women were and are much more than supports or props for male leadership. For example, the women's club movement of the early twentieth century trained leaders and met to set their own agendas and enact them, with or without the support of men. Cheryl Townsend Gilkes, Evelyn Brooks Higginbotham, and Barbara Savage's work, among many others, collectively reclaims the significance of the leadership and social change organizing of women during the late nineteenth and early twentieth centuries. They offer accounts of the masses of Black women who were participants in local and national clubs like the National Association of Colored Women's Clubs and the National Council of Negro Women, as well as denominational bodies, such as the Woman's Auxiliary of the National Baptist Convention.[87] They also foreground the complex legacy of leadership and activism among key women, such as Ida B. Wells-Barnett and Nannie Helen Burroughs. For example, Wells-Barnett is best known for her ability to create space and give voice to women's leadership and ideas on social crises, in her writings and national anti-lynching campaign. Wells-Barnett was one of few Black women of her era who created space outside of the church for women's leadership and voices.

Burroughs, working within church structures initially, also became a force for social transformation as she advocated for and created a separate women's convention as an auxiliary to the National Baptist Convention, which was (and remains in a large part) run by only male clergy. Burroughs outlined a type of interconnection of Christianity and social transformation that many today reject. In part, her understanding of racial uplift and overcoming oppressions intricately connected "respectability" and social justice politics. Higginbotham outlines the innovations of Burroughs's politics of respectability, which placed equal value on the Bible, self-help strategies, and social justice. According to Higginbotham, "the Baptist women emphasized manners and morals while simultaneously asserting traditional forms of protests, such as petitions, boycotts, and verbal appeals to justice."[88] While Burroughs's emphasis on respectability has been criticized, she created methods of working to advance the causes of African Americans in an era where their worth and dignity were being undermined constantly; respectability politics was only one of these methods. Burroughs also did not limit her protests to White American society at large; rather, she focused much of her critique on the structures and methods within Black churches and institutions. Like Du Bois and others, Burroughs was not uncritically Christian. Instead, she began her career offering a speech to the National Baptist Convention in 1900, entitled "How the Sisters Are Hindered from Helping."[89] In this speech, she expressed her "righteous discontent" with the new convention of Baptists, which resulted in their authorization of the formation of the Women's Convention.[90]

But in the midst of the sometimes-contentious battles with male clergy and leadership, Burroughs's work in Black women's club movements brought about tremendous change—empowering Black women to value their worth and work, and to find their own ways of creating change that would support the rest of the community, but which did not necessarily or primarily have to rely on the affirmation of it. They held themselves to higher standards and advocated for an understanding of Christian faith and witness, such that any version that did not set equality and justice as one of its ultimate goals was not Christian or faithful in their opinions.

In the subsequent generations, women's organizing continued to hold in tension faith in God, work in churches, and work in communities. For example, the story of rural grassroots organizing and social change during the Civil Rights Movement includes the work of women like Fannie Lou Hamer. Hamer was born to sharecroppers and would have been the product of much of the rural religion proponents of the social gospel. Hamer's faith was formed by her parents, who "were devoutly religious" and who "taught her that hatred would destroy her spirit if she gave in to it."[91] Hamer counters many perceptions of who should be able to lead and advocate for change, because she was not able to finish school and was only able to improve her reading skills through Bible study at her local Baptist church. Nevertheless, Hamer stood up against the oppression of Black sharecroppers. She became a local change agent, even before she took opportunities to attend mass meetings hosted by the Student Nonviolent Coordinating Committee (SNCC) and the Southern Christian Leadership Conference (SCLC), who were in rural Mississippi to conduct citizenship education and to help adults learn and register to vote. Hamer also broke church protocol by challenging Black male pastors who she thought were derelict in their responsibilities to lead people to work for change or even to vote.[92] Hamer is notable for standing up during the middle of sermons to ask questions about why these preachers were not advocating for change and social reform.

Beyond her willingness to call out religious leaders, she did not stop speaking up even when she was arrested and brutally beaten after attending a citizenship training program hosted by other fearless women activist and educators like Annelle Ponder and Septima Clark. Barbara Savage describes the work of Hamer and other activist women like her as *religious rebels*, writing that the women became "a part of an activist minority . . .

whose courage and persistence and faith fomented a racial revolution and a religious movement."[93] Savage is not alone in describing the protests, marches, and sit-ins of the Civil Rights Movement as religious. Despite the unyielding patriarchy among many African American men and religious organizations, Black women were able to carve out space to effect change—change that held together their deeply held convictions of faith and social transformation.

Ongoing Barriers to Black Christian Social Witness

This chapter has both a hopeful and a cautionary tone. Recounting the narratives and histories of freedom fighters and contemporary activists reminds us of the ongoing struggles for freedom and liberation for all; at the same time, it also reminds us of the power of their lives as public Christian witnesses. These contemporary and historical young activists not only effect change; they also inspire others to do the same. This chapter places young activists in relation to their historical predecessors, and it will hopefully remind and inspire adults and other young African Americans of what is possible in every generation. However, part of inspiring young Africans Americans to connect with the contemporary and historical exemplars requires that we both attend to what we learn from African American Christian social witnesses and that we address the many barriers that inhibit young African Americans from connecting their struggles for social transformation with current and historical Black churches.

First, it is important to note that Black youth activism is not simply a corrective to the spiritual experiences of Black youth (or a symptom of fragmentation); rather, the activism of young African Americans has already begun to transform the world, churches, and religious scholarship. Thus throughout this chapter, I have sought to show how youth activism is an animating force for continued faith and growth. For example, the activism of young Black people is reminding the Black Christian community of a larger, nobler version of itself and enlivening the tradition to push forward and add to the categories of Black church social teachings, social witness, and Black public theology. In addition to the surge in activism by young African Americans, there has been a parallel surge in social and political commentary by scholars of religion and clergy, alike. In fact, Black religious academics have come alive in ways that I worried was not possible anymore.[94] Pastors too have preached more about issues confronting their communities (not in lieu of, but alongside personal narratives of salvation and hope for something better, be it material wealth or an afterlife). Certainly, not all Black religious academics or clergy are responding to the events and activism of young African Americans, but more are, and the responses have been striking.

In part, there is still significant theological reflection presented in the traditional formats of texts written for seminarians and other scholars, but there has also been a resurgence of the role and import of the public intellectual who must bridge the academy, church, and community. In many ways, this attempt to connect religious scholarship with the work and actions of Black people has reminded many Black religious academics of the reality of the lived experiences of Black people and the role that Black clergy and intellectuals can play in it. However, it has also forced scholars and theologians, who for generations overlooked the contributions of youth and young adults, to take seriously what they are saying to the world and at times to the Church. Some academic theologians are even writing about the ways that the movements of young African Americans are making them theorize and do theology differently. For examples, Black religious scholars such as Yolanda Pierce, Pamela Lightsey, Eddie Glaude, Kelly Brown Douglas, Leah Gunning Frances, Cornell West, and Brittney Cooper, among so many others, have offered reflections on the activism of young African Americans and/or have personally engaged with these young people. They are embodying the best of the Black scholar-activist tradition and recentering the significant contributions and leadership of African American youth to the development of Black political and religious discourse.

However, Black youth activism also comes with a reminder that there persist barriers both to youth working for change and to youth connecting their faith (and contemporary religious institutions) with this change. The idea of young people protesting and advocating for their rights should offer their communities a senses of pride and encouragement. However, we recognize that in addition to concerns and perceptions of young people as thugs, criminals, and so on when they dare to assert their authority and voices, within African American communities there are still many obstacles to Black youth activism.

In particular, religion is not and has not always been a source of joy and healing on which to build one's understanding of liberation and which propels one forward. Religion is complex, and Black Christianity is equally so. Therefore, even as we attend to the ways that it interconnects (and that it should interconnect with movements for change), we must also acknowledge that it can serve as a barrier to youth activism.

Myopic Theology

Even as I affirm faith-based youth activism as an example of that ways that Black youth are already countering narratives of fragmented spirituality, I note that it is not as simple or unidirectional as this. In truth, faith-based activism is a reminder of what is possible with young people, but it is also a reminder of the limits of much lived and popular Christian practice and theology. For the most part, the initial understanding of Christianity and even Christian theology is not the call of Christ to work for change in the world. Often the perception is that Christians (and Black Christians) are rule-bearers and caught up with telling young people what not to do and how not to act, instead of actually offering values and encouragement for ways to live that directly affect their lives and communities.

Often this narrative has been named in the growing irrelevance of Black churches and Christianity to the experiences of Black youth (often barriers include outmoded worship styles, language, and a generally unwelcoming atmosphere), but more than irrelevance, there are actual limits within the theology that Black churches teach that are making them increasingly ineffective. If all we offer is "fear God so you can go to heaven when you die," then young people will rightly note that they have enough to fear right now and the promise of heaven does little to help overcome their current struggles. Likewise, since death is real and prevalent (as discussed above), theologies that do not offer ways of dealing with death and questioning why or how Black death is so pervasive become a barrier to youth taking action and to an integrated spirituality. Young people are demanding more than myopic, one-dimensional theology.

Hierarchy, Gender, and Respectability as Barriers to Youth Activism

Reinforcing many of the obstacles are questions of leadership and whether young people can lead or whether they should just "participate" and fall in line with the vision and work of the adults and elders. Even within community organizations and protests, there are often clashes between the work and vision of young people and adult activists. At times this includes a divergence of agendas and methods, and other times it includes outright disagreements and inability to collectively move forward.

I have so often resisted focusing on issues of gender (over and above race)—even as I attempt to carefully attend to the intersectionality of all oppressions—but repeatedly the places where Black Christian activism and young people appear to be clashing most heavily in this generation is around the pull/push of hetero-normativity and gender-conformity as a prerequisite for "respectable" leadership. As noted above, Black Christian women's organizing is crucial to the success of religious and political transformation. However, this history is only partially embraced. Even when we acknowledge the importance of students, for example in the sit-ins in Nashville and the groups of students working with Reverend James Lawson, we often fail to attend carefully to the interconnections of gender, class, and colorism. David Halberstam, in *The Children*, carefully notes the gender and class strata that governed the life of most college students in Nashville during the 1950s and '60s.[95] It was therefore an unlikely feat for the core leadership of the sit-ins in Nashville to emerge with a young woman, Diane Nash, at its center and poorer, darker male students from the poorest of the Nashville colleges, American Baptist, like John Lewis and James Bevel.[96] However, Halberstam's 2005 work remains the story that is often overlooked or underemphasized, and therefore the dominant narrative of historical Black religious activism remains that of King or the SCLC and not the myriad women, young and old, who were essential to the work of transforming their worlds in both traditional and non-traditional roles (e.g., as both teachers and as leaders of direct-action). Therefore, in imagining what Black Christian youth activism looks like, there is both an assumption that the historical models do not include women and girls and an assumption that the issues of women are secondary or only discussed when connected to how they impact the life of the larger community.[97]

To be certain, this chapter reminds us that so often even our religious histories and typologies of moral leadership focus on an ideal, solitary, and male religious leader. With the few recent exceptions noted above, these histories and typologies have often neglected communal, collaborative models of leadership and change. These more communal models of change are important to the work of sustained change and Christian social witness. Assuredly, diversity persists in the models of social change in the continued efforts of youth today. For the most part, Stephen Green is continuing in the work and world of Black male clergy leaders, while Quita is continuing in a model of collaborative advocacy and organizing.

Likewise, the #Blacklivesmatter movement is more of the latter, while we see efforts to make it the former. In part, there is a theoretical simplicity in focusing on singular leaders and models. Indeed it is harder to theorize and describe collaborative leadership and organizing. Thus so much of the historical work, even about Black Christian witness, is connected to ideals of "great men." It is, however, historically inaccurate to esteem only the work of singular male leaders; Black youth are resisting this type of framing in contemporary models. With the presence of more women writing history and the accessibility of new technologies, such as social media, that do not require the same institutional gatekeeping. Young, queer, Black women collectives are coming to the forefront as leaders of social change and exemplars of a very different type of social change, as well as Christian social change. As such, we must be careful to honor and include all models of leadership and activism.

An expansion of the historical voices is helpful in offering a better, more accurate understanding of how African American Christians have engaged social issues; however, among young African Americans, this alone will not be enough. For example, even when we note the dominant historical moves, we note that the methods of protest from different eras do not directly translate to today's struggles or technology. While I honor the communal racial uplift of Black Baptist women and women's movements as described by Higginbotham, most of the efforts of these churchwomen aimed at a politics of respectability. And respectability alone does not hold for young African Americans today because they have witnessed first-hand that how one dresses or the manners and morals one uses does not protect one from the insidious effects of White supremacy and oppression. There is no longer an assertion that being respectable or going to the correct church can afford youth advancements and freedom from oppression. Therefore, the history and even the expansion of who we include as historical exemplars expands our understanding of how faith and activism are interconnected; but what is required is an ongoing invitation for young African Americans to continue building on this history, to see the story as their story and to creatively add their ways of being and protesting to this narrative.

Conclusion

Each of the snapshots offers very different understandings and models of Black youth activism, but they collectively model for us and push us further into the history of Black public theologians, intellectuals, and activists. They also push us to explore current social changes movements lead by Black youth to ascertain if or how religion plays a part and what the current barriers to Black youth activism are. These young people have pushed the contours of how I theorize about fragmented spirituality, but they offer counternarratives to fragmentations as well as complex and diverse models of what an activist strand of a more integrated spirituality could entail. Reflecting on the lives of these young people, in conversation with the complex and diverse narratives of Black churches as political organizations and religious leaders and activists, we see that they open up another chapter in this complex history and tension. But they also offer correctives to the somewhat unrealistic expectations placed on African American churches. Black youth are countering the notion that this is the only institution that Black people have. Instead, their abilities to organize and build coalitions across a range of non-profits, civic organizations, and churches—primarily through social media-driven connections—points to young African Americans working for change in ways that does not simply lament the dearth of organizing power and leadership within African American communities.

These snapshots also push practical theologians to explore how these young people emerged as Black public theologians and activists (even if they would not self-identify as such). Beyond honoring the work that they are currently doing, there is additional interest in exploring the experiences and influences that propelled their work. Some young African Americans, like Newsome and Fort, have clear narratives of why they are working for change now, and they are beginning to make sense of how their early experiences as Black people, as people of faith, and as humans who were conscious of the suffering of others shaped them and pushed them to take public stances. It is also important to note the layers of networking, mentoring, and education that each of these young people has undertaken. They did not simply see the injustices in the world, but they were exposed to groups and models as well who helped them see that they could make a difference and how to start. So as a religious educator, I then step back and wonder if there are ways that we can replicate this formation or at least begin to be more attentive to offer youth and young adults access to models, if they want to respond and begin to connect their faith with the injustices they see in the world.

6

Choosing Life with Youth

VISION AND STRATEGIES OF ABUNDANT LIFE

ALIVE! I WONDER *if I will be alive*. Death, violence, oppression, and racism have become part of the narratives of all young African Americans, whether they are experiencing these firsthand or just reading about them on social media. Parents and youth workers are also struggling and wondering how to walk with young people in a world such as this. For some youth, there is not a longing for a brighter future; rather, they simply wonder if they will get a chance to grow up and if they will be alive. As I reflect on this reality, I too often wonder if raising awareness about the issues facing young people is enough, or if we must also look at what life for them should look like and what type of vision calls people out of the cycles of death and violence and into the co-creating roles esteemed in chapter 3. Is there more to life than death and suffering? And what does life, and even a practice of choosing life, look like for young people?

In this chapter, we return to the narrative of one of the youth introduced in chapter 1. And it is in listening to the wisdom of Kira that we begin to see a vision of life where violence and death are not the totality of existence. In truth, Kira's story helps us to explore the paradoxical vision of abundant life that God offers to humanity through Jesus. It is a vision that is not simply utopian, but an invitation to a way of life that is *not* defined by death and oppression. Ironically, Christianity is a religion that focuses on death and resurrection. And in some strands of the religious tradition, discussions of Jesus's death and dying far overshadow his life. But in this chapter we wrestle with an invitation to live and choose life.[1] In this chapter we reflect on what it means for young people to live in a world surrounded by death, to have a dominant religion, Christianity, steeped in death (and violence), and to find within this same tradition hope and life. This is the work young African Americans are requiring both of themselves and of the communities and traditions that nurture them—to both see a vision of life and live into it. Therefore, that is the task before us.

Taking the Limits Off: Kira's Story

At the time of her interview, Kira was a rising high-school senior who grew up in a fairly impoverished and crime-infested neighborhood in Florida. Her parents divorced when she was younger, her schools were labeled "failing," and many of her teachers were afraid to push too hard or try too much because it might attract more negative attention to an already bad situation. Kira was more than aware of the perceptions of her community. She was also attuned to the cycles of the violence and death around her. She recounted one set of incidents vividly:

> We were coming home from church and saw a whole bunch of police and everything and I just overlooked it. And when I got to school, it was like, Michelle got shot in the head.
>
> But I think people get so used to hearing about death that they become numb. So it wasn't any coming together to cry and moan. It wasn't that. It was just like, here, we're going to put a big old piece of paper up here and give a shout out to [Michelle]. . . . Miss You.
>
> But then after that, another girl got shot walking home, but she didn't die . . . so people get so used to hearing about death, especially young death, being at the wrong place at the wrong time. There wasn't any remorse, it was nothing like, let's come together. . . .
>
> And if I don't watch out, I kind of get numb to it, too.

During Kira's interview, I was brought up short listening to her observe that people get used to death and her concern that she might become numb also. So I asked how she resisted. Amazingly and somewhat unexpectedly, she said she actively "witnessed," and she attempted to build community and show her friends that they were loved.[2]

I came to the interview with Kira with many preconceptions about "witnessing" (given the history of evangelicalism and conservative Christianity in the United States and because of Kira's more conservative religious background); however, Kira's main message to her friends was that there was more to life than "what was immediately around them." She wanted to share that there was more than failing schools, ineffective teachers, and cycles of death, fear of retaliation, and more death. The cycles of violence and poverty were not the most significant part of her story. Kira exuded joy and positive energy that I could not quite figure out.

In addition to her vivid recounting of the violence in her community, Kira also embodied a faith that was so strong, and her hope in God was so secure that all of the gloom around her paled in comparison. Again, her strong faith and language such as "we are not fighting against humans, but against spiritual things" raised suspicions in me and a desire to push back against Kira's faith affirmations. In particular, one can question whether Kira's faith empowers her to address her immediate life circum-stances.[3] I initially thought, as have many others, that her joy and hope were merely naïve, otherworldly spiritualizing that might keep her from working for the change needed to correct systems of violence and pov-erty in her community.[4] Kira was somewhat of an anomaly among the students I interviewed over the years, in that she was part of a more theo-logically conservative religious community. Her mother was a pastor of an Apostolic church, and while her religious conservatism was evident in her style of dress and her language—she also often pushed beyond stereo-types of religious conservatism to offer complex theological reflections on the world around her. In other words, she was already embodying much of the work that I hope all youth will do in terms of spiritual practice and theological reflection (and her actions proved to be equally informative for my reflections on responses to fragmented spirituality).[5]

One of the ongoing challenges in taking seriously the lives of African American youth is to learn to listen *with* youth. Instead of prescribing or criticizing how young people should respond, it is important to see the possibilities in their theological reflections and to discern what theological truths and practical strategies emerge. It is necessary to reiterate this strat-egy here, because I too did not fully grasp what Kira was describing and embodying at first. Her work and witness only made more sense when I placed it into the context of other social change and non-violent move-ments. For example, I noted that when a sixteen-year-old says she wanted to walk around her community and her school, getting to know people and telling them that she loves them and God loves them, I got suspi-cious. But when we read about clergy walking the streets in Boston or Los Angeles, we herald it as innovative responses to systems of violence. In Boston, it was called a "miracle," and in Los Angeles it became "Homeboy Industries."[6]

Kira, along with the other students interviewed in this project, also challenged many of my initial assumptions about the types of injustices that were most prevalent for African American youth. For example, I came to their interviews imagining that race and racism were the most salient category of oppression that they were experiencing. In reality, the young people most often did not name racism, but they gave examples of violence happening around them every day and their fears about violence locally and globally. To be sure, there is a strong connection between systemic racism and violence, but it was significant that each of the African American youth I interviewed described some sort of violence against other youth and young adults as part of their lived realities or concerns for their communities and the world.

In other words, their narratives collectively have forced me to expand the categories of what we imagine young people are dealing with and what types of systems and cycles of oppression remain most pressing in their lives. The narratives of my interviewees predated and in some ways predicted the growing attention that violence against Black youth would take in the recent years. Contemporary protest against vigilante violence and police brutality against African American men and women have seen a parallel increase in youth-led activism and protests (recounted in the previous chapter). However, the perpetual questions persist concerning the connection (if any) between religion and the concerns of young people and even their protests against violence around them.

In addition to expanding the categories of what African American youth are dealing with, Kira reminded me of the power of hope, faith, and community building in the face of violence, poverty, and innumerable injustices that many adults will never fully understand. For example, when I asked her about her "understanding of the role of the church or God in the community or in the world," I expected nihilism or uncertainty (for that was what most other youth expressed, and it was often what I was feeling in the face of overwhelming systems of injustice). Instead, Kira boldly stated that

> we are just vessels of God, and if we want to see a difference in the world, we got to let God fully work through us. Like we have to take the limits off, to go all the way out.... We got to let [God] fully use us to let a change happen.

Beyond being unexpected, Kira's response is both simple and complex. There is a level of parroting of larger themes of allowing God to work, but there is also something more here than a response to youth violence. Kira's response reminds us of a larger theological (and practical) corrective to fragmented spirituality among African American youth. Her statement is both a confident affirmation of the power of God and the agency of humanity (youth in particular), but it also points toward a larger way of being, which I argue is expressed in the idea of the *Abundant Life*.

The Way of Life Abundant

Kira's admonishment to "take the limits off" pushes youth and adults to wrestle with an alternative vision of life that does not start with violence, but that embraces life and life more abundantly. As I listened with Kira, I also listened to the wider Christian tradition for understandings of abundant life or the reign of God that might have influenced her or that resonate with her vision. The concept of abundant life has a long and complicated history. Far from being a fully articulated doctrine or theology, it draws on varied interpretations of words attributed to Jesus in John 10:10, where Jesus states that his purpose for coming to earth was so that all could have life, abundantly: "The thief comes only to steal and kill and destroy. I came that they may have life, and have it abundantly."[7]

However, during the mid-twentieth century, the idea of abundant life became synonymous with teachings about spiritual growth, material prosperity, and physical healing.[8] And while I am not certain that Kira's personal theology would contradict this interpretation of abundant life, I argue that material prosperity or simple individualistic advancement contributes to fragmented spirituality, while a larger interpretation of the abundant life serves as a corrective.[9]

Abundant life, or a way of life abundant is not simply a set of truths to espouse or a theology to believe in, but it is our best approximation of what we are called to as Christian communities. Thomas Groome argues that in John 10, Jesus is echoing the same wisdom offered to his disciples when Jesus taught them to pray "thy kingdom come on earth as it is in heaven." In other words, Jesus is pointing toward the ultimate vision of God. This vision includes communion with God in the reign or kingdom of God— and this is what Jesus is calling for on earth. According to Groome, abundant life, or the fullness of life, is what God intends for all. Groome writes, "God intends the best of everything for everyone, all the time, and the integrity of God's creation."[10] Similarly, Dorothy Bass and Craig Dykstra, in their introduction to a volume on practical theology, begin by affirming that "God in Christ promises abundant life for all creation. By the power of the Holy Spirit, the church receives this promise through faith and takes up a way of life that embodies Christ's abundant life in and for the world."[11]

However, these seemingly simple statements of what God intends for our lives are overwhelming. If one follows and agrees with Groome's statement that this is what God wants for us and that the church has to take up this way of life in and for the world, then we have to follow it through to completion. This includes recognizing that "what God wants us to have is how we should live."[12] For example, if God's will is the integrity of creation, then we have to be good stewards of it. If God's will is justice and peace, then we must do the work of justice and promote peace in society. If God's will is that all be fed, then we have to do the work of eradicating hunger. If God's will is peace with justice, then we have to work toward ending cycles of violence. And this is overwhelming primarily because it is hard to imagine this reality or even this aspiration. In other words, a theology of abundant life so often gets co-opted and reduced to material wealth or health because we can see that, but we cannot see a world that might work in harmony for the good of all and with creation.[13]

Both Groome and Bass offer this vision and outline the role of ministers and leaders (and theological education) in this process. But they seem to forget that a necessary first step is helping people *see* and embrace the idea that abundant life is an option for them. It is the hard but necessary work of doing ministry with African American youth, and other oppressed communities, which first requires re-affirmation that abundant life is a way of life they can walk in right now.

Thus, in reflecting on recent literature on the way of life abundant, I also remain frustrated. My critique of earlier reflections on abundance was its narrow focus on the material or physical dimensions of abundant life. However, in the recent literature, the impetus for conversations about abundant life, and even the telos and urgency of empowering people toward life-giving ways of life, is very different. For example, some works focus on theological education and the role of practical theology or even the purpose of education. Other conversation partners start with a question of whether "faith will exist on earth." All are commendable questions and foci, but I come to the discussion of abundant life through the narrative of a young woman (and communities of young people), for whom living is not something that can always be realistically imagined happening beyond the age of twenty-five. For many youth like Kira, life is not just a spiritual construct or a set of middle-class values. Life is survival. Life is the day-to-day breathing in and out and being grateful for your very next breath. And so I am cautious and wonder what it means to proclaim abundant life in the midst of the news that another young person on America's streets or around the globe has been gunned down. What does it meant to read John 10:10 for Hadiya Pendleton (or any other list of young people who have died violently over the past few years)?[14]

Therefore, many articulations of abundant life remain insufficient as well. I, with Kira, am asking, How do we foster a way of life abundant that addresses the realities of violence, poverty, and dehumanization, among African American youth? A 2008 editorial reflecting on the harsh realities of poverty and material insecurity among the working poor reminds us of these tensions in our discussions of Christianity and traditions. Kristin Largen offers a sharp reminder that there is tremendous work to be done among Christian communities in responding to the economic crises that so many Americans (and others around the globe) encounter. She outlines the ways that Christian communities can spiritualize practices such as praying the "Our Father" without fully considering those who request "daily bread" not as a reminder that God provides all that we need, but as a desperate cry for food and daily sustenance. She concludes her editorial writing,

> The church has a moral responsibility to address those places, to bring the grace of Jesus Christ into those situations, and to be a prophetic voice for life; and not just life, but abundant life.[15]

Largen's reflections, like Kira's, offer a stark reminder of the ways that religious communities have limited God and failed in their work to fully imagine and work toward helping all of creation experience the abundant life promised by Jesus.[16] Howard Thurman, in his seminal text *Jesus and the Disinherited*, writes,

> I can count on the fingers of one hand the number of times that I have heard a sermon on the meaning of religion, of Christianity, to the [person] who stands with his [or her] back against the wall. It is urgent that my meaning be crystal clear. The masses of [people] live with their backs constantly against the wall. They are the poor, the disinherited, the dispossessed. What does our religion say to them? The issue is not what it counsels them to do for others whose need may be greater, but what religion offers to meet their own needs.[17]

While Thurman does not use the language of abundant life, he does push us to consider the lived realities of the dispossessed and disinherited of this generation. The indictment is that religion has often failed to explicitly offer any direct response to questions of how we live now and what a life worth living looks like, in which all have the ability to meet their basic needs. Thurman wrestles with the constant reality that Christianity has often been implicated in the death-dealing forces of modern society and the systems in which African American youth are having to fight simply to survive. However, Thurman also holds on to the *religion of Jesus* as a reminder that beyond the history of Christianity there is a vision offered by Jesus (and the way he lived) that offers the masses who find themselves up against the proverbial walls of life, a better way to live. Writing about an impoverished Jesus who knew the insecurities of living on the margins of society, Thurman affirms that

> [Jesus] knew that the goals of a religion as he understood them could never be worked out within the then-established order. Deep from within that order he projected a dream, the logic of which would give to all the needful security. There would be room for all, and no [one] would be a threat to [their kin]. "The kingdom of God is within."[18]

Abundant Life Is . . .

So what does it mean to practice or live life abundantly?

Abundant life is not a life without problems or with material prosperity, per se, but it is a way of life that opens all to full participation in the work and blessings of God and God's community. A theology of abundant life propels religious communities to wrestle with and try to understand what God intends and how we must act in the world. If Jesus says, "I come that you might have life and have it more abundantly," then we have to try to embrace life and abundant life.

I have often thought that it was disingenuous to declare abundant life in the face of despair. But Kira, like Thurman, pushes us to see that Jesus is defining abundant life within an insecure, occupied, and oppressive state. From Jesus's articulation, we learn about abundant life, not in the absence of pain or death, but in the face of it. It is in the juxtaposition of life and death that Jesus proclaims the abundant life: "The thief comes to steal, kill and destroy; but I [Jesus] come that you might have life." Jesus is hinting at the fact that abundant life is the ability to keep living in the face of death. It is the ability to thrive and experience the fullness of life, even when death, corruption, and violence are ever present.

In a world that loves death, or at least where death and the threat of violence are daily occurrences, life is a radical concept. Exploring the many ways that abundant life has been employed throughout the past century is helpful, but it also requires that we do more than rehearse this history— that we also articulate what abundant life can mean for African American youth today.

While I appreciate Groome's hopeful faith claim that *God intends the best of all things for everyone at all times and integrity of creation*, this requires a great deal of unpacking for Black youth. Looking specifically at the lives of young African Americans, abundant life is a life worth living, a life that does not require youth to grow up too fast. It is life that demonstrates that young people are beloved by God, and that counters the harsh reality that young African Americans live in a world where they are not always loved and where they are constantly judged as deviant or delinquent. Abundant life is a life where young Black women and men get to dream and aspire toward a vision of themselves, as whole and in community with others. It is being able to articulate ideals of life not simply in terms of "working for change" and fighting injustice, but actually being able to benefit from structures that they helped design to empower all to flourish.

Abundant life requires a healthy sense of agency, in that youth will be empowered to critically reflect on their communities, and if they see a wrong or feel that things should be done differently, they will feel capable of taking direct action in response. Abundant life includes a level of security within one's self and in one's community. This is where the discussions of food insecurity and material needs are important. Environmentalists have taught us the need to care for creation and to be better stewards of the limited natural resources on earth. However, we have often heeded their warning with fear that there is not *enough* to go around and that therefore we must fight over and hoard the little resources that are available. We have also been tempted to perpetuate environmental racism, out of fear that we will not have enough resources for the community that we live in, if we care for all communities. In environmental debates, fear can be helpful, but it cannot be the only solution. Instead, it is important to push past the fear of *scarcity* to redefine abundance in terms of the creativity of responses that one can make given finite resources. Abundant life requires

a reorientation of all, alongside of an acknowledgement of our interconnectedness with others around the globe and with our environment.

Abundant life also requires a mindset shift, in which we push beyond
the limits of how things have always been done, to a place of being
secure in the future and to spaces where we are because we are participating in creative ways of living and operating now, such that we are not
constantly depleting all that is around us or allowing others to do the
same. Declaring abundant life with youth requires that we address the
fears, but that we also work together to push youth and ourselves beyond
the limits of seeing ourselves only as targets of violence, to a place of
being secure in our future because of the creative solutions to violence
that we are enacting now. Declaring abundant life with youth requires a
complete mindset shift in which society must shift to see the interconnectedness of young people, particularly minority youth, with the rest of
the global society—and to see that their lives are directly influenced by
adult policies.

Declaring abundant life with African American youth is not an easy
task or one that simply requires Black youth to "think differently," but it
is a complete reorientation of our way of life, in response to the promise of God given in Jesus Christ. In essence, abundant life with African
American youth involves the following:

- It proclaims *life as an option* in a world that loves death.
- It opens youth to a sense of *security* within one's self, one's community,
  and God.
- It attends to the material and physical realities of their lives.
  - This includes a balance of care for the earth and others with ability
    of individual flourishing. It shifts from a mythology of scarcity to a
    mindset of abundant life—as abundance of creative solutions to the
    problems around us.
- It requires *agency*.
  - Youth must be willing and able to act for change for a better world.
- It embodies *limitless hope* in God, in one's self, and in the world
  around one.

Declaring abundant life with youth requires a level of hope that I often do
not possess alone (which is why Kira's reminder was so important to me
and has in many ways sustained my work for years since she first shared it).
It also entails much more than simply wishing that things could be better.

The essence of abundant life rests in one's affirmation that God offers us more than the current reality (security, healthy relationships, mutual concern, cooperation, a more just community/world, etc.). Abundant life also rests in our ability to live in such a way that aspires toward this vision and gift that God offers. Proclaiming life more abundant with youth calls youth to live (as Kira noted) without the limits of what is expected or without the restrictions of a death-loving, hopeless, and corrupt system. It is amazing that it took a sixteen-year-old to remind me of what was promised by the revolutionary Messiah centuries ago. However, it reflects the power of adolescents and the work required in each generation, so that we can begin to truly experience life more abundantly with each young person in each generation.

Strategies for Abundant Life
A Critical Pedagogy of Integrating Spirituality

Responding to fragmented spirituality among African American youth and walking with youth into a vision of abundant life also requires rethinking pedagogical strategies in African American churches. The review of educational curricula in African American churches and interviews with African American youth demonstrates the ways that educationally communities of faith are perpetuating and failing to challenge fragmented spirituality. Therefore, in addition to offering a vision of abundant life, I outline the goals and strategies of a *Critical Pedagogy of Integrating Spirituality*. As outlined in the introduction,

> *Integrating spirituality is spirituality that empowers youth to hold together the seemingly disparate areas of their lives, to tap into the resources of their faith communities, and learn from historical and current faith exemplars, in order to see themselves as capable of living abundant life by effecting change on individual, communal, and systemic levels.*

Hopefully at this point, it is clear that an integrating spirituality is not simply a reaction to the problem of fragmentation in society and among young African Americans; it is also a vision and an invitation to a way of being that empowers young people and adults to live well in the here and now (even as they remain assured of the life to come). It is also a reminder of the best of African American Christianity. And with any invitation to a way of being, there is a need to review how communities and churches have functioned in the past and to offer possibilities and practices that foster this alternative way of life, this vision of abundant life.

Therefore, in the second half of this chapter we turn to pedagogical strategies with young African American Christians. However, questions may arise regarding why one should offer a ***critical pedagogy*** of integrating spirituality, as the practical response of a vision of abundant life, or even why one should affirm the ability of religious education to help young African Americans. For starters, pedagogy includes both strategies and practices, but critical pedagogy also includes a philosophy or orientation that affirms the potential for both positive transformation and oppression within educational endeavors. Critical pedagogy requires that we wrestle with the power of education (and religious instruction) for good and evil. As such, I find myself attending to the larger traditions of radical religionists and educators, many alluded to earlier in this text (see chapters 3–5), who affirm the need and ability to take seriously the lived realities of people, particularly marginalized and oppressed persons, such as young African Americans, and who see within these same communities the resources to effect change for their own lives.

Critical pedagogy often includes processes of unlearning and learning, reflection, and empowering students to seek and create knowledge, not to simply passively receive it.[19] Embedded within the history of critical pedagogy are links to both Marxist thought and critical theory; however, for me there are also links to religious and social change movements that intricately connect the efforts of individuals and communities to strategies of uncovering practices, beliefs, or ways of being that have served to keep people(s) from living fully and freely. In addition to the grounding in critical theory and educational theories, I build on the historical models of connecting religious education with social change. In fact, pedagogy, or even an understanding of religious education as essential to social change, predates the emergence of critical pedagogy by Freire and others in the 1960s. For example, the early religious educator George Albert Coe wrestled with the purpose of education and faith, asking, "Shall the primary purpose of Christian education be to hand on a religion, or to create a new world?"[20] Coe argued against any understanding of a "private relation with God" but sought to remind Christians of their role in transforming society. Thus, as early as 1929, scholars were naming the goal of *religious education* as "the reconstruction of society, continuous growth, and formation of the whole child."[21] This interconnection of religious education and societal transformation reflects the theological trends of that era, including the social gospel movement and liberal theology. Likewise, the early Sunday school movements, as well as the central roles of religious organizations and women's clubs in establishing and supporting educational endeavors among African Americans in the late nineteenth and early twentieth centuries demonstrate the power of religious education in supporting a vision of abundant life.

Historically, religious education among African American Christians has been as diverse as the religion itself—with varied foci and efforts to promote social change *and* criticism that it has failed to attend to the needs of the people. The earliest independent African American churches often were the sources and locations of educational uplift and literacy training for previously enslaved and illiterate persons. The establishment of publishing houses for religious education curricula often accompanied the growth of independent churches and later denominations.[22] Over time, however, these efforts toward literacy and religious instruction were not always well received. Carter G. Woodson, in the *Miseducation of the Negro*, offers harsh critiques of both church and clergy in their educational efforts. Likewise, later liberation theologians like Albert Cleage lamented the fact that one could not turn to Black or White religious education curriculum if one wanted anything that would affirm the liberation of Black people and an understanding of Jesus's work in that liberation struggle.[23]

At the same time we see a diversity of positive emphases within African American religious education. For example, religious educator N. Lynne Westfield in her discussion of womanist practices of hospitality and pedagogy asserts that the "bottom line" among African American women and their practices of religious education is justice. Westfield writes, "In retrospect, it seems rather clear to me that what the women are most interested in, engaged in, and invested in is justice. . . . We want justice for our families, our friends, and ourselves. Our bottom line is justice."[24] Similarly, religious educator Anne Wimberly, in her discussion of intergenerational African American Christian education, names "liberation and vocation" as the central purpose or quest of religious education. In particular, she argues,

> Persons are searching for forums in which they can address who they are and can become in their everyday social contexts. . . . Whether persons attend church school, Bible study groups, youth groups, or other Christian education settings in church, home, or community, African Americans often tell of a deep inner yearning. This yearning is their soul's search for liberation and vocation.[25]

Looking at the history of religious education, religious educator and historian Kenneth Hill argues that there has been a threefold emphasis in African American Christian religious education "to form, inform, and transform people in Christ."[26] Undoubtedly the purposes and functions of religious education have changed over time—at times supporting the abundant life of communities and at times failing to include any engagement with society at all. However, standing within the early emphasis of religious education to "transform society," I assert that rethinking our educational practices and pedagogy are essential in offering a framework for empowering young African Americans to realize a vision of abundant life. Therefore, I offer a *critical pedagogy* of integrating spirituality that helps young people both learn and unlearn, and create anew ways of living abundantly.

Religious Education and the Way of Life Abundant

Looking across the historical articulations of the purpose of religious education, the larger framework of religious education includes both "forming" persons in the traditions and practices of a community of faith and as transformative of individuals, communities, religious traditions, and society as a whole. However, each of these foci also feels diffuse without the overall orientation toward a vision of life offered by Christ (and espoused in the wisdom of Kira). Therefore, here I further explore the formative and transformative functions of religious education and the ways that they foster integrating spirituality and help youth embrace a vision of abundant life. In part, it starts with noting that formation and transformation are not mutually exclusive goals, but both are required for a critical pedagogy of abundant life. In spite of the fact that throughout the history of religious education, as well as within particular religious communities, it can become difficult to hold these goals together, I offer this dual framework of formation and transformation as a scaffolding that surrounds a pedagogical response to fragmented spirituality and that empowers youth to integrate divergent goals, without becoming overwhelmed by them.[27]

In order to address the specific concerns of African American youth who are experiencing fragmented spirituality in the ways illumined in this research, I underscore the formative goal as one of reconnecting African American youth with the legacy of African American spirituality and forming them in the traditions of the Black church and of Womanist resistance.

Intricately connected to helping youth *tap into* this legacy, I also describe the transformative goal of this pedagogy as building on the critical and radical pedagogical structures that address issues of conscientization, liberation, and vocation.

Religious Education as Formation: Renewing the Shared Practices of African American Spirituality

Kenneth Hill describes the task of *forming* in African American Christian education as the formation of communal identity, both by participation in a community of faith and as part of a shared legacy of overcoming oppression in the United States.[28] Religious education as formation thus requires connecting African American youth with communities and practices of African American spirituality, both within and beyond Black churches, and inviting them into the renewal process of these communities and practices. A critical pedagogy of abundant life and integrated spirituality does not simply need to "reconnect" youth with historical practices. In truth, there is no genuine participation in the life of faith and communities that allows practices or communities to remain unchanged. Therefore, *reconnecting* should not imply that youth simply take on static traditions—when in fact the invitation is for young African Americans to share in these practices as full participants.

In the previous chapters, I outlined elements of African American spirituality and theology that have empowered African American Christians to survive, resist, and remain faithful in the midst of oppressive structures and individual struggles. I also point to examples of young African Americans who are calling for changes in contemporary practices in Black theology and churches, as well as reminding us of the best of African American Christianity and social witness. However, in many cases, contemporary youth have not benefited from the best practices of Black churches or communities. One of the major criticisms often recited in assessing the spiritual lives of contemporary adolescents is that their spirituality does not reflect the totality, complexity, or the richness of their religious traditions. For example, Evelyn Parker argues that the fragmented spirituality of African American youth is "historically inconsistent with the spirituality of African Americans of years past." Parker contrasts their spirituality with exemplars of African American spirituality, such as persons like Fannie Lou Hamer.[29] On the other hand, my own research and the research findings of Christian Smith's National Survey of Youth Religion demonstrate that the religious lives of contemporary youth are direct reflections of the religious lives of the significant adults in their lives (namely parents). I do not lift this up to "blame parents or adults" for inconsistencies in youth spirituality; however, I recognize that in order for youth to fully live and embody an integrating spirituality, they must be exposed to this type of spirituality *and* nurtured in it.

Many African American youth struggle to connect with or even see the value of African American Christian spirituality, because of a lack of exposure to this history and because of the larger trends toward individualism that in many ways impedes any embrace of a communal legacy or ethic.[30] For example, in an interview conversation on diversity within religious communities, one young woman, when asked what she was taught about African American history or whether she learned about the Civil Rights Movement in her school or church, responded,

> My school, no way. I mean it's [African American history is] never really emphasized. I mean we don't even really celebrate Black History month. For that matter any other ethnicity's holidays.... I mean at church we do touch upon it. But I think they're almost kind of like well you know about that, you know. [*Interviewer: They assume that you know.*] Yeah, and so I mean like I know I can see that, but then it's definitely not emphasized as much as it probably could be.[31]

Her response summarizes a typical approach within communities of faith toward connecting youth to the legacy and history of African Americans. Living and being a part of racially similar groups does not equate explicit teaching and knowledge of one's history and traditions. Many predominately African American faith communities (particularly where the larger community is also African American) assume that youth already know the history, and therefore communities of faith do not need to rehearse that history as well. Likewise, other predominately African American faith communities do not fully acknowledge or affirm the complex history of African American Christianity, either because the larger community does not know it either or they have chosen to adopt a generic Christian history and narrative. However, as the young woman's interview indicates, African American youth recognize that much more can be said and taught about African American history in their schools and churches.

I suggest that despite this lack of ongoing exposure to African American history, a critical pedagogy that helps youth integrate their spirituality and live a vision of abundant life requires strategies for empowering youth (and adults) to participate in and benefit from the larger historical and spiritual legacies of African Americans. Here I outline two pedagogical strategies: "Re-telling the Story" and "Re-imagining Worship Practices" of African American Christian communities.

Re-telling the Story: Formation in the Narratives of African American History and Faith

One of the foundational methods of inviting African American youth into the shared legacy of African American heritage and spirituality lies in reconnecting youth with the narratives of African Americans and "reminding" youth of the legacy of faith, resistance, survival, and liberation that permeates their communities of origin. Part of this process also includes developing ways of inviting youth into these larger communal stories, such that they not only learn or know the history but that they begin to see the narrative as *their own*.[32] Many scholars affirm the significance of reconnecting African American youth with these narratives;[33] in particular, religious educator Anne Wimberly's *story-linking* methodology centers on the significance of narratives for the vitality of African American Christian Education. Wimberly describes story-linking as "a process whereby persons connect components of their everyday life stories with the Christian faith story found in Scripture ... [and] connect their personal stories with Christian faith heritage stories of African Americans found outside Scripture."[34] In this process, the sharing of narratives connects or reconnects the lives of youth with the historical and biblical narratives of African American and Christian communities.

Womanist religious educator N. Lynne Westfield further affirms the significance of narratives and storytelling in a liberating (or liberation-focused) educational process. She describes the practice of "tell[ing] the story" as the first of many specific tasks within a Womanist pedagogy for both religious communities and seminary classrooms. Westfield writes,

The power of story to teach and transform cannot be overemphasized. The dynamic possibilities of teaching are revealed in the practice of storytelling.... The stories gave them new perspectives and reminded them who and whose they were.... Storytelling allows students, Black and White, male and female, to discover that

they are not alone in their struggle for liberation.... Stories give
us exemplars and encourage us towards actions of resistance and
justice.[35]

While Westfield emphasizes the power of storytelling and narrative in general, Wimberly is clear that there is something powerful about linking the stories of our lives with the stories of our ancestors and faith exemplars. Wimberley's practice of story-linking itself serves as an example of reconnecting African American youth with their history and heritage as it is modeled on the story sharing practices of Africans and African Americans from the early slavery period.[36] Wimberly's method also reminds us of the importance of intergenerational story sharing. For Wimberly, the narrative process is essentially intergenerational, exposing youth both to the stories (the historical data) and to the embodied narratives (the exemplars of faith and wise persons within the community). In other words, telling their individual stories and affirming their own voice as youth is important; but it begins to counter fragmented spirituality (and the trends toward individualism) when youth are invited also to share in the stories that define who they are as part of a larger community. Thus building on both the heritage of Africans in the United States and upon the biblical witness that many embraced, it becomes imperative to "tell the stories"—the narratives that affirm the central identities of who African Americans are and how they have survived and resisted.

Building upon the Hebrew Bible narratives that admonish the Israelites to build monuments and to encourage their children to ask questions such as "what do these stones mean?" biblical scholar Walter Brueggemann also affirms the significance of "telling the story."[37] His work outlines the way that story serves to form a foundational communal identity and articulate the normative claims of a community (not in a strict catechesis mode), by inviting the young and old into a dialogue.[38] More specifically, in the biblical tradition as well as in African American heritage, the method of inviting youth into the narratives of the community are typically initiated by the questions of the young—a process that encourages wonder and imagination, all in the form of asking "why?" Brueggemann points out that the response to the questions of young people is not a detailed or direct answer, but the response remains simply, "Let me tell you a story"—inviting youth into the identity-shaping stories of the community.

As noted above, in reference to the work of educator Kenneth Hill, forming a communal identity *has* been part of African American religious education; however, it must remain at the forefront as well. The continu-ing emphasis on communal identity and narratives persists even as we resist essentialist narratives and notions of Black experiences. Instead, resisting essentialism and naïve simplifications does not mean that communal identities that hold a diversity of sharing and relationships together are not possible and prevalent. Part of the invitation to shared narrative rests on complexity and nuances that emerge in the telling and re-telling of narratives. In other words, it is imperative that communities of faith share their communal history with youth and encourage youth to learn what it means to be part of the community if they want to persevere as a community and to ensure that youth know who they are and what resources (in terms of legacy and shared wisdom) are available to them.[39]

FORMING FUNCTIONAL THEOLOGY

Furthermore, when we invite youth into dialogue around the normative stories of the community or encourage their questions of what things mean, we are also affecting the "functional theology" of youth (or attempt-ing to affect youth spirituality on a functional level). Womanist theolo-gian Monica Coleman defines functional theology as epitomized by the statement "I don't know how this works, but it makes me feel whole."[40] Here, Coleman is quoting an African American woman as she gathered to participate in an African traditional religious practice. Coleman builds on this statement in her description of a postmodern Womanist theology and writes that the woman's statement

> reminded me [Coleman] that, even when we don't understand it, most of us default to a functional theology—a theology that works for us at our most crucial moments. A functional theology cares little for systems and consistency; it's the rock-bottom faith we cling to at two o'clock in the morning when we can't sleep.[41]

Recognizing our propensity to cling to a "functional theology," I have often wrestled with how persons of faith develop this functional theology and how we help young people develop a functional theology that can speak to and hold them in the face of their experiences, particularly those of violence and racism. Thus, I posit that telling and re-telling the normative stories aids in the development of functional theology; however, often it is not what we explicitly know or think that sustains us or pushes us onward in the midst of struggle. It is what we *do* that reflects our deepest beliefs, core (often tacit) knowledge, and understandings of who God is and how God is working in our lives.

Therefore, the second crucial method involved in the formation of youth into the history and spirituality of African Americans centers on reconnecting youth with the *practices* of African American individual and communal worship. In addition to the practice of telling the stories, youth have to be surrounded by and mentored into religious practices and disciplines that will form (and possibly challenge) their core and functional theology.[42]

Re-imagining Worship Practices: Formation in the Disciplines of African American Spirituality

While I would be hard-pressed to remember ever receiving a coherent set of beliefs or tenets of Christianity and/or African American history in my early experiences of religious education, undoubtedly my earliest memories center on worship and the many ways that the "kids" were invited to participate in worship. Every Sunday, we sang, prayed, read scriptures, listened to sermons, gave tithes and offerings, and engaged in fellowship for what felt like hours after worship. The core of my training and memories in religious education and the experiences that served to form my "functional theology" emerged from my participation in the communal practices of worship. However, beyond my experiences and anecdotal evidence, here, I briefly explore the ways that formation in the practices of worship also helps youth develop an integrating spirituality. As noted above, Coleman argues that it is the functional theology that helps women continue to survive and work toward salvation—to continue to make a way out of no way. Reflecting on this concept, I emphasize that formation in worship practices empowers youth to participate in practices that communities have found to be reliable and helpful in resisting oppressive structures. Here again, I do not romanticize African American religion or Black churches or argue that these practices are the panacea for all that concerns young African Americans; however, one should not overlook a tradition and set of practices that have sustained communities for centuries through horrific experiences. In part, several of the young people interviewed and presented above note the ongoing significance of worship practices and communities in their lives—even when they desire more from them. For example, Nyle Fort longed for a worshipping community that could create space for him to cry, pray, and cuss in the wake of ongoing tragedy and violence against Black people. He saw that this space was

lacking and had to take action to create it—embodying the urgency of rei-
magining worship practices with young African Americans so that they
can speak to their current concerns.[43]

In an effort to reconnect youth with the legacy and tradition of African
American spirituality, we have to invite youth into the daily life and practice (spiritual disciplines) of African American spirituality and worship. In
her description of the pillars of Afro-Christian worship, sociologist Cheryl
Townsend Gilkes outlines the centrality of Black Preaching, the Prayer
Tradition, the Musical Tradition, and the Testimony Tradition.[44] Gilkes
also writes that these traditions have historically centered on the usage of
the English Bible and by extension have enabled the formation of a biblical imagination. Expanding upon Gilkes's articulation of the function and
purposes of practices of African American worship, I suggest that reconnecting youth with worship practices will serve as the foundation from
which youth can develop an integrating spirituality and begin to live into
a way of life abundant. In many ways, I see the practices of worship as
the elements that will hold youth even as they critically engage and reflect
upon their experiences in the world around them. Part of the formative
goal of religious education centers on connecting youth with the following
practices and traditions of African American religious experience.

BIBLICAL READING
The Bible historically and currently remains a central focus in African
American Christianity. Within African American churches there is a long
tradition of reading, listening to, and even memorizing and reciting passages from the Bible. In each of the educational resources analyzed above,
biblical texts and images served as the core narratives and content upon
which the lessons were formed. Even though one of my major criticisms
of the sermons and Sunday school lessons was their lack of diversity and
complexity in terms of the theological themes espoused, the materials still
offer evidence of the importance of the Bible within African American
Christianity. Part of the focus on biblical texts connects historically with
the struggle for literacy among enslaved African Americans and the reality that if one knew how to read during the slavery era, one was most
likely reading the Bible.[45] Beyond the availability of Bibles (more than
other texts), in early African American communities, the biblical themes
of exodus, liberation, promise, and hope resonated with the experiences of
African Americans and persist in their contemporary religious language.[46]
Noting the prevalence of these themes and the way that the Bible continues

to function in other practices, such as preaching, prayer, and singing, in African American churches, I argue that any discussion of spirituality and pedagogy needs to include an invitation for youth to connect with and embrace these themes and narratives. Furthermore, in order for youth to fully engage the resources of their religious lives, they must begin with a core practice of their tradition, which focuses on biblical readings.[47] As noted above, it is imperative for youth to know and rehearse the story— and the African American Christian story is one heavily interwoven with the biblical narratives.

PRAYER

Building upon the significant role of reading and hearing the Bible within African American Christianity, the "prayer tradition" forms another essential practice for youth. Prayer, in African American Christianity, is formal and informal, public and private, communal and individual. However, beyond the modes of prayer, it is more important to note that within African American Christianity, prayer is not simply a means of communicating with God, of asking God for "stuff," or even a passive response when more direct action is not taken.[48] Instead, prayer goes hand in hand with working for and actively expecting God's change and transformation in tangible ways in their current situations. Gilkes describes many narratives of the ways that women, often referred to as "prayer warriors," prayed fervently for God's direction and provision as they were actively engaging in various social struggles. For example, Gilkes recounts a narrative from an early church that was purchased by freed slaves in Charleston, South Carolina at the end of the Civil War. In this narrative, the prayer warriors prayed as the members of their community transported the money to the bank. They prayed during each leg of the journey that their life savings would not be stolen and that the payments would make it on time, so that their dream of owning their church could be realized.[49] Similarly, contemporary young African American activists like Bree Newsome and Jonathan Butler name prayer as part of their processes of organizing and preparing for direct action—actively seeking God's presence as they worked for change.

In these examples, we see the individual and communal dimension of prayer that youth can reconnect with and that will empower youth to embrace the interconnection between prayer and action for individual and communal struggles and concerns. In particular, looking back at Kira's example, we saw a young woman of tremendous faith who still struggled to connect her faith with a more nuanced strategy for acting in response to the violence in her community. In her interview, Kira starts her discussion saying, "Two things that I worry about ... and something I forget I need to pray about." This stands out as a reminder that even youth with a strong foundation in their worship community and with a strong individual prayer life need to be continually invited and reminded of the practices of prayer and the ways that it goes hand in hand with responding to issues in their communities. Examples from the interviews and other narratives on the lives of African American youth demonstrate that African American youth are participating in the practice of prayer. However, in order to foster a more integrated spirituality and one that empowers youth to continue integrating new experiences, youth must be reminded of the myriad ways that prayer functions.

SINGING

Music remains an essential element of African American worship, and while there is great diversity within communities of faith regarding styles and genres of music, African American worship—from the earliest slave traditions to the contemporary evangelical megachurches—is almost synonymous with music and singing. Religious educator Yolanda Smith reflects on the powerful role of spirituals historically and for ongoing religious education. Smith outlines the ways that Negro Spirituals offer a framework for religious education that embraces a "triple heritage": connecting youth with their Christian, African, and African American heritage.[50] However, beyond the theoretical framework, the practice of communal singing impacts a bodily way of knowing that connects individual worshippers with a larger community and experience of God's presence.

Looking broadly at the practice of singing, Don Saliers describes the ways that communal singing shapes and produces a type of embodied and lived theology. Recounting the responses of a group of women when asked about their favorite hymns, Saliers writes, "Over time, participation in the practice of lifting their voices to God had worked in subtle and complex ways to shape basic attitudes, affections, and ways of regarding themselves, their neighbors, and God."[51] He points to the ways that the power of singing goes beyond the words of the song—the practice also informs a communal identity and ethic. The experience of singing also goes far beyond the moments when the songs are sung communally; it connects people with the memories and experiences where they first learned the songs and other experiences in which the song was sung or heard. Music becomes part of the body's memory.

Saliers also reflects on the role of music within African American traditions and describes another dimension of singing, in that music has the power to "sound prophecy—to ring out in opposition to injustice."[52] Saliers lifts up the example of James Weldon Johnson's 1921 hymn, "Lift Every Voice and Sing," which was later adopted as the Negro National Anthem. The song draws on biblical imagery while also testifying to the "powerful, graced experience of God discovered ... in the midst of their suffering."[53]

In addition to the powerful legacy and educative role of spirituals and hymns for forming communal identities and sounding protest, it is also significant to encourage youth to explore all genres of music, historical and contemporary, in African American Christianity and culture. For in music youth are taught essential biblical narratives and theological truths, connected with other communities and moments of protest, and empowered to express their embodied knowledge of God, self, and their neighbors.

There is also powerful music of protest, which goes beyond worship music. In particular, many youth have been influenced by hip-hop (culture and music) and rap. While the history of these genres is quite complex, it is important not to overlook the cathartic and prophetic nature of early hip-hop—as a means of expressing the concerns of urban youth. To be certain, one of the challenges to reconnecting African American youth with the worshiping traditions of Black churches will be helping them integrate the variety of music traditions that speak to their experiences and remind them of their abilities to protest and be strengthened by communal acts of creative expression.

TESTIMONY

Alongside the traditions of music, prayer, and the central role of scripture in worship,[54] African Americans have continued a tradition of testimony and testifying.[55] From my childhood in rural Virginia, I remember many testimony services—characterized by an elder standing to tell what the Lord had done for her. The testimony services prepared the congregants for the remainder of the service and served as a forum for sharing struggles and transforming individual concerns into communal concerns. As sociologist of religion Cheryl Townsend Gilkes notes in her discussion of pillars of Afro-Christian worship,

Testimony transforms the collection of worshippers into a community. Oppression and suffering make testimony important for psychological survival. Testimony does not resolve black problems but
does transform them from private troubles of distressed individuals
into public issues of a covenant community.... Testimony can be a
form of protest.[56]

Gilkes discusses the ways that testimony is essential to forming community and creating the "shared experience" that Black religion addresses.
She also argues that testimony served as "antecedents to movements for
social change." [57] Thomas Hoyt also notes the community-building and
change-producing functions of testimony sharing in his discussion of testimony as a practice of Christian faith:

Although only one person may be speaking at a time, that person's
speech takes place within the context of other people's listening,
expecting, and encouraging. In testimony a believer describes what
God has done in her life, in words both biblical and personal, and
the hands of her friends clap in affirmation. Her individual speech
thus becomes part of an affirmation that is shared.[58]

Here, Hoyt points to the two dimensions of testimonies: to testify to the
church and world about the action of God, and to testify to God, telling God
the truth about themselves and others. The dual dimension of Christian
testimony illustrates the many functions testimony has in African
American churches.[59] Hoyt also illustrates the transformative power and
call to action of the testimony. Hoyt asserts that, in the preaching moment,
"testimony requires a response from those who receive it. Preaching is a
witness intended to evoke other forms of witness.... The testimony of
preaching is a prophetic testimony, one that makes compelling claims on
both preacher and hearers"—calling communities to respond to God's
blessings *and* mandates for justice.[60]

Although many churches no longer include a testimony service in
their weekly worship services, the practice persists in many and varied
ways. Reflecting on the practice of testimony, I argue that it is essential
to nurture youth in this practice, as the practice of sharing testimonies
models for youth ways of sharing and addressing individual and communal concerns. I also found that practicing testimony sharing with youth
serves to nurture youth in the legacy and narratives of African American

communities and empowers youth to participate in transforming and renewing the traditions of African American communities.

The tasks of empowering African American youth to reconnect with the communal history and story of African Americans and nurturing youth in the practices of African American worship, however, serves as only one dimension of a pedagogy that fosters integrating spirituality. Essentially, while it is imperative for youth to know their history and to be shaped by the practices that aided their ancestors, religious practices and spirituality are never static. To educate with a goal toward dynamic spirituality and abundant life, pedagogy that pushes for transformation is also required.

Radical Pedagogy: Religious Education as Transformation

bell hooks's introduction to *Teaching to Transgress* describes her understanding of the transformative dimensions of education; she writes, "I celebrate teaching that enables transgressions—a movement against and beyond boundaries. It is that movement which makes education the practice of freedom."[61] For hooks, education as transformation is transgressive, pushing beyond normative and acceptable boundaries, and a practice of freedom or liberation. When reading hooks's definition of "teaching and transgression," I initially struggled to explain how religious education should also be about transgression. Beyond the historical, biblical, and popular religious usage of the word "transgression" to connote sin, the idea of teaching people to transgress remains problematic in religious circles. Often the perception is that one must teach people to conform or assimilate into the life and traditions of communities of faith. In the previous section, I too make the case that youth need to be nurtured in traditions and practices of African American communities and should learn *the story*—the normative claims and the canonical narratives that identify African American Christian communities. Recognizing the almost oxymoronic nature of teaching to transgress within religious communities, I find that hooks's work is invaluable to my understanding of the purpose and function of religious education with African American youth.

Even as I stress the need for youth to connect with and draw upon the rich resources and legacy of African American communities, the process of being formed in these communities includes being formed in a community that also includes a history of fighting against oppression. Connecting with the heritage of African Americans includes connecting with the long and ongoing tradition of transgression—of not conforming to what was or is expected of African Americans or Christians as a people. Being formed in the heritage of African American Christianity includes being educated to transgress and to see education as transforming the traditional structures and boundaries of religious communities and society.

Therefore, in defining the transformative dimensions of religious education, I focus on religious education as (1) transformative of individual lives in community; (2) transformative of society and structures; and (3) transformative of religious norms and structures. The transformation of individuals, religious institutions, and society is intricately connected; however, I look at each individually and outline strategies that attend to the ways that each interconnects as part of a critical pedagogy of transformative religious education.

Religious Education as Transformative of Individual Lives in Community

Anne Wimberly, in the preface to *Soul Stories*, discusses the many dimensions of liberation and vocation, which emerge from her research and ministry in African American Christian communities. She includes the narrative of one African American man who states, "When I think of liberation, what comes to mind, first, is the feeling of being all right inside myself."[62] His statement reminds us of the profound reality that at the heart of discussions of transformation, liberation, and radical or revolutionary education, are the people who are struggling to "be alright" with who they are and how they are living in the world. In particular, Wimberly reminds us to attend to the personal (as well as systemic) dimensions of liberation, and to the ongoing process of liberation. Wimberly writes, "For this man and other participants . . . liberation is not a singular or one-time accomplishment. Rather it appears to be a multidimensional process that doesn't stop."[63] This understanding of liberation and the need to attend to the personal dimension of liberation and freedom is echoed in the work of young activists like Quita for whom personal wholeness is essential and interconnected with communal wholeness.

Wimberly's articulation of the multiple dimensions of liberation further demonstrates the interconnection between the individual's quest for liberation and the systems and communities that must also be part of the ongoing process of liberation. Wimberly gives significant attention to the individual's role and the effects on each person in their quest for liberation. She describes her understanding of liberation as a view "from the inside"—indicating both that she develops this definition from the narratives of African Americans (insiders to their experiences) and that the definitions of liberation take seriously the prior, often internal reflections of each person regarding liberation.

Wimberly reiterates the ways that religious education that seeks to foster liberation and transformation must start with the yearnings and reflections of the "insiders." She writes,

> The presence of these "views from the inside" underscores the importance of acknowledging the very real reflective activity in which participants are already engaged. It suggests that persons' liberation and enactment of vocation begin with them. . . . The guidance leaders/teachers give to participants ... should build on the participants' prior reflection processes.[64]

Essentially, Wimberly argues that liberation begins with the person and builds on his or her reflections. The role of the teacher in transformative, and liberative education is not to impose the process of liberation; neither does the teacher bring about liberation for or outside of the reflections of the participants.

Similarly, Paulo Freire begins his seminal work outlining the vocation of all people as "humanization"—the process of being and remaining fully human, despite the many attempts to thwart this process, such as "injustice, exploitation, oppression, and the violence of the oppressors."[65] In his discussion of dialogical and liberative education, Freire also affirms the need for any efforts toward liberation and transformation to begin and connect with the people and their questions. Freire offers "problem-posing" education as a corrective to educational practices that further reify oppressive structures, by depositing narratives and knowledge that continue the mythology that the oppressed are less than human or that humanization is not a viable possibility.[66] Freire's understanding of liberative education is built upon the acknowledgment of men and women as "conscious beings"—as beings who are both capable of and already engaged in reflection on the world around them. Thus, Freire rejects the dichotomy between teachers and students. Like Wimberly, Freire sees teachers and students as together in the learning process, jointly responsible for the learning and liberation; and there emerge teacher-students and student-teachers.[67] Furthermore, for truly liberative education that leads to transformation of the world, Freire argues that there must exist "a profound love for the world and people" and faith in humankind.[68] Freire describes this faith as

> faith in their [humanity's] power to make and remake, to create and re-create, faith in their vocation to be more fully human (which is not the privilege of the elite, but the birthright of all). . . . Without this faith in the people, dialogue is a farce which inevitably degenerates into paternalistic manipulation.[69]

In other words, Freire recognizes that transformative education not only begins with humans, but must truly demonstrate love for humans and faith that they can participate in their own liberation and transformation of the world.

From Wimberly and Freire's discussions of the vocation and liberation of humans, I lift up one essential strategy of transformative pedagogy related to the particular goal of transforming individuals in communities. Affirming the value and humanity of each youth is essential for transformation to take place. Therefore, transformative religious education includes empowering youth in the development of healthy identity and self-esteem.

DARING TO BE SOMEBODY: AFFIRMING YOUTH HUMANITY
One of the recurring issues in working with young people is whether youth should also be included in the quest for liberation. This recurs even within paradigms that value liberation and within communities that have been historically oppressed. In particular the issue arises of whether youth, as children and adolescents, should be full participants in their vocation of humanization, as outlined by Freire. While there are differences in development, maturation, and responsibilities of youth and adults, these differences should not result in the domestication of youth or serve to relegate youth to the role of observation or mere recipients of information and faith traditions.[70] Instead, truly transformative religious education takes seriously the process of empowering youth to know and value who they are, right now as young people, as well as connected to a larger community and history. As noted in the previous chapter, youth have taken and continue to take the lead in liberation and activist movements. However, these actions by youth are not always included in what we expect of them and/ or what they always expect of themselves. The narratives of young activists and faith leaders are not celebrated enough; thus, it must become part of

a critical pedagogy to affirm the humanity of young people and by extension their ability to participate fully in their own liberation and flourishing.

Womanist theologian Jacquelyn Grant, in her discussion of theology and ministry with youth, writes that Christian education and theology with youth must help instill a sense of *somebodiness* in youth. Grant
describes the idea of somebodiness as an affirmation of the humanity of
Black people, but particularly of youth.[71] Religious education as transformation must overturn notions that youth are not fully human. For the
most part, this is not stated explicitly, but in many cases churches and
the larger society treat youth as "almost humans" because of their ongoing biological, social, and psychological development.[72] However, Grant
reiterates that despite this development, children and youth are already
fully human.[73] She writes, "While a black theology affirms the humanity
of blacks in general, I would argue that special attention must be given to
the humanity of youth. Black theologians must be willing to examine and
challenge the church's assumptions about youth."[74] In other words, Black
theology and religious education should work to remind youth and others
of their *somebodiness*. Especially given the context of state-sanctioned violence against Black youth in the form of police brutality and unprosecuted/
under-prosecuted cases, it remains imperative that churches and religious
leaders in particular affirm the humanity of Black youth. In many ways the
rallying cry of Black Lives Matters is an echo of the 1960s and '70s cries
of "I am somebody" or "I'm a man." Sadly, the message that Black youth
are neither subhuman nor unable to participate in their own liberation
struggles still has not been received by the wider society or by religious
communities.

Grant, along with hooks, Wimberly, Freire, and others, describes the
essential role of education in the process of affirming *somebodiness*. In particular, Grant argues that even though the vast majority of public schools
lose African American children at a very early age,[75] Black churches have
a responsibility to educate youth and empower youth to resist efforts to
dehumanize them or limit their understanding of who they are and who
they can become. Likewise, Wimberly defines the interconnected dimensions of liberation from self-denigration, from dehumanization, and from
miseducation and lack of vision.[76] Liberative and transformative education
must continuously affirm the humanity of the participants and the value of
young people as they currently are. In the Christian context, this includes
reminding youth of their value to God, but it also includes empowering
youth to understand what they are capable of. Reaffirming the humanity

and value of young people also includes the difficult task of empowering youth to work through the myriad myths that adults and larger society often perpetuate about youth.

Often, developing one's self-esteem and identity is seen as purely individual and personal work. However, Womanist scholars call attention to the ways that encouraging youth to be womanish—or "outrageous, audacious, courageous or *willful* ... Wanting to know more and in greater depth than is considered 'good' for one. Interested in grown up doings. Acting grown up. Being grown up.... Responsible. In charge. Serious"[77]— directly challenges hegemonic structures.[78] For example, for African Americans and women, particularly young African Americans and young women, to be educated—engaging in the processes of knowledge acquisition and production—has historically been an act of resistance and a direct challenge to hegemony. Hegemonic structures often attempt to uphold the myths that youth, African Americans, women, and others cannot be educated or should at best stay in their "place." Thus, religious education as transformative of individuals does not simply affect the spirits and identities of individuals, but also affects the ways that each individual works together in the larger community and world.

Transformation of individuals includes much more than simply changing how they see and understand themselves; however, this is an essential step in the process of transformation. While youth have to participate in their own transformation by acquiring skills and resources to succeed, alongside acquiring skills for success in the current system, youth must also learn to *read* and ask questions of whether the *world-as-it-is* is how it should be. Therefore the transformation of individuals—including helping youth to recover their individual and collective voice, transforming youth self-perception, and encouraging youth toward personal achievement—also challenges and transforms institutional and societal myths and structures.

Religious Education as Transformative of Society and Structures

All education is political, especially religious education, in that all education has implications for how we live in society and how we engage the structures and systems around us. In this section, I continue to explore hooks's description of education as the practice of freedom by pointing to the ways that the social and political practices of education empower youth and undergird a vision of abundant life.[79] In the previous chapters, I describe some of the theological claims that present alternatives to fragmented spirituality, such as public theology and cooperation with God.

Building on these concepts, I describe the ways that religious education is also about empowering youth to work in the world, with God, to transform that world. However, historically the idea that society, institutions, systems or structures could be changed has eluded adults and youth alike.

The possibility of transforming the world is daunting. It is in the best interest of oppressive powers and structures for young people to buy into the idea that "there is nothing that they can do," or that all they can hope for is survival in a world that they have no control over. However, many critical theorists and radical educators have worked for centuries to remind students that the world and humans are interconnected. Brazilian revolutionary educator and critical theorist, Paulo Freire writes, "Education as the practice of freedom—as opposed to education as the practice of domination—denies that man [woman] is abstract, isolated, independent, and unattached to the world; it also denies that the world exists as a reality apart from people."[80] The significance of this interconnection is that it reminds us that the world can be changed and influenced by the collective work of individuals. Freire, who is best known for his criticism of the banking model of education, in which students are simply the depositories of expert knowledge and narratives, underscores the ways that that liberative education transforms the world. As noted above, Freire pushes for "problem-posing education," which builds on the questions and critical reflections of persons in community as the basis for education. This method of education resists any notion that the world, systems, or society is an unchangeable reality.[81]

The tension of holding together humans and society (and by extension the personal and private with the communal and public) in education is also echoed and wrestled with in the work of educator Henry Giroux. In a critique of both traditional and radical approaches to education, Giroux argues that we can never abandon the dialectic between human agency and societal structure.[82] Giroux notes that while radical educators expose the relations between schools, society at large, power, domination, and liberation, they often fall into the traps of either *idealism* or *structure and domination*. Giroux defines the trap of idealism as the trend to "collapse human agency and struggle into a celebration of human will, cultural experience, [to create] classrooms of happy social relations."[83] Likewise, the trap of structure and domination removes human agency from the equation. Instead, it presents the perspective that "history is made behind the backs of human beings" and that in the course of such domination human agency virtually disappears.[84] Neither of these positions is sufficient or accurate for Giroux; instead, he draws on critical theorists who provide a "mode of critique that extends the concept of the political not only into mundane social relationships but into the very sensibilities and needs that form the personality and psyche." He argues that critical theorists refuse to abandon the dialectic of agency and structure. Instead, critical theorists take seriously the claim that *history can be changed and that the potential for radical transformation really exists.*[85] Essentially, Giroux is arguing for a way of thinking about transformation that takes seriously humanity's ability to work for change on individual and systemic levels.

Beyond asserting that humans have the ability to transform society, religious education as transformation also pushes us to educate youth in ways that bring about transformation. Allen Moore, in his work *Religious Education as Social Transformation*, expounds upon the interconnections between religious education and transformation within society and societal structures. Moore's vision is that religious education is an ethical way of life that serves to transform religious platitudes into concrete social structures that are just and serve the welfare of all people.[86] In other words, the transformative elements of religious education with youth requires inviting youth into the practices of critical reflection and imagining or dreaming of an alternative reality and acting to achieve these alternative visions. This is also seen in the work of Giroux and Freire. Freire outlines the practice of critical consciousness in conjunction with his idea of dialogical education. The process of coming to critical consciousness about the world and being in the position to truly transform the world requires both reflection and action, or *praxis.*[87]

CONSCIENTIZATION AND ONGOING CRITICAL
REFLECTION AND ACTION

Directly connected with the work of transforming the ways that young people see themselves and form or transform their identities is the need to engage youth in the process of *conscientization*, or coming to critical consciousness. Coming to critical consciousness is not just raising awareness about issues in the lives of young people. Critical consciousness includes transforming how youth perceive the world around them and awakening within youth the ability to critically reflect on and take action in their worlds.[88] In his discussion of dialogue and dialogical education, Freire writes that "there is no true word that is not at the same time praxis."[89] For Freire, dialogue is significant because it points to a reordering of the educational and societal structures by placing two equals, two subjects, into conversation or dialogue with one another. Thus for Freire, to truly be in dialogue or to "speak a true word is to transform the world."[90] It is incorrect to read Freire's discussion of dialogue and dialogical education and assume that he is referring simply to encouraging people to talk with one another or even encouraging young people to speak their minds. Instead, in order to understand what Freire is calling for, we have to see that true dialogue is not common and does not take place without essentially being transformative. Freire states that dialogue, or speaking a true word, cannot be done for another person, nor can it be done alone. Dialogue and coming to critical consciousness is a mutual process.[91] When true dialogue takes place, it turns structures and systems of domination on their head. Similarly when people engage in the process of critically reflecting on the systems of injustice, in which they are surrounded, and begin to act in response to their new understanding, structures are transformed.

Religious educator Katherine Turpin expands Freire's understanding of conscientization, recognizing the difficulty in directly translating Freirian pedagogy to a US consumerist context. Turpin argues that "Freire was able to assume that once participants in culture circles become able to name their own oppression, they would be motivated to resist this oppression through collective action." However, reflecting on her context of working with middle-class American teenagers, Turpin found that often "awareness of our 'caughtness' in this system [of consumer capitalism] . . . seems to engender feelings of guilt or powerlessness rather than motivation for resistance."[92] Turpin instead proposes the idea of *ongoing conversion*—emphasizing the idea that within each youth there remains a paradox in what one is aware of and how one chooses to act in the world. Ongoing conversion instead emphasizes the way that transforming the world, and how youth act in the world, is not a "one time thing." Turpin argues that conversion requires a "deeper change." Turpin defines conversion, writing, "Conversion, then refers not just to a change in awareness and understanding, but to a change in both our intuitive sense of the way the world is (imagination) and our capacity to act in light of that intuitive sense (agency)."[93] Building on Freire's understanding of conscientization and Turpin's understanding of ongoing conversion, I argue that transformative religious education, specifically education geared toward transforming society and structures, must include an understanding of *ongoing praxis*: an ongoing process of critical reflection and action in the world around them.[94]

Religious Education as Transformative of Religious Institutions, Norms, and Practices

In addition to empowering youth to know and tap into the history and legacy of African Americans, education that fosters an integrating spirituality requires that youth are also empowered to ask questions of this history, to critically reflect on it and to even move beyond the historical trends and accomplishments to do "a new thing." As we encourage youth to critically reflect on the world around them and on myriad social issues and structures, it is equally important to encourage youth to critically engage religious institutions, norms, and practices. In tandem with inviting youth to participate in religious communities and practices, we must also fully include youth in the constant transformation of these practices. Youth must resist oppression, including the oppressive narratives and practices within communities of faith. The idea of transformative religious education becomes farcical if or when we put limits on what youth can question, critically engage, or work to transform. While, presumably, religious institutions are included in any analysis of society and social structures, I want to pay attention to the specific ways that transformative religious education must include ongoing critical reflection on faith traditions and practices—to ensure that the traditions that we espouse as affirming life do not morph into dehumanizing ones. In other words, truly critical pedagogy must also include room for reflection on the pedagogy and the tradition.

Ongoing critical reflection is a good practice in general; however, the need for critical reflection on religious norms and traditions is necessary because of the many places in history where religion and religious institutions have not been on "the right side" of struggles for justice. Religious institutions have often perpetuated and maintained the status quo, or have been at best reluctant to intervene in breaking down systems of oppression. It is important to also note that contemporary scholars continue to launch this critique of religious institutions in general, but also of the Black church. For example, Womanist religious educator N. Lynne Westfield offers a scathing critique of the domestication of both public and religious education in the post-civil rights era. Westfield writes,

> Too many Black churches are intoxicated by the post-civil rights malaise and entombed into a misguided, sanctimonious capitalistic funk.... I am suggesting that the domestication (the taming,

the acculturation of a post-slavery mentality of passivity, steeped in capitalistic values that demand compliance with our own oppression) of our churches and our church education must cease.... The educational agenda must reflect the reality of oppression, and equip students, of all races and each gender, for the battle of liberation.[95]

Within this critique Westfield suggests that religious education in African American churches should take seriously the lives and practices of its members and resist the temptation to overlook the existence of oppression and injustice within their lives. In other words, by remaining silent, religious institutions become complicit, if not the direct agents of oppression. Thus it is imperative that part of any educational plan that seeks to truly encourage youth to integrate their spirituality with their concerns for the world and struggles to live into their vocation must also include space for reflection on and questioning of the tradition.

Walter Brueggemann, in addition to his discussion of the centrality of narratives, or Torah learning, in biblical education, points to the ways that the Hebrew canon and model of religious education includes elements that guard against traps that come with educating in only one mode. He writes,

> If a community educates only in Torah, it may also do a disservice to its members. It may nourish them to fixity, to stability that may become rigidity, to a kind of certitude that believes all of the important questions are settled.... That is why alongside of the Torah, there is a second division of canon.[96]

Brueggemann argues that the prophetic writings introduce an element of "disruption for justice."[97] In contrast to the Torah, or normative narratives, which are the foundational consensus elements of the communal identity, the prophetic word is "immediate, intrusive, and surprising. It is not normative. It is not known in advance.... It is not known until it is uttered."[98] The prophetic word represents a break from the norms and "transgression" of normative narratives, practices, and even communities. Prophetic education is intended "to nurture people in an openness to alternative imagination which never quite perceives the world the way the dominant reality wants us to see it."[99] Thus, religious education that takes seriously prophetic breaches and disruptions must include openness to "new revelation" and a faith that "God is still speaking."

However, Brueggemann cautions that "new revelation" is by its very nature problematic. It raises the question of authority and how we determine what is "true" or legitimate. For example, many of the biblical prophets were considered marginal or peripheral characters—representing sources that were not legitimated. However, it was often because of this marginal status that the prophets were able to see or make such proclamations. Brueggemann argues that

> we are immediately pressed to recognize that new revelation must come from unlegitimated sources because there is a closed circle between old revelation and its proponents. That circle will be broken and shattered only by a new voice which has no such vested interest. . . . New truth is likely to be a *cry* from "below," not a *certitude* from "above."[100]

In a sense, Brueggemann is reminding communities of faith that, while prophetic words are rare and hard for us to comprehend (or accept even when we receive them), religious education needs to nurture within youth an awareness of attending to the marginal voices and speaking up when and if we feel our voices are being marginalized.

SPEAKING AND BEING OPEN FOR A PROPHETIC WORD

Therefore, connected with the goal of transformation of religious institutions and traditions, I suggest that a critical pedagogy of integrating spirituality includes the strategy of encouraging youth to speak and hear prophetic words. I am careful not to victimize or romanticize youth, suggesting that young people do not have a vested interest in the old or normative traditions. Neither do I suggest that all youth, or even all African American youth, perceive themselves as living on the periphery, particularly within their faith communities. However, I assert that youth should participate in the practices of speaking truth to religious power. This practice empowers youth, as well as adults, to constantly listen for and expect God's new and ongoing revelation—a revelation that is often revealed in the cries and deep passions of the people. For example, Evelyn Parker discusses the ways that African American youth experience rage and anger. These emotions do not fit well within the religious or cultural norms; however, in many cases this rage is an indication of the passions and outrage of Black youth and their responses to perceived and real injustices. Parker argues that youth should not be forced to simply tone down their anger; rather, transformative pedagogy should foster listening and encourage youth as they experience these moments of truth within systems of injustice and oppression.[101] Parker outlines a framework of *holy indignation*, which she defines as a "form of constructive rage. It is the freedom to express anger against injustice in the sacred space of the Christian church and also the public square of North American society."[102] Similar to Brueggemann, Parker's framework opens the sacred space of religious institutions to also include the prophetic and sometimes enraged testimonies of African American youth.

Along similar lines, many religious educators also emphasize the many ways the mere act of listening can be transformative. In particular, Jennie Knight discusses the often troubling and problematic nature of listening with youth.[103] This is in part because adults are not prepared for what they hear and in part because youth may not feel confident or free to truly speak. Furthermore, prophetic words are not easily reintegrated into the norms of the community—they create a breach. By encouraging youth to speak and listen for these prophetic words, we are attempting to awaken in them a strategy for not only seeing issues in their communities, but also working to change them. In truth, the examples of young Christian activists in chapter 5 remind us of the ongoing prophetic roles that young African Americans are taking and must take. As such, we also note that part of the educational curriculum and even practices that we encourage young people to participate in must include the Christian practices of public social witness, or speaking a prophetic word, which interrupts the status quo.

FOSTERING AND NURTURING an integrating spirituality, which empowers young people to live into a vision of abundant life, is an ongoing, arduous, and complicated task. However, just as young people are pushing us to explore theological norms that offer alternatives to fragmented spirituality, they are reminding us (and requiring religious communities) to engage the robust pedagogy and methods of educating young people in a more holistic and integrated spirituality that also exists. In many ways, the pedagogy offered here summarizes the chapters above. The dual focus of forming and transforming parallels the focus of chapters 3–5, where we discuss at length the elements of Black Christianity and theology, which youth should hold to and which are essential to countering fragmented spirituality. Similarly, chapters 4 and 5 demonstrate the transformative religious education foci that youth are already engaged in and that young

African Americans require in order to have a more robust spirituality. For example, critical and creative reflection is exemplified in the poetry of Black and Brown youth and even in their critical questions for God. The activism of young African Americans also represents the best of strategies of religious education as transformation—as it empowers youth to speak truth to power and to take direct action in response to the issues that they are facing daily. In sum, these strategies together help young people to envision and live into a way of life abundant—and not simply a life of fear and despair.

Reflecting on the five contours of abundant life above, we see the critical pedagogy of forming and transforming attempts to answer how congregations and scholars can participate with young people in this vision of abundant life. There is not a one-to-one parallel between the strategies and contours of abundant life, but the strategies serve to empower youth and strengthen this vision of abundant life in them. For example, inviting youth into the narratives of African American Christianity is essential to proclaiming life and connecting young people with a vision of God who offers life and a community that affirms life in the midst of death. Creating communities where young people are both nurtured and heard also supports the ability of young African Americans to become more secure in their own identities, their communities, and God. The strategies for individual and social transformation, particularly embracing their *somebodiness* and coming to critical consciousness, can only take place as young people are attending to their material realities and seeing not only the problems around them, but the actions that they can take in response. At each turn, the critical pedagogy outlined above requires that young people fully act and participate in their own faith development and liberation. It requires an almost herculean strength to hold together and attend to all that they are confronted with, but these processes take place within community and only with the ongoing affirmation of who God is and how God can and does move within young people.

Conclusion

I just didn't know churches like this existed.

—BAILEY

I AM STILL haunted by Bailey's words and tears. She is a young woman who spoke of simply not knowing that churches existed that took seriously the lives and struggles of young people.[1] As she struggled to compose herself before she could share her poem about the lives of urban youth, what was made tacitly clear in her statement (yet remained unspoken) was that she had been looking for this type of community. She wanted the type of church that valued the experiences of young people, and also faith and justice. There was such emotion and longing in her words that they stood out for me even more than the poem she shared. However, her confession that she did not know that churches were creating space for young people is an indictment of the church. Either churches have a "PR" problem and therefore are not getting the message out to young people that church is this kind of space, *or* by and large churches are not places where young people feel that their concerns and voices are valued and affirmed. Both of these possibilities are problematic, and they speak to the heart of the research in this book.

As I listened deeply to the lives of young African Americans, I was repeatedly reminded of the ways that they continue to wrestle with injustices—such as violence, poverty, and racism—in addition to their ongoing development and processes of determining who they are or want to be. I encountered the stories of youth who were "successful" and those who were struggling for mere survival; all were feeling overwhelmed by senseless crime and harassment around them. I overheard stories of young Black men who were stopped and searched by police as they were walking through their own subdivisions, on the way to spend the night with friends. I observed youth as they fought daily against the impulse to give up in the face of the "craziness" around them. And often blaringly absent from their experiences and reflections were discussions, or even evidence, of their spirituality. Even among young people who were actively involved in churches (as a significant majority of young African Americans are), there was little interconnection between what took place in church and what young people were most concerned about or struggling with.

In exploring the spiritual lives of young African Americans, I observed that young people were not integrating different areas of their lives and were experiencing fragmentation in their spirituality and at times in their identities. Fragmentation was not an indicator that young people were less concerned about their worlds, or disinterested in God (or attending churches), or even an indicator that they were inactive in their communities. Instead, there was a disconnect between or fragmentation in the ways that these areas of their lives intersected. The youth interview and survey data pointed toward the ways that fragmented spirituality, though functional, limits the prophetic potential and power of young African Americans today.

As I paid particular attention to young people, I noticed that African American youth are concerned about the world around them. When simply asked to describe their communities and schools, youth offered vivid descriptions and did not shy away from discussing the problems that exist around them. These young African Americans were both excited about their friendships and families, and frustrated with their schools or communities. Overall, these young people were not blind or unaffected by issues going on around them.

I started with the concerns of young people, not simply because I assumed that all youth have issues; but I wanted to step back and not impose my list or concerns on youth. I wanted to hear firsthand what was significant to this group of African American youth. However, I also started with their concerns, because I wanted to pay attention to how their concerns connected (or did not connect) with their spiritual lives and their action in the world.

Across the discussions of their concerns and their understandings of God, the youth interview and survey data demonstrated many dimensions of fragmented spirituality. The youth described positive experiences of God and confidently described God blessing them in individual and personal ways. However, their language and responses were less confident when describing God's activity in their communities, particularly in government. Many youth even stated that while God may be or might try to be in politics, politicians do not acknowledge or do not demonstrate any evidence of God's activity in the political realm. Furthermore, in the narratives, youth were clear that contemporary politics does not reflect their understanding of how God should be connected with government. However, the youth had difficulty naming and outlining effective examples of God's activity in the governmental arena.

Beyond their understandings of God's activity in the world, the youth also described various experiences in communities of faith. In particular, most youth had positive experiences of their faith communities and described their churches as extended families and significant communities of support. Few of the youth also named the ways that their churches emphasized the need for action in the world around them. However, other youth found their churches to be ineffective in fully welcoming and encouraging them, and often irrelevant to their concerns. Specifically, these youth described the ways that their churches did not offer help in making sense of many issues that were taking place in their schools and communities—such as racism or violence.

The youth also demonstrated fragmented spirituality in the ways that they understood and described their agency in their communities. Commendably, the youth were very active in their communities. They volunteered their time tutoring and doing community service projects. However, mirroring their lack of confidence in God's work in political arenas, youth were not equally confident in their abilities to take action on larger societal or political issues. As noted, the youth were often very aware of the problems in their local communities and governments, but the many issues that youth named did not connect with the work that they were currently doing in their communities. In other words, their awareness of current events and politics demonstrates the ways that youth are paying attention to their communities; however, their awareness did not translate to direct action or even awareness of the interconnectedness of individuals, communities, and governments.

Additionally, the youth interviewed did not see themselves as fully capable and effective agents right now. Many youth narratives were filled with statements such as "when I get older," "when I finish college," or "I know that one day I will do something great." Each of these responses emphasized the hope for what youth would accomplish *later*, but did not convey a strong sense among the youth themselves about what they were currently able to accomplish. Thus, I observed youth who were faithful, aware, and actively preparing for a future, but not actively working to address their real concerns in the present.

Furthermore, even when youth were clear that they felt a need or a calling to respond to concerns in their communities, there was a disconnection for many youth between their work in the community and their spirituality. While the notion of God calling them to respond to issues in their community resonated with many youth—many named particular future professions that they felt drawn to because of this "calling"—other youth rejected or remained uncertain about a direct link between their religion and their motivation to make a difference in the world.

To summarize, fragmented spirituality among these African American youth was evidenced in the following:

- an overemphasis of the personal (in that God and religion were most often connected with their personal lives, and there was a very limited view of God working in society at large and the government);
- a lack of confidence in their ability to effect change in the present or beyond the personal domain; and
- a disconnect between their spirituality, their faith communities, and their communal involvement.

While wrestling with the disconnects and the narratives of so many young African Americans, the easiest answer is to blame youth for having fragmented spirituality. But the research does not support this posture. In fact, *blame* is not the most helpful posture. And if we were to blame any one group, the blame for fragmented spirituality and identity more fully rests with the adults (and more general societal structures). The larger societal context and religious communities foster an environment where fragmentation is more functional and where the most prevalent understandings of God and faith are only concerned with the personal and intrapersonal (not as leading to the communal or political, but stopping at the personal).

The youth narratives reflect larger trends and sources of fragmentation and fragmented spirituality in American society and within African American Christianity. For example, discussions of religion and religious temperaments from the early twentieth century onward include discussions of divided selves and double consciousness, indicating a centuries-old presence of fragmentation in spirituality and identities within the larger context. Furthermore, contemporary understandings of the self and identity development center on concepts of multiple selves, or multiple narratives and identities that make up a person's identity. Also, from a sociological perspective, American society in modernity and postmodernity includes both an emphasis on a public and private sphere and by extension differentiated expectations of the types of actions that can take place in each sphere. Along with the trends toward privatization and role differentiation, a key component of American society is American individualism, which focuses primarily on the individual in terms of the rights of individuals and in the ways that the individual is treated as fully autonomous, and in a sense disconnected from communities and institutions. In relationship to these trends, I also explored the ways that American individualism impacts American religions and youth spirituality. Looking at the work of sociologists Robert Bellah and Christian Smith, I noted the ways that contemporary youth spirituality includes trends to focus on God's personal connection to youth and to emphasize religion as being primarily concerned with making individual youth feel good. These trends thus demonstrate a larger context in which fragmentation and individualism are rampant, and in which religion is designed and expected to remain private and individualized. Religion thus is not expected to require much of its adherents.

Furthermore, the sample of educational resources in African American churches included religious language and practices that focused primarily on the personal and interpersonal. These educational resources did not greatly demonstrate communal or societal dimensions of Christianity or spirituality. The emphasis was on a less active spirituality, which focused on reflection and religious actions such as prayer and trusting in God. They excluded discussions of God's work in society or even the need for active engagement in communities and society as a response to experiencing the presence of God. Likewise, the educational resources included complex understandings of God, but still emphasized God's work with individuals and in personal lives above other types of action.

In other words, in exploring the larger societal and religious contexts I should not be surprised by the narrative of the young woman at the beginning of this chapter. In truth, the young African Americans interviewed in this book were like Bailey: they too did not have models of an integrating spirituality or of religious communities that supported them in the ways that they most often desired. What I found in listening with young people and in observing several larger contexts in which their spirituality develops is that the spiritual lives of young African Americans are complex and messy (like the larger contexts), and what they are most struggling to find is a way of integrating or unifying their myriad experiences. The young African Americans in this research have not given up on God or even religious communities. They affirm traditions and practices that may seem surprising to outsiders. These include witnessing, singing hymns and in choirs, and being part of a church community (either a youth group or a larger community). They also wrestle with whether these practices and their churches are relevant to their understandings of the call of God for their lives and for the concerns they have about their community.

Beyond the young African Americans interviewed, I also listened for the places where African American youth were wrestling with larger theological and social quandaries. These included exploring whether or not God cares for them in the face of the myriad injustices they encounter and whether or not their faith can speak to the activism that many young African Americans are also engaged in. What emerged is that religion and churches are still important to the spiritual lives of young African Americans. Christian Smith and Melinda Denton, looking at all American teens, noted that just because young people were not actively involved in churches did not mean that they did not want to be or "would not become active under certain circumstances."[2] Similarly, looking specifically at *disconnected* African American youth, Anne Wimberly also noted that young people were looking for churches to speak to their concerns. Young people, particularly young African Americans, still have expectations that the Christian church should be a positive part of their lives. And yet, there are many "Baileys" who get emotional at the realization that "churches like this" exist. One of the young activists interviewed in this book recounted the African American teens who also shared with him that *if* their churches were like this (a place where the death of young Black men and women could be discussed and where people spoke truth to power, even if it meant cursing in church), then they would go *more*.

These statements from young African Americans are a cause for Black churches to hope and a call for them to *do better*. As such, this book has attempted to explore the lives of young African Americans (in all of their complexity and messiness) and to start the conversation about what Christian communities can and should do in order to be better models for young people and to nurture young African Americans into an integrating spirituality and an abundant life. However, instead of pointing to one precise model or vision of integrating spirituality with young people, this book explores glimmers of hope and places where young African Americans, interviewees at a summer academy, poets, and young Christian activists are already leading the way in terms of the types of discussions they are pushing society to have and in naming the issues that are at the forefront of their lived realities now. Young African Americans (those interviewed and in the larger society) are pushing communities, parents, and religious leaders to rethink even how we discuss our faith and what role faith can and should play in public discourse. Young activists, Christian and otherwise, have led the way for a type of public engagement that many have never experienced since (or even in) the Civil Rights Movement of the mid-twentieth century. In truth, young African American activists have broadened the conversations of civil disobedience and Christian social witness, to the point where they are pushing academic theologians and local congregations to re-imagine what is possible.

I have outlined the role of religious education and critical pedagogy in helping young people realize a vision of abundant life that does not start with violence or death. And in my understanding of religious education, we move away from perceptions of religious education as primarily education for conforming to a particular tradition or denomination, to a practice of teaching and engaging in dialogue with young people such that they embrace a way of life abundant.

However, it is not enough for this work to demonstrate that many young African Americans, who are involved in and inspired by a variety of movements, media, and organizations, still seek churches that encourage their spiritual formation and reflective action in the world around them. It is not enough to outline practices and theological insights that are available to foster integrating spirituality among young people. Instead, a commitment of religious leaders and churches to wrestle with whether they actually want to be places where young people gain insights and encouragement for a better way of life is also required.

I often get into trouble, because I remain clear that my ultimate goal in my research (particularly as a practical theologian and Christian) is *not* to increase membership in churches. I would love for more young African Americans to be present in religious communities, but my ultimate goal is the wellbeing and flourishing of young African Americans. This flourishing includes spiritual wellbeing, and I affirm it emerges in living up to the promise of Christ who offers to all a way of abundant life. However, *if* churches fail to fully embrace them and their lived realities (and fail to affirm their abilities to lead and shape the shared life of faith already, right now), *then* young people can and will create communities of hope and flourishing apart from churches. These young African Americans leave us to wrestle with whether religious communities can encourage youth to live life abundantly, to embrace an integrating spirituality. They leave adults to wrestle with not only whether adults are capable of doing this work, but if they actually want to. They leave churches to wrestle with whether they are willing to count the cost of holding onto ways of being that alienate young people or whether to fully embrace the powerful witness of youth.

Are Our Expectations Too High?

I have been asked repeatedly if my expectations are too high or if my standards for the type of integration of self, faith, and action are so extraordinary—such that no young person or adult fully embodies it. Honestly, in some way I agree with the implications of this question. My standards for what the life of faith and a way of life abundant could be are not widely present or even readily apparent in the lives of African American Christian youth or adults. In part, I am guilty of years of hope and optimism in what Black churches could be or should be. There are traces of the trap of seeing the political and social engagement of the Civil Rights era as ubiquitous and just the baseline of what Black Christianity could be. However, at the same time, with a more tempered set of expectations, I resist the inference that if it is not readily possible, we should not aspire toward it.

Undergirding my high expectations are a lifelong conviction that religion, and particularly Christianity, should *do something*. Recently the language of active faith has pointed toward my understanding that the Christian tradition is not simply a belief system, but it is a way of being, living, and acting. In this work, I have challenged Christian practices or educational resources that would focus narrowly on individual or interpersonal actions, while neglecting communal and societal transformation. However, in this challenge, I again hear the critique that maybe my standards are too high!

Part of the assertions that my standards might be too high also rests in two somewhat erroneous assumptions and pitfalls that require a final word of clarification. This first is the erroneous belief that any one individual alone can "perfect" this type of integrating spirituality. Throughout this work, the lives of young people have inspired us to think carefully about what communities of faith, which support young people, can look like. It is worth repeating here, that while individual development and discernment is important, realizing a vision of abundant life and integrating spirituality is never a solitary or individual effort or achievement. This is not an individualistic spirituality, so how could we expect young people or adults alone to experience this type of spirituality without community and supports? This also requires an understanding that even the spiritual lives of young people are not only shaped in churches, but in families and culture, through creative expression and action.

Likewise, the second potential pitfall lies in the erroneous assumption that this work of integration is purely or primarily the work of humanity. What I am calling for in this work is a renewed spirituality. As such, our discussions of cooperation with God and the work of the spirit as a partner in this work is important. We should never look at the lives of young people, spiritual or otherwise, and assume that we have the power to transform them through any singular effort. Certainly, we point to the best practices and systems of supports and solutions to help young people flourish. But as a religious practitioner, I must always attend to the work of God in bringing about this transformation as well. Thus, we must remember that God also participates in and stretches our spiritual lives far beyond what we can accomplish alone. Ironically, pushing people of faith to trust that God also has something to do or say in how they live out their faith should not be a cop-out, but often it is read this way. However, for me the truth is that any response to fragmented spirituality or vision of abundant life that does not rest on the cooperation between God and humanity becomes another manifestation of fragmentation.

To be certain, one of the lessons of this research is that *not* everything is possible. A single church or pastor, or even a single religious tradition, cannot offer youth all that they need to respond to the systemic injustices that they encounter on a daily basis. However, it is in the collective and creative expressions and outlets of young people that we see models of the types of communities and supports that will help youth integrate their understandings of self and God and their communities.

Hoping against Hope

Throughout the research I have been shocked and amazed by the many issues named and responses given by the youth. In their narratives, I glimpsed the myriad joys and concerns that youth wrestle with on a daily basis, in their friendships and relationships, academic lives, and in their future plans. I also saw the problems they experience with gangs, violence, low expectations from teachers and peers, and even ongoing inequality in how Black youth are viewed and treated in schools. However, I also saw youth who were actively seeking God's guidance and presence in their lives and youth who were making plans for future success and yearning to respond to issues around them. Beyond helping me to further explore and research their spirituality, listening to the narratives of young people and paying attention to the very real concerns, and at times tragedies, that are part of their daily lives serves as a clarion call for communities of faith and concerned adults.

Admittedly, the task of addressing the myriad concerns that African American youth face remains overwhelming. Likewise, the task of helping religious communities better equip youth to respond to these issues looms large. I am also aware that any type of solution will seem inept and limited. Nevertheless, I am encouraged to continue the work of building the capacity of institutions and communities of faith, so that they become part of a collective network of resources that can empower youth development. In other words, in this work I am not arguing that a different type of spirituality will change or ameliorate *all* youth concerns; however, I assert that spirituality should be among the resources that youth can turn to in their efforts to address their concerns. Hence I am excited about the possibility of nurturing an integrating spirituality with youth—as they are empowered to hold together the seemingly disparate areas of their lives, tap into the resources of their faith communities, learn from historical and current faith exemplars, and see themselves as capable of effecting change on individual, communal, and societal/systemic levels.

Moreover, I am excited and energized because nurturing youth in this type of spirituality and making the space for youth to be "outrageous, audacious, courageous or *willful* . . . [and] to know more and in greater depth than is considered good"[3] will not only improve their way of being in the world, but will challenge us in new and exciting ways.

Returning to Bailey's statement that "I just didn't know churches like this existed" and to Kira's call to "take the limits off," I am reminded that together they offer us hope. It is a hope that young African American Christians (and even non-believers)—in the midst of violence and poor schools, and in the middle of adults and churches that have not modeled for them the rich messiness of an integrating spirituality—have not given up on communities of faith, and that if only we would respond in kind, tremendous strides could be made as we collectively choose life and walk in a vision of abundant life!

Youth Interview and Survey Questions

Part I: Exploring Daily Activities

1. Tell me a little bit about **a typical day** in your life.
   a. What types of things do you do?
      i. Do you have particular passions or hobbies that you do (or like to do) daily?
   b. What people do you see or hang out with?
   c. What places do you go to?
      i. Do you have to go to school? To work? Do you stay home often, go to friends' houses, church, or the mall?
   d. Are there questions or things that you typically think or worry about?
2. Tell me a little about **the place you grew up**.
   a. What made it unique?
   b. What would you want to tell someone about it who had never been there before?
   c. Can you think of one event or experience that represents what you think of when you think about where you grew up?
   d. Who makes up the majority where you grew up? The minority?
3. Tell me a little bit about where you go to **school**.
   a. How large is it?
   b. Describe a typical day at your school. What are some of the events that make up this typical day?
   c. What do you like best/least about your school?
   d. Who makes up the majority at your school? The minority?

4. Tell me a little bit about your **primary group of friends**.
    a. Who is part of the group?
    b. Where do you know them from?
    c. Have you kept in touch with them since coming to YTI? How have you done so (e.g., cell phone, Facebook, e-mail, etc.)?
    d. What similarities do you share? What makes you different from each other?
    e. What hot topics or political issues does your group of friends agree about? What hot topics or political issues do you disagree about?

5. Tell me a little bit about your **family**.
    a. Who do you live with?
    b. What are some things you like to do with your family?
    c. Tell me about a time when you were proud to be a part of your family.
    d. Are there religious practices that are a part of your family life (e.g., prayer before meals, devotions, etc.)?
    e. What values do you think your parent/s most want to pass on to you?
    f. If I were interviewing your parents today instead of you, what would they say they most want for you or is their greatest hope for you? What would they say is the worst thing that could happen to you?

6. Are you a part of a religious tradition or faith community? Let's talk about **your faith community**. Can you describe it for me?
    a. Is the faith community you are a part of now the same one that you grew up in? When/how did you get involved in this community?
    b. Tell me about a time when you felt passionate about being involved in your faith community or a time when you had a particularly powerful experience in your faith community.
    c. How would you summarize what happens at your church for someone who's never been to your church?
    d. What would your church say is the message of Christ?
    e. What would you say is the most important for others to understand about your faith? What has been the most important for you?
    f. How does your church understand "God's work" in the world?
    g. And how is God calling your church to be a part of that work in the world?
    h. Can you think of a way your faith community has helped you to become who you are today?
        i. Are there things that your faith community would not want you to do or people they would not want you to associate with?

Part II: Exploring Youth Concerns, Struggles,
and Actions in the World

1. Tell me about some of **the concerns and struggles, both personal and social,** that you or other youth face.
    a. What are some things that you or other youth talk or worry about?

b. When you look around your **school and community**, what kinds of concerns do you have?

    i. What things do you want to see changed?

c. Similarly, as you look in the **larger society**—are there things in the news about other parts of the country or world that concern you?

    i. What things do you want to see changed?

d. Can you describe how you respond when you encounter these particular struggles?

e. What are some of the resources (beliefs, people, practices) you turn to in order to help with these struggles?

f. What types of things are you doing in your community, government, world?

    i. What would you like to do? See done?

2. Do you feel a particular need or "calling" to respond to some of the crises and social concerns you see in the lives of teenagers or in the world?

a. If so, what are the reasons for working for change?

b. Do you have a sense of God/church/family/friends/school calling you to work for change?

c. Have you ever learned about a problem in the world that has motivated you to change something about how you live, or to encourage other people to change something about how they live? Tell me about the problem and what changes you made.

3. How does your church, faith, or understanding of God help you to think about or make sense of the struggles that you or other youth have? To make sense of the concerns you have for the world?

a. Are there particular practices (e.g., prayer, meditation, Bible reading, etc.) that help you in making sense of troubling situations in the world?

b. Do you have specific people that you take your questions and struggles to? (Can you talk to a leader in your church, a friend, or others?)

c. How have you come to find these people and/or practices? Was it a process of trial and error? Was there something particular about these practices/people that clued you in to the fact that they would be good in times of questioning, fear, or struggles?

4. Where/how do you experience God working in your life, community, and, government?

a. Do you think of God as working or acting in your life or the lives of other people?

b. Do you think of God as being involved in your community, politics, and government? If so, how?

5. Also, what would you say is your church's perspective and response to issues of race, poverty, gender, and class?

a. Tell me about what your church teaches about these issues.

b. For many, discussions of race, class, poverty, gender and sexuality can be difficult.

      i. What is your response to discussions about racism, classism, and so on?

      ii. Do you still see/experience such issues?

  c. How important is race to your self-understanding/identity?

      i. Can you give me an example of why or how race is/is not important or has shaped your life so far? OR How important is your ethnicity (Euro-American, African, Irish, etc.) to your sense of self?

  d. In what ways do the categories of race, class, gender, or sexuality enter your daily life?

  e. Do you think about your race, ethnic background, class, or gender on a regular basis?

  i. When does it come up most, if ever?

  f. Can you reflect on how you think God is calling you to respond to these issues? Does God have anything to say?

  g. Do you see racism, poverty, and sexism ending in the near future? Why or why not? How?

6. Can you describe someone you admire for how he or she **makes a difference** in the world?

  a. What made this person stand out for you?

  b. Are there other people whom you know personally who are making a difference in your community?

      i. What types of work are they doing?

      ii. How are they making a difference?

  c. Have you seen a clergy person or member of your congregation involved in the community (making a difference in your community)? Describe when/how.

7. Similarly, can you give some examples of **the ways young people make a difference** in your community?

  a. What types of activities are you currently involved in, and how are these activities making a difference in your community, government, or world?

  b. What types of things are youth in your school or community currently doing?

  c. What types of things can young people do?

  d. What would you like to do? See done?

  e. Give an example of how this activity impacts your community and youth.

  f. Are there barriers that limit the ways young people can make a difference in your community? Explain.

  g. Who/what in your community is supportive of young people and their efforts to make a difference?

*Part III: Exploring Youth Hopes and Dreams for Their Future
and World*

1. As you think about yourself finishing high school and moving on to what is next, what are your goals/dreams in life? How do you plan to achieve them?

2. What are your dreams for your community and world? How do you plan to help them happen?

3. When you think of your life five or ten years from now, what place will some of the experiences you have told me about have in your life? What place will faith/religion/church have in your life?

Conclusion

1. Is there anything else you wish I had asked about that I did not ask about?

2. Is there anything else you wish to add to our conversation or anything you said earlier that you would like to go back to?

3. Thank the scholar for taking part in the interview and sharing his or her stories with you.

4. After turning off the audio recorder, ask the scholar one last time if it is ok to use the interview in the research. If the scholar says no, erase the interview while the scholar watches.

SAMPLE SCHOLAR SURVEY

Part I: Information About Yourself

1. Gender: ____ Male ____ Female

2. Age _____

3. Race/ethnicity _____

4. Region of the country with which you identify or in which you have spent most of your life
   ____ a. Southwest
   ____ b. Northwest
   ____ c. Midwest
   ____ d. Northeast
   ____ e. Southeast

5. State in which you now live _____

6. Please list the people you live with (e.g., Mom, Grandparents, 1 sister, cousin) and include pets if you want.

7. Religious denomination or affiliation _____

8. On a scale of 1 to 5, with 1 = not involved and 5 = very involved,
   a. How involved were you in a faith community growing up? _____
   b. How involved are you in a faith community now? _____

9. Please explain your answer to #8 a and b. (For example, "I was not very involved in a faith community growing up because I only went to worship once a month with my family. Now I am very involved because I go to worship, Bible study, and youth choir each week.")

10. Please briefly describe each group below. Think about what you would want someone who knows nothing about this group to know about it. Also include

information about the dilemmas or concerns you encounter in each group, if any. This can include any type of concern you wish (personal, social, political, etc.):

a. your hometown

b. your school

c. your main group of friends

11. Have you ever learned about a problem in the world that has motivated you to change something about how you live, or to encourage other people to change something about how they live? ___yes ___no If yes, briefly describe the problem and what changes you made.

12. Please describe someone you admire for how they make a difference in the world.

13. Please describe someone you know personally who is making a difference in your community.

14. Have you seen a clergy person or member of your congregation making a difference in your community? Please describe when/how.

15. Give some examples of the ways young people make a difference in your community.

16. Are there barriers that limit the ways young people can make a difference in your community? Explain.

17. Who/what in your community is supportive of young people and their efforts to make a difference?

18. Please check the types of activities you are currently involved in in your community. Please check all that apply and feel free to write activities not listed in the space below.

- ☐ Volunteering at a nursing home or hospital
- ☐ Volunteering at a homeless shelter or soup kitchen
- ☐ Delivering meals to homebound persons ("Meals on Wheels")
- ☐ Volunteering in a community center
- ☐ Trash pickup (cleaning up parks, playgrounds, streets, highways, etc.)
- ☐ Rebuilding houses (Habitat for Humanity, Christmas in July, etc.)
- ☐ Recycling
- ☐ Organizing recycling at home, school, church, and so on.
- ☐ Educating peers and/or adults on environmental concerns
- ☐ Member of an environmental community organization
- ☐ Community gardening
- ☐ Writing letters or making calls to elected officials and politicians regarding a community concern
- ☐ Participating in a mock government (mock general assembly, mock senate, etc.)
- ☐ Signing a petition or letter addressing a community concern
- ☐ Registering voters
- ☐ Tutoring
- ☐ Mentoring

☐ Coaching community sports teams

☐ Teaching adult literacy, ESL, or GED classes

☐ Peer educator about sexual health and relationships (unprotected sex, HIV/
   AIDS, STIs, relationship abuse, etc.)

☐ Peer educator about community violence and conflict resolution

☐ Protesting or picketing _____

☐ OTHER _____

Part II: Faith, Community, Your Family, and You

19. What was the approximate racial/ethnic makeup of the faith community or
    church in which you grew up? (Please use percentages.)

20. My faith community thought faith was important for people's lives because . . .

21. Please place an "X" next to all that apply:

    ____ a. My faith community seemed to stress that people were evil, bad, or
          deeply flawed.

    ____ b. My faith community seemed to stress that people were mostly good and
          trustworthy.

    ____ c. My faith community seemed to stress that people are a mixture of good
          and evil and need to be reflective about how we participate in both good
          and evil.

    ____ d. My faith community seemed to stress the need for God to escape the evil
          of this life.

    ____ e. My faith community seemed to stress the need to acknowledge how
          God is working in hidden and subtle ways through ordinary people and
          creation.

22. Please describe a time when you felt the presence of God in your life.

23. What theological perspectives or alternative faith practices did your faith com-
    munity warn you against? Please explain the rationale they gave for this.

24. Judging not merely from what was said by leaders in the faith community, but
    also from what you observed from the lives of members of the community,
    guess the most important values of your religious community. Mark an "X" next
    to only five:

    ____ a. To be a respectable member of the middle class

    ____ b. To work hard and stay out of trouble

    ____ c. To send their children to college

    ____ d. To own the right homes, cars, or clothes.

    ____ e. To be reflective about how our lifestyles might participate in systems of
          injustice

    ____ f. To be patriotic

    ____ g. To love Jesus

    __ h. To love others, even those unlike ourselves

    __ i. To worship every Sunday and to tithe

    __ j. To work as a movement toward creating a society of peace, equality, and justice

    __ k. To care for each other as family

    __ l. To work to end injustices in the world such as poverty and racism

    __ m. To _____

25. Please place an "X" next to all that apply:

    __ a. My pastor and faith community rarely discuss the responsibility of religious communities to the poor.

    __ b. My pastor and faith community sometimes talk about the responsibility of religious communities to the poor, but it is most often framed as a condition of people far away and in another country.

    __ c. My pastor and faith community sometimes talk about the responsibility of religious communities to the poor, and our faith community sometimes sends work teams to offer charity to those in need.

    __ d. My pastor and faith community feel so strongly about the responsibility of religious communities to the poor that not only do we send work teams but we also regularly discuss legislation that impacts the poor and collaborates about how to act on their behalf.

    __ e. My pastor and faith community feel so strongly about the responsibility of religious communities to the poor that we have made efforts to invite the poor into our worship and our homes.

26. Are issues that have to do with class, poverty, or socioeconomic status discussed in your faith community? If yes, what actions have been taken in light of these discussions?

27. Please place an "X" next to all that apply:

    __ a. My faith community took consistent and concrete steps to create more racial/ethnic justice and harmony.

    __ b. My faith community sought ways to put our members into relationships with those of other races or ethnicities.

    __ c. My faith community, through sermons and lessons, often affirmed the importance of viewing all races and ethnicities as equally part of God's family.

    __ d. My faith community seemed altogether to ignore issues of racial and ethnic prejudice or justice.

    __ e. My faith community seems to view racial matters as important, but only has a limited perspective that does not take into account the many subtle ways people are ignored or oppressed.

Please rate the following statements:

28. My faith community seems generally open and affirming of gay, lesbian, bisexual, and transgendered persons.

1	2	3	4	5
true	somewhat true	neutral	somewhat false	false

29. I know of at least one openly gay, lesbian, bi-sexual, or transgendered person in my congregation.

1	2	3	4	5
true	somewhat true	neutral	somewhat false	false

30. The preacher and teachers of my faith community often speak of the importance of openness to gay, lesbian, bi-sexual, and transgendered people in biblical or theological terms.

1	2	3	4	5
true	somewhat true	neutral	somewhat false	false

31. My faith community generally avoids the subject of alternate sexual orientation altogether.

1	2	3	4	5
true	somewhat true	neutral	somewhat false	false

32. My faith community is openly hostile to gays, lesbians, bi-sexual or transgendered persons.

1	2	3	4	5
true	somewhat true	neutral	somewhat false	false

33. Complete the following sentences:
    a. "My family taught me how to be a good _____."
    b. "My family taught me to be suspicious of _____."
    c. "In my family, it would have been weird to talk openly about _____."
    d. "My family warned me against these theological perspectives or alternative faith practices: _____."

34. Please name the religious practices, if any, that your family does at home.
35. If you had to name the three things your family valued most, what would they be?

Part III: Challenges to Faith Community and Family
Perspectives

36. Place an "X" on the line next to the statement that best describes you:
    ___ a. My view of the world, God, and my place in the world has changed significantly in the past two years.
    ___ b. My view of the world, God, and my place in the world has remained much the same as it was a couple of years ago.
    ___ c. My view of the world, God, and my place in the world has not fundamentally changed, but I have many more questions about it than I did a couple of years ago.
    ___ d. I have so many new questions and problems that have become real for me in the last two years that I am not sure if my view of the world has changed or not.

Please explain your choice the statement in question 36. For example, why did you state that your view of God changed or remained the same?

37. Currently, what is your most burning question that leaves you unsettled about how you view the world, God, or your place in the world?

38. When it comes to making sense of your burning questions and life experiences, what activities, people, and resources are most helpful or supportive (e.g., prayer, friends, books, etc.)? Please explain.

39. What issues are you hearing about in the news that have to do with questions of community and diversity? How are these issues talked about and/or dealt with?

APPENDIX B

Curriculum and Sermon Review Methodology

METHODOLOGY OF CURRICULUM REVIEW

The sample of Sunday school curriculum includes 106 lessons from the Urban Ministries, Inc. (UMI) adolescent curriculum line. This includes fifty-three lessons (or the equivalent of a little more than one year of lessons) from the *J.A.M.* (Jesus and Me) curriculum (designed for ages twelve to fourteen) and the *InTeen* curriculum (for youth ages fifteen to seventeen). UMI's curriculum for young adults is not included in the analysis.

UMI curriculum follows the "International Uniform Lesson Series"—a series of biblical texts and themes set by an ecumenical and national committee. This series outlines a six-year cycle of Sunday school lessons.[1] The sample reviewed includes four quarters across two years, in an effort to get a sense of the range of Biblical texts and the supplemental lesson development offered. The 106 lessons come from the *J.A.M.* and *InTeen* curriculum for Summer 2007, Fall 2007, Summer 2008, and Fall 2008. Each quarter includes thirteen to fourteen lessons dated for each Sunday in that three-month quarter. Each quarter is also designed around a particular theme that emphasizes a theological topic and/or practical area of knowledge or concern in the lives of young people.[2]

Quarter	Curriculum	Theme	Theological Themes and Biblical Texts
Summer 2007	*J.A.M.*	"Fine Print" African American literary publications	Justice Old Testament prophets
	In Teen	"Doing It Right" Obeying God and doing what is right	
Fall 2007	*J.A.M.*	"Weather" Genesis creation stories	Creation/beginnings/ covenant/ promises/
	In Teen	"Sculpted by God"	dreams/visions/family genesis narratives
Summer 2008	*J.A.M.* *In Teen*	"I Can See Clearly Now" "Images of Christ"	Images/attributes of Christ, Gospels/Hebrews/James
Fall 2008	*J.A.M* *In Teen*	"Generation Christ" "The New Community"	Community/New Testament

This sample of lessons represents the last full cycle of Universal Series lessons from 2004–2010; therefore we get a representative sample of the biblical text used, but it does not fully represent the most recent themes set forth by the Universal Committee or possibly contemporary issues that the UMI authors put in conversation with the biblical text and themes. The next six-year cycle, 2010–2016, also included eight themes: God, hope, worship, community, tradition, faith, creation, and justice. Each theme is addressed in three quarters. For the full scope and sequence, see http://standardlesson.com/scope-sequence/.

My methodology for reviewing the UMI curriculum included reading through each lesson carefully and then answering the guiding questions:

- THEOLOGICAL THEMES: What are the major topics or theological themes presented?
- PRACTICAL ISSUES: What issues or practical situations are addressed? (E.g., are personal sin, sicknesses, wealth, or other personal, communal, or systemic/societal issues addressed?) Are issues such as racism, poverty, sexism, heterosexism, or homelessness named or explored in the sermon/curriculum? Do the topics/themes presented include calls to personal piety or behavior? Communal action? Social justice? None? All?
- UNDERSTANDING OF GOD: How is God described? What attributes are ascribed to God? How and where is God understood to act? What is God expected to do?

- CHANGE OUTLINED: What types of change does the preacher/curriculum call for? (Personal? Communal? Systemic?) Is there a call to collective civic engagement or political action?
- HUMAN ACTION: How are humans encouraged to respond or act in the world? (Charity? Good works? Prosperity? Advocacy? Justice-building?)
- ADOLESCENTS: How are adolescents referred to in the sermons or curriculum? (Are they referenced or included? If so, how?)
- RACE/ETHNICITY: Is there any reference to race or ethnicity in the sermon/curriculum? If so, how?
- AFRICAN AMERICAN: How are African Americans discussed and described?
- HOPES: What hopes are named for the community? The African American community? For the world?
- EXPLICIT AND IMPLICIT CURRICULUM: What conclusions might be drawn about what is being taught explicitly, implicitly, or by being ignored?

After the initial reading, I did a second reading of the notes and responses to my eleven guiding questions to see if there were any patterns or clustering of particular themes or topics addressed in the curriculum. In order to facilitate my analysis and to offer a more succinct review of the curriculum, I used a random number generator to select a sub-sample of my larger curriculum sample of 106 lessons.[3] The subsample is not completely random, in that I chose to select four lessons from each quarter and each curriculum; and I chose to review the same four lesson numbers for each curriculum.[4] Thus I reduced my original data set from 106 lessons to thirty-two lessons. In my statistical analysis I refer to percentages of my subsample of thirty-two. However, in my discussion of particular qualitative characteristics of the curriculum, I also draw from the larger sample.[5]

METHODOLOGY OF SERMON SELECTION

The sermon sample includes sermons from predominately African American churches across the United States. The sermons collected were all preached over the past nine years and span the years of 2006–2009 and 2013–2015. This range reflects two separate sermon samples (one which was originally part of my dissertation research and another more recent, which has also attempted to look at any possible changes in the theology of Black preaching in light of more recent activism and social unrest in response to ongoing violence against Black and Brown people).

My general criteria included selecting

- sermons from diverse African American Christian traditions or denominations;
- sermons from a broad geographical area; and
- sermons from congregations of varying sizes.

	2008	2015	Total
Sermon Demographics			
Sample Size	10	19	29
Gender of Preacher			
Male	8	14	22
Female	2	5	7
Type of Ministry[6]			
National	6	14	20
Local	4	5	9
Membership Size	Small: 1	Small: 2	Small: 3
	Medium: 2	Medium: 0	Medium: 2
	Large: 2	Larger: 6	Large: 8
	Megachurch: 5	Megachurch: 16	Megachurch: 21
Denominations	Baptist: 4	Baptist: 9	Baptist: 13
	Nondenominational	Methodist: 3	Non: 6
	(Non): 4	Non: 2	Methodist: 4
	Methodist: 1	United Church of	United Church of
	United Church of	Christ: 2	Christ: 3
	Christ: 1	Disciples of Christ: 1	Disciples of Christ: 1
		Episcopal: 1	Episcopal: 1
		Pentecostal: 1	Pentecostal: 1

The sermons analyzed here do not statistically predict trends within the larger constellation of African American churches. But in attending to the sermons from a sample of churches, we were able to see specific examples of Black preaching and theology. This sample of sermons is a strategic convenience sample and thus reflects some biases and limitations. The first sample of sermons focused on ten churches primarily in the Atlanta area. (Five of the sermons are from churches in the Atlanta metropolitan area, with two churches in Texas, one church each in Maryland, Florida, and New York.) The second sample of sermons focused on a broader sample from nineteen churches across the country. The sample includes churches in Atlanta, Chicago, New Haven, New York, and from various parts of California, the Washington, DC metropolitan area, Tennessee, and Texas.

In addition to regional diversity, I attempted to ensure a slightly more representative sample by choosing sermons from a combination of local and national ministries. I define local and national ministries based on whether the preachers and churches focus mostly on local or national audiences and on whether the preachers claim national recognition and prominence in the African American Christian community—as evidenced in their preaching itineraries, their publications, their multimedia broadcasts, and in general, the size of the church. The local sermons were obtained by contacting local pastors and requesting their participation in the research by submitting sermons. The national sermons were collected using multimedia downloads from YouTube, Christian media outlets, such as *Streaming Faith*, and directly from the church or ministry websites.[7] In selecting the national sermons, I decided to use sermons that were the most popular—that is, had received the most "hits" or purchases—on the multimedia outlets. While popularity does not indicate the exact impact of the sermons, it does give a sense of the influence (in terms of the number of persons listening to and purchasing) of the particular sermons. The first sample includes four local churches and six national ministries. The second sample includes nine local churches and ten national ministries.

Also, in selecting sermons from both popular national preachers and local congregations, I am attempting to show some of the range of preaching and ministries that currently make up the African American church. Initially, my research protocol only included sermons from local pastors; however, I soon realized that this sample would not address or reflect larger trends in African American Christianity.[8] While the majority of African American churches are still in the small-to-medium membership range (with less than one thousand members), there is an increasing desire and trend toward megaministries that is impacting even the ways that smaller churches are conducting their ministries and presenting their theology.

Looking at the demographic data of the sermon sample, I note that the sample is skewed toward Baptist and nondenominational ministries. Of the churches sampled, there are thirteen Baptist churches (including Full Gospel Baptist), six nondenominational churches, four African Methodist churches, three churches affiliated with the United Church of Christ, and others from Episcopal, Disciples of Christ, and Pentecostal traditions. The sample includes churches that can be characterized as part of the historically Black denominations, as well as inclusive of contemporary trends within African American Christianity—which includes a waning emphasis on denominationalism and a continued emphasis on the role of the charismatic preacher or leader within the spiritual community.

The sample is also skewed toward larger and megachurch-sized ministries and is also heavily skewed toward male preachers.

The sample represents some balance in church history and organization, in that half of the national ministries are very new, with the ministries emerging in the last twenty years. In these churches, the pastors also tend to be the organizers as well. However, the sample also includes churches that have been established for generations and can be viewed as pillars within the national and local African American community.

In selecting sermons, I only selected sermons from "regular" African American worship services. I intentionally do not focus on sermons specifically designed or created for African American adolescents, such as sermons from youth groups, youth churches, or youth revivals. While many larger African American churches are developing specialized ministries for the youth, the prevalence of youth group and/or youth church among African Americans is still considerably less than in European American or mainline denominations. Christian Smith, in his seminal research of the religious lives of adolescents, notes that African American youth participate in youth groups at rates of 44 percent, less than the national sample average of 52 percent, and considerably less than the 64 percent of youth group attendance among conservative and mainline Protestants.[9] While youth worship services and revivals play a very significant role in the religious lives of African American youth, these events tend to be an annual, or at best a monthly, occurrence. The infrequency of youth revivals or special youth Sundays does not diminish my understanding of their significance in the overall development of youth in African American Christian communities; however I see it as only one part of a more complicated calendar of youth spiritual development. In most cases, active youth participants in the African American church spend the majority of their time in "big church" or "regular church" with the adults, listening to and being exposed to the sermons and influence of senior pastors. For this reason, I chose to analyze the sermon content of "regular," non-youth-specific worship services. Additionally, analyzing non-youth-specific worship sermons offers some insights into how African American adolescents are viewed and fit into the larger experiences, expressions, and theology of African American churches.

Anonymity

In my research, I do not reveal or publish the sources of the sermon information as to neither skew nor promote the materials of any pastor, local or national. Instead I created a coding system that identifies pertinent demographic information about the church and preacher—while protecting their identity and copyrights.

SERMON ANALYSIS METHODOLOGY

The methodology for reviewing the sermons parallels the process of analyzing the UMI curricula. It included listening to each sermon carefully, taking notes on the general content and structure of the sermon. After listening and note-taking, the research team answered the guiding questions regarding the theological themes, practical topics, understandings of God and adolescents, types of change and/or human action included in each sermon. After completing the analysis worksheets and answering each of the guiding questions, I summarized each response, creating a combined analysis chart, from which I sought to see if there were any commonalities and general trends among the sermon content.

Notes

INTRODUCTION

1. I first encountered the term "fragmented spirituality" and the general content of the definition in Evelyn Parker's *Trouble Don't Last Always: Emancipatory Hope among African American Adolescents* (Cleveland, OH: Pilgrim, 2003), 35–36. Parker specifically defines the problem of fragmented spirituality in terms of African American adolescents' discourse about their faith and racism. I build on her initial findings by exploring the disconnection of adolescent spirituality from discourse around other systemic ills—looking at the intersectionality of systemic ills such as racism, classism/poverty, sexism, and youth violence.

2. See Kenneth Gergen, *The Saturated Self* (1991; repr. New York: Basic Books, 2000). Gergen is somewhat apocalyptic about the demise of the coherent/traditional self, but points toward a concept of a relational self. Gergen does not simply see humans as chameleons (being whatever is required in a particular setting), but describes the self as emerging in relationships with others.

    See also Dan P. McAdams, Ruthellen Josselson, and Amia Lieblich, eds. *Identity and Story: Creating Self in Narrative* (Washington, DC: American Psychological Association, 2006). The authors in this volume also point to the contradictions sometimes inherent in postmodern/multiple selfhood, but they also begin to point to how these contradictions are neither completely "bad" nor the entirety of the identity story. In many ways, these multiple and contradictory identities function better than a rigidly coherent identity and serve to expand particular categories. For example, this volume contains an essay on the identity of homosexual orthodox Jews; for many, this is a contradiction in terms, but the authors explain how they have come to construct/narrate their identities to include both.

3. Philippians 4:13 (paraphrased). Also see Parker, *Trouble Don't Last Always*, 29–51 for a fuller discussion of her interviews with youth actively involved in churches, but still not finding the resources within their Christian communities to redress systemic ills.

4. See David White, *Practicing Discernment with Youth* (Cleveland, OH: Pilgrim, 2005), 53.

5. Parker, *Trouble Don't Last Always*, 43.

6. Many sociologists of religion and ethicists point to these trends in their attempts to characterize the Black church. Du Bois pointed to the communal and social roles and functions of the Black church, while at the same lambasting the church/pastors for not helping to improve the personal piety/morality of Blacks in American. See W. E. B. Du Bois, *The Souls of Black Folks* (1903; New York: Vintage Books, Library of America ed., 1990). See also E. Franklin Frazier, *The Negro Church in America* (New York: Schocken Books, 1964); C. Eric Lincoln and Lawrence Mamiya, *The Black Church in the African American Experience* (Durham, NC: Duke University Press, 1993), 12–15; Evelyn Brooks Higginbotham, *Righteous Discontent: The Women's Movement in the Black Baptist Church, 1880–1920* (Cambridge, MA: Harvard University Press, 1993).

7. Peter J. Paris, *The Spirituality of African Peoples: The Search for Common Moral Discourse* (Minneapolis, MN: Fortress, 1995), 22.

8. Alister E. McGrath, *Christian Spirituality: An Introduction* (Malden, MA: Blackwell Publishers, 1999), 9.

9. William Stringfellow, *The Politics of Spirituality* (1984; repr., Eugene, OR: Wipf and Stock, 2006), 22.

10. Similarly, George Ganss, SJ, in his introduction to *Ignatius of Loyola: Spiritual Exercises and Other Writings* (New York: Paulist Press, 1991), 61, writes, "Spirituality is a lived experience, the effort to apply relevant elements in the deposit of Christian faith to the guidance of men and women toward their spiritual growth, the progressive development of their persons which flowers into a proportionately increased insight and joy." Ganss, like Stringfellow, points to the ways that Christian faith should and can apply to every aspect of life and should affect one's development.

11. Paris, *The Spirituality of African Peoples*, 22.

12. Paulo Freire, *Education for Critical Consciousness* (New York: Continuum Books, 1974), 5

13. Dale P. Andrews, *Practical Theology for Black Churches: Bridging Black Theology and African American Folk Religion* (Louisville, KY: Westminster John Knox, 2002), 1.

14. Ibid.

15. Here I am careful to note that discussions of practical theology or even the "nomenclature" of practical theology are still widely absent in the lived communities and daily parlance of some participants in communities of faith.

16. Albert G. Miller, "What Jesus Christ and African American Teenagers Are Telling the African American Church," in *The Princeton Lectures on Youth, Church and Culture 1997*, 37, http://www.ptsem.edu/lectures/?action=tei&id=youth-1997-04

17. Ibid. See also Lincoln and Mamiya, *The Black Church in the African American Experience*, 309–10.

18. Miller, 37, 41. Miller supports his conclusion by citing a study by C. Eric Lincoln and Lawrence Mamiya that asked why youth and young adults were missing in Black churches.

19. See Anne Streaty Wimberly, Sandra Barnes, and Karma Johnson, *Youth Ministry in the Black Church: Centered in Hope* (Valley Forge, PA: Judson Press, 2013).

20. See Kenda Creasy Dean, Chap Clark, and David Rahn, eds. *Starting Right: Thinking Theologically about Youth Ministry* (Grand Rapids, MI:.Zondervan, 2001), 19. Here, Dean asserts that youth are already practicing theological reflection, and thus she invites youth workers to more intentional theological reflection on the lives and religious practices of and with youth. Dean writes,

    Approaching youth ministry from the perspective of practical theology assumes that youth are called to take part in every practice of Christian ministry.... All Christians are called to be practical theologians, disciples whose obedience to God in the church and world puts our truth claims into practice. (19)

    Dean also intentionally blurs the lines between professional practical theologians and the tasks of "theologically reflecting on our Christian action" required of each Christian in order to emphasize the collective and intentional work of practical theology to which we must invite children and youth (19–21).

    See also Andrew Root, "Practical Theology: What Is It and How Does It Work?," *Journal of Youth Ministry* 7, no. 2 (Spring 2009): 55–72. Root writes, "Youth ministry is a practical theological discipline that seeks to construct a theology of action/practice for younger generations of people" (71). Root further argues that scholars of youth ministry "are those in the theological faculty that attend to reflection on God's action in concrete locations where young people are present, seeking to construct theories born from practice that lead individuals and communities into faithful performative action in the world" (71).

21. Mary Elizabeth Moore, "Children and Youth Choosing Life," in *Children, Youth and Spirituality in a Troubling World*, eds. Mary Elizabeth Moore and Almeda M. Wright (St. Louis, MO: Chalice Press, 2008), 13.

22. It is also important to note that many scholars are now coming to see the pedagogical nature of interviewing youth (beyond simply gathering research data). For example, see Dori Baker and Joyce Mercer, *Lives to Offer* (Cleveland, OH: The Pilgrim Press, 2007), 73–74. The authors note that conducting interviews with youth can be a type of "holy listening," and youth ministry in which youth come to make meaning through narrative. Therefore I remained open to the information I gleaned in the interviews as well as the pedagogical function of the interviews in fostering an integrating spirituality.

23. Ada Maria Isasi-Diaz, *En la Lucha/In the Struggle: A Hispanic Women's Liberation Theology*. (Minneapolis: Fortress Press, 1993), 68.
24. Ibid. 87–88
25. Christian Smith with Melinda Lundquis Denton, *Soul Searching: The Religious and Spiritual Lives of American Teenagers* (New York: Oxford University Press, 2005), 162–64. See their work for a more complete discussion of their theory about moralistic therapeutic deism as popular religion among American adolescents.

CHAPTER 1

1. All youth in this chapter are real. Their names have been changed and identifiers have been removed from their quotes to protect their anonymity. Also, I try to stay as close to their words as possible, editing them as needed for readability.
2. See Parker, *Trouble Don't Last Always*, 35–36. As noted in the introduction, Parker developed her understanding of fragmented spirituality by drawing upon interviews with African American youth in the 1990s in the Chicago area. Her interviews gave examples of youth who were very confident and passionate in their descriptions of God working in their individual lives. However, the youth used the language of "wishful thinking" in discussing their experiences of racism. The youth did not exhibit the same confidence or describe God working in their lives regarding racism.
3. All youth except one young man from the Atlanta community were YTI participants. I opened my research sample to include non-YTI students after noting the limited pool of African American males attending the 2008 YTI summer academy. Also, none of the 2008 male participants chose to participate in the interviews. However, expanding my research pool did not produce a tremendous influx of willing African American male participants.
4. My research does not look at the spirituality of African American youth in non-Christian religious traditions and thus does not make any assumptions about their views and/or struggles to integrate their spirituality with other areas of their lives. Neither have I researched what this phenomenon looks like in non-religious, atheist, or seeking African American youth.
5. These interviews (conducted summer 2008) were also complemented by interviews conducted during YTI Summer Academy 2004–2007. The earlier interview years focused less specifically on questions that point to fragmentation in one's spirituality, but many of these issues emerge without asking specific questions. Of particular significance is that one of the male interviews was conducted in 2007, using a similar interview protocol; however, this protocol did not ask explicitly about the role or work of God in politics and society. The second male was interviewed in Summer 2009, following the 2008 interview protocol.

Also, while there is some overlap in the survey and interview participants, methodologically I treat each survey and interview response as a discrete piece of data. The survey responses were collected anonymously via an online survey product, and only requested demographic information such as age, race/ ethnicity, gender, region, and denomination. Thus it is impossible to directly match survey responses with the responses of the youth interviewed. Also, not all youth surveyed were interviewed and not all interview participants completed the online survey.

6. See Appendix B for the full listing of youth interview questions.

7. I make this assertion about the data sample because it is not sufficiently large (N = 22; 14 surveyed and 8 interviewed) and it is not a random sample. It is rather a sample of convenience because the majority of the youth are selected from YTI applicants.

8. While I do not want to label her pessimistic in her understanding of racism, she does not feel empowered to stand up for herself and call out racist teachers. I also note that her church is not a place where she can find or would seek help with this.

9. Kira uses the language of "witnessing" throughout her interview. Witnessing often refers to the practice of going through a particular neighborhood, walking "door-to-door," or simply having a conversation with another person about one's beliefs as a Christian. Witnessing may also include sharing of "testimonies" or narratives that recount the ways that being a Christian have affected the lives of the testifier or witness.

10. However, I wonder if there is room in her theological understanding for concerns about how to make things better now. I tried to discuss this with her, but it was harder to ask about this, since I am not sure I even know what a more theologically robust or "here and now" response would look like. Even as I wonder if her approach of witnessing and Bible study—so that her peers will get saved before they die—is sufficient, I wonder more if a protest, rally, or a movement to end youth violence in her community, is sufficient either.

11. In the total survey population, 35 percent of the youth named violence or gangs as an issue of concern, 25 percent talked about different groups (races, classes, ethnic or religious groups) as being divided or segregated, and 16 percent named concerns about racism. 75 percent of African American youth list violence as a concern, while only 35 percent of the larger sample list violence as a concern.

12. These responses among youth of African American descent for YTI 2008 are somewhat surprising, in that I expected their level of religious involvement to be on par with or above the overall average (including all ethnic groups); however, the overall survey sample showed that 80 percent of all the youth were either regularly or very involved in their religious communities.

13. And this is very different from the experiences of youth regarding the church's influence in their lives.

14. See Appendix A for a summary of the full survey questions.

15. An allusion to Philippians 4:13.

16. Q: And do you think that God is calling to work for change?

    A: At one point I did. I forgot when. I mean ... at one point I felt like I should become a pastor or something like that. I forgot why. I forgot how it happened. But I really did feel like it to the point that if my grandpa is a pastor, and so I was like, oh, it must be in my blood. But then I've decided to become a psychologist. And I figured I could work—you can do psychology with religion in it. And so I figured I can work both of them together to help people.

17. I characterize her statement as pessimistic because she relays the ways that her community is reluctant to get involved or see the ways that they can respond to the suffering around her. However, I also note that other youth interviewed were less inclined to talk about or did not identify with the idea of being called to respond. For example, Muwasi responded that she did not think it was her concern to respond to the crisis and social concerns of other youth or in the world.

18. An alternative question could also be why these dimensions of the youth's lives should connect. There are continued debates about the feasibility of integrated identities or even consistency in our lives and decisions. Beyond the question of whether we can be consistent, the question remains: even if we do not hold every aspect of our lives/selves in tandem, can we at least develop the skills to draw on the resources in each arena? Particularly, I hope that the youth who are "on fire for God" could use that same fire and energy and hope in God to address concerns in other areas of their lives.

    Kira's narrative is really helpful and pushes me to think about what this looks like. For example, Kira is making things happen and is working for change in ways that most mainline youth are not (however, most mainline youth were not quite as passionate about God either).

19. Later in this work, I also attend to the ways that contemporary protest movements and events are increasingly serving as catalysts for youth communal involvement; I argue that they must therefore be included in the influences on their spirituality.

20. See Christian Smith and Melinda Lundquist Denton's *Soul Searching: The Religious and Spiritual Lives of American Teenagers*, which notes this trend also among the responses of Black youth, and youth attending historically Black protestant churches.

21. Jacqueline Trussell, "The Convention Movement of the Black Baptist Churches," *BlackandChristian.com*, accessed May 20, 2009, http://www.blackandchristian. com/articles/academy/trussell1.shtml.

    For more information on the interconnection of publishing boards and Black Baptist denominational development see also Leroy Fitts, *A History of Black Baptists* (Nashville, TN: Broadman, 1985); and James Melvin Washington, *Frustrated Fellowship: The Black Baptist Quest for Social Power* (1986; repr. Macon, GA: Mercer University Press, 2004).

22. For the history and fuller discussion of the development of the Sunday School Publishing Board (SSPB) in 1915, after a split over the governing of the Boyd Publishing Company (then named the National Baptist Publishing Board), see their website. Like the Boyd Publishing Company, the SSPB continues to produce Sunday school curricula and educational resources for African American Baptists. "Our Story," *Sunday School Publishing Board*, accessed July 21, 2016, https://www.sspbnbc.com/about-us/our-story/

23. Kenneth Hill, *Religious Education in the African American Tradition: A Comprehensive Introduction* (St. Louis, MO: Chalice Press, 2007), 18.

24. Ibid.

25. Du Bois, *The Souls of Black Folk.*

26. Also see W. E. B. Du Bois, *The Negro Church* (1903; repr. New York: AltaMira Press, 2003).

27. Although many argue that the power of the Black church and clergy is waning among this generation of youth, I still affirm the power of clergy within African American churches and communities. It is my opinion that while the many youth are exposed to innumerable images and potential role models from the media and internet, clergy and other community leaders still have a significant role to play, as they offer tangible role models and influence in the lives of youth. The significance of clergy is also indicated in the YTI survey results. When asked whom they admired in the community for making a difference, the youth in the sample mentioned many clergy persons.

    Also see Andrews, *Practical Theology for Black Churches*, 16–22. Here Andrews offers a description of the significance and function of preaching in African American religion. While Andrews is focusing on the role of sermons and Black preaching in pastoral care and ecclesiology in the African American church, his work still offers tremendous insights on the role and significance of preaching and sermons in the African American church.

28. Lincoln and Mamiya, *The Black Church in the African American Experience*, 175 (emphasis added).

29. Please note that the percentages do not add up to 100 percent because some lessons included discussions of more than one issue.

30. This analysis schema draws upon other schemas that analyze the types of change and transformation that people and institutions can go through/make. In particular, I am indebted to Ronald Ferguson at the Kennedy School of Government. In assessing the levels and locations of action of youth development organizations, he starts at the level 0 and works up, notating 0–grassroots organizing; 1–schools/local direct service agencies (such as clubs, community centers, tutoring programs afterschool); 2–local government agencies (the ones that offer oversight or funding for direct service agencies, city council, school board, etc.); 3–state; 4–federal (where laws are made that dictate the types of programs or funding that can be provided to support youth; also, this macro level must include national heads of major organizations, such as the national

boards of Big Brother Big Sister and national think-tank organizations, such as the Annie E. Casey Foundation, etc.). I am further indebted to the Women's Theological Center's curriculum development team that developed another schema that looks at the type of individual and communal change that people and institutions make.

31. Hill, *Religious Education in the African American Tradition*, 20. This trend noted by Hill also connects with trends noted by Gayraud Wilmore in *Black Religion and Black Radicalism: An Interpretation of the Religion of African Americans*, 3rd ed. (Maryknoll, NY: Orbis, 1998), 163–95.

32. Hill, *Religious Education in the African American Tradition*, 24. While Hill lifts up the fifty-plus lessons over the ten-year span that dealt explicitly with racism and prejudice, this is somewhat problematic for me, in that that still amounts to five lessons per year. Similarly, it is not clear whether other justice issues are also addressed and how Black Christians were expected to respond to these discussions of religion and racism.

33. It is important to note that during the 2015 sermon sample I made a conscious choice to include more women and denominations beyond the historically Black denominations, as well as to include explicitly affirming ministries. Therefore, while I argue that there is a shift in terms of Black Christianity in general with regards to the importance of working for justice as well as personal faith and piety, the presence of less traditional Black denominations also opens the door for the inclusion of these themes in the landscape of Black theology.

34. It is important to note that UMI has begun to fully address the intersections of faith and communal/systemic issues. While the content of specific biblical lessons continues to lean toward the personal arena, I want to note the efforts to address faith and broader social concerns. Again, I cannot point to a specific reason for the shift in emphasis, but the larger social contexts as well as activism of young people of faith is a possible source of influence.

     One particular addition to the UMI resources includes a new online magazine, *Urban Faith*. Recent publications from one of my former students point to the expansion of resources and the added attention to the integration of faith and justice. See Allen Reynolds, "How to Put Your Faith to Work in Response to Today's Violence," *Urban Faith*, July 15, 2016, http://www.urbanfaith.com/2016/07/put-faith-work-response-todays-violence.html/.

35. I am careful and somewhat hesitant to place these two actions in a separate category because the argument can and might be made that all of life is connected with the Spirit of God, and therefore it is misleading to separate these actions out as "non-spiritual." Thus I struggle with the nuance of language and not the specificity of the particular actions called for.

36. Luther Smith, "When Celebrating Children Is Not Enough," in Moore and Wright, *Children, Youth, and Spirituality in a Troubling World*, 28.

37. However, Lincoln and Mamiya assert, "Sermon content may well be one of the indicators most revealing of black consciousness" (*The Black Church in the African American Experience*, 175).

38. Ibid. 169. The authors note that their "study is one of the first systematic empirical attempts to begin charting the influence of the black consciousness movement upon the black clergy since the civil rights period" (169). They argue, "Given their strong leadership role in the African American congregations, we assumed that this clerical elite will have an influence upon lay members through their sermons, personal theology, and educational methods. Our study was limited to the views of the clergy, and a further examination of the views of the congregational members needs to be done in the future" (167).

39. Ibid. 175–76.

40. Ibid. 176.

41. This confirms and connects with Evelyn Parker's earlier findings, in that she noted that the students she interviewed had most of the elements of a robust and complex faith, but still struggled to put it all together.

CHAPTER 2

1. William James, *Varieties of Religious Experience: A Study in Human Nature* (1902; repr. Mineola, NY: Dover, 2002), 78–188.

2. Ibid. 167.

3. Ibid. 171.

4. Ibid. 175–83. While, I am not affirming James's understanding of the *divided self*, nor using it as a major theoretical lens through which to view fragmented spirituality among African American adolescents, I find it significant to mention his work as an example of the ways that fragmentation and division of souls/self/personality have been historically connected with religious temperaments and experiences.

5. Du Bois also interchangeably spoke of religion as the inner ethical life.

6. Du Bois is critical of both temperaments. He is wary of the radical nature of the northern Negro, in that it often leads to bitterness when even as one becomes educated and one's mind is expanded, one is better able to see the limitations of one's power and the inability to affect change. He is equally wary of the southern Negro who recognizes that only by lying and deceiving is there any opportunity for economic growth or advancement. In a sense, the southern Negro had to both lie to him/herself as well as perform for his/her employer (e.g., ex-master). Du Bois, describing the condition of the southern Negro, wrote,

   To-day the young Negro of the South who would succeed cannot be frank and outspoken, honest and self-assertive, but rather he is daily tempted to be silent and wary, politic and sly; he must flatter and be pleasant, endure petty insults with a smile, shut his eyes to wrong; in too many cases he sees positive personal

advantage in deception and lying. His real thoughts, his real aspirations, must
be guarded in whispers; he must not criticize, he must not complain. Patience,
humility, and adroitness must, in these growing black youth, replace impulse,
manliness, and courage. With this sacrifice there is an economic opening, and
perhaps peace and some prosperity. Without this there is riot, migration, or
crime. (Du Bois, *Souls of Black Folks,* 147–48)

7. Du Bois, *Souls of Black Folks,* 8.
8. Ibid., 146.
9. Both James and Du Bois describe the experiences of the divided self and double
consciousness as a conflict in one's inner thoughts that cause one to struggle to
remain whole or even sane. James describes the heterogeneous personality of
the divided self, writing,

> Their spirit wars with their flesh, they wish for incompatibles, wayward impulses
> interrupt their most deliberate plans, and their lives are one long drama of
> repentance and of effort to repair misdemeanors and mistakes... [Referring to
> St. Augustine, James writes that he was] distracted by the struggle between the
> two souls in his breast, and ashamed of his own weakness of will, when so many
> others whom he knew and knew of had thrown off the shackles of sensuality.
> (*Varieties of Religious Experience,* 169–71)

10. I want to reiterate that *in most cases* there is an incongruity between the ideals
and experiences of the youth. This tension is helpful in that it points to the
ways that youth have not become complacent with their negative experiences
and are still able to determine when/if situations do not meet their expectations. However, the interviews do suggest that youth feel empowered to act upon
some of their complaints or concerns. In some ways, the interviews served as an
intervention: helping youth themselves become more aware of the incongruity
in their lives and pushing them to ask more questions of their surroundings and
community members.

Even though the purpose of the interviews is to obtain more information concerning the spirituality of youth, James Fowler (*Stages of Faith*
[New York: HarperCollins, 1981]) and Joyce Mercer and Dori Baker (*Lives to
Offer: Accompanying Youth on Their Vocational Quests* [Cleveland: The Pilgrim
Press, 2007]) point to the ways that the interview process of intentional and deep
listening to the voices and concerns of youth in many ways serves to empower
youth (beyond the agenda of information gathering initially sought by the
researcher).

However, I am aware that not all of the youth demonstrate this incongruity,
for many youth have complaints about their lives, cities, schools, and the like,
but a few do not *really* expect that anything should be different—and in most
cases I argue that they cannot imagine how things would/could be different;
they thus resign themselves to the notion that this is the way that things will
remain.

11. Fowler, *Stages of Faith*, 77. I draw on Erikson's original writings in other parts of this chapter; however I found Fowler's summary of the tasks and outcomes of Erikson's theory of identity development to be most helpful in starting the conversation on how identity development connects with spirituality among adolescents.

12. Ibid. 72. Here Fowler refers to the work of Lawrence Kohlberg on moral development and Robert Selman's work on perspective taking in interpersonal relationships, as he outlines the foundation for his stage theory of faith.

13. Sharon Deloz-Parks, *Big Questions, Worthy Dreams* (Danvers: Jossey-Bass, 2000), 63.

14. Fowler, *Stages of Faith*, 72–73.

15. Janie Victoria Ward, *The Skin We're In* (New York: Fireside, 2000), 126. In chapter 1, we looked at the ways that youth were portrayed in educational materials in the African American community—pointing to the fact that youth can be empowered to live, act, and believe in particular ways according to the images and models that are reflected back to them. This earlier assertion draws on the fact that within adolescence, youth are developing the capacity for mutual interpersonal perspective taking. This capacity makes youth more open and susceptible to the views and images others have of them. Therefore, I assert that it becomes even more essential for youth to both see examples of other youth working and living in certain ways, participating in the life of the church and community in meaningful ways, but also for youth to receive specific and generic feedback on how they are viewed and valued in the community, the church, and by God.

16. Michael Nakkula, "Identity and Possibility," in *Adolescents at School*, ed. Michael Sadowski (Cambridge, MA: Harvard Education Press, 2003), 7–8 (emphasis added).

17. Erik Erikson, *Identity, Youth, and Crisis* (1968; repr. New York: W. W. Norton, 1994), 23–24.

18. David Gortner, *Varieties of Personal Theology: Charting the Beliefs and Values of American Young Adults* (Burlington: Ashgate, 2013), 11–12.

19. Ibid. 1.

20. Ibid. 10.

21. Erikson, *Identity, Youth, and Crisis*, 23.

22. Gergen, *The Saturated Self*. Gergen continues exploring the shifts in understanding of selfhood in his more recent text, *Relational Being: Beyond Self and Community* (New York: Oxford University Press, 2009).

23. Gergen, *Saturated Self*, 19.

24. Ibid., 11. He writes, "Many historians find the Western preoccupation with the unique individual both extreme and restricting. How did our culture come to place such importance on individual selves? In one fascinating account of the development, John Lyons proposes that the centrality of the self was largely a product of late-eighteenth-century thought" (11).

25. Gergen, *Saturated Self*, 69.

26. Ibid., xix.

27. Ibid.

28. Gergen is writing in 2000 before the boom of social networking, but in some ways his understanding of technology, social saturation, and relational selves has much to bear on an analysis of technologies such as Facebook (and MySpace in earlier years). These technologies attend to both the growing connections between humans and technology and the ever-growing realization that relationships are essential for human existence. I doubt, however, that he could have imagined that relationships would have been established or maintained via web-based communities. These communities are showing increasing significance for adolescents, post-adolescents, and adults.

29. Gergen, *Saturated Self*, , 73.

30. Ibid. 74–76. Gergen is careful not to define multiphrenia as an illness and notes the increasing normalcy of such experiences.

31. Gergen, *Saturated Self*, 80.

32. Kenda Creasy Dean, *Practicing Passion: Youth and the Quest for a Passionate Church* (Grand Rapids, MI: Eerdmans, 2004), 85.

33. Ibid. 86. Dean and I are more aligned in her assertion that the plural self requires integrity. She argues, "Youth tend to solve the problems of pluralism by relativizing truth to 'whatever,' compartmentalizing the self by carving life space into discrete cubicles" (86). However, we also diverge somewhat on her understanding of what this integration looks like. She argues, "Even plural selves require enough traction to create an affinity between roles, a 'stickiness' that allows the partial self to cling to a governing center" (87). I am more optimistic that there are means of integrating plural selves that do not involve one part/self needing to become the dominant role or voice in the process. In this way I revert back to my assertion of the need to balance many dimensions of self and youth spirituality—hence the need for integrating and integrated spirituality.

34. Ibid. 86.

35. For example, Marissa's experience of racism and favoritism with one of her teachers is not viewed as something to which she needs to respond. She asserts that this thing cannot be changed and that her church/religion has nothing to say in response to this either.

36. YTI in many ways represented a break in the norm, in that it limited access to and usage of cell phones, internet, television, and other technologies of "saturation."

37. Dwight Hopkins, *Being Human: Race, Culture, and Religion* (Minneapolis, MN: Fortress, 2005), 81.

38. Ibid. 82.

39. Ibid.

40. Ibid. 82–83. Hopkins also seems to be expanding Smith's conceptualization of the relational self, because Hopkins is moving more into a discussion of the

nature of human beings and not focusing only on how individuals interact in community—in other words, his work seems to imply an ontological connectivity.

Hopkins's definition of the self/selves resonates with my understanding, as I embrace his discussion of communal selves and connections to prior legacies, as well as spiritual dimensions of identity. However, I remain reticent to endorse an a priori spiritual ontology for human beings, both as espoused by Hopkins and Dean, in her discussion of youth identity as full integration and identity as *homo religiosus.*

41. Ibid. 83.

42. See Gergen, *Relational Being.*

43. This discussion of relational and communal selves includes myriad theological as well as cultural and psychological predecessors and interlocutors. Some noteworthy examples from theology include Schleiermacher's description of ultimate dependence and Martin Buber's I-Thou discourse, and Womanists' ethical considerations of the communal nature of Black women's theological reflections.

44. For example, much of nineteenth- and twentieth-century US Christianity grew out of revivalism and personal conversion narratives of autonomous individuals, who could know God for themselves.

45. Further elaborations on these theological distinctions emerge in the next chapter. For many point to the solitary work of Jesus in "saving" the world. However, I argue that even in an atonement theology paradigm, the work of Jesus did not and could not take place without the rest of the Trinitarian Godhead, pointing to a communal nature of the divine. Likewise, Jesus's salvific work would also be unnecessary without a relationship with humanity.

46. Fragmentation is not simply the presence of a variety of ways of responding to issues in society, but fragmentation speaks to the ways that many people demonstrate a disconnection between their actions, beliefs and experiences in the world.

47. Robert Bellah, Richard Madsen, William Sullivan, Ann Swidler, and Steven Tipton. *Habits of the Heart: Individualism and Commitment in American Life* (1985; repr. Los Angeles: University of California Press, 2008), 220.

48. Jose Casanova, *Public Religions in the Modern World* (Chicago: University of Chicago Press, 1994), 11–35.

49. Ibid. 35.

50. Ibid. 36.

51. Ibid. 36. See also Thomas Luckmann, *Invisible Religion* (New York: Macmillian, 1967), 9–12.

52. Casanova, *Public Religions in the Modern World,* 36.

53. Ibid.

54. Ibid.

55. Casanova, *Public Religions in the Modern World,* 37

56. Ibid. 221.

57. See Mark G. Toulouse, *God in Public* (Louisville, KY: Westminster John Knox, 2006).

58. Nancy Koester, *The History of Christianity in the United States* (Minneapolis: Fortress, 2007), 27–48.

59. Bellah et al., *Habits of the Heart*, 221. Also I am always interested in what people state outright and what ideas are tempered with "I don't know." In looking at Sheila's quote, it is illuminating to see that she is certain that she should love herself and be gentle to herself, but she "guesses" God wants us to take care of other people.

60. In some ways this parallels Patricia Davis's research findings with adolescent girls who placed a strong emphasis on "being nice" and not on finding or com-mitting to the truth about themselves or their religious traditions. See Patricia Davis, *Beyond Nice: The Spiritual Wisdom of Adolescent Girls* (Minneapolis, MN: Fortress Press, 2000).

61. Bellah et al., *Habits of the Heart*, 221.

62. Ibid. 222–23.

63. Ibid. 224.

64. Ibid. 226.

65. Ibid. 233.

66. Ibid. 248, see also Parker Palmer, *Company of Strangers: Christians and the Renewal of America's Public Life* (New York: Crossroad, 1981), 155.

67. Andrews, *Practical Theology for Black Churches*, 56.

68. Lincoln and Mamiya, *The Black Church in the African American Experience*, 227.

69. Ibid. 234.

70. Christian Smith with Melinda Lundquist Denton, *Soul Searching: The Religion and Spiritual Lives of American Teenagers* (New York: Oxford, 2005), 162.

71. Ibid. 148.

72. Ibid. 149.

73. Ibid.

74. Ibid. 162–64. See their work for a more complete discussion of their theory about moralistic therapeutic deism as popular religion among American adolescents.

75. Ibid. 162–63.

76. Ibid. 165.

77. Ibid. 120.

78. Ibid.

79. Ibid. 163.

80. Ibid. 167

81. In some ways, Smith's findings are less optimistic than Evelyn Parker's. Parker, as noted above, saw within most of the youth interviews the essential elements of a more robust spirituality, but she did not see them as fully connected and functioning in liberating ways in the lives of youth. Smith instead points to both a lack of theological language and conceptions of God who would actively demand and encourage action on behalf of the common good.

CHAPTER 3

1. Charles H. Long, *Significations: Signs, Symbols, and Images in the Interpretation of Religion* (Aurora, CO: The Davies Group, 1999), 165. Please note that while I capitalize Black throughout the text, I honor the preferences of authors quoted.

2. Barbara Savage, *Your Spirits Walk beside Us: The Politics of Black Religion* (Cambridge, MA: Harvard, 2008), 2.

3. Ibid.

4. Peter J. Paris, *The Spirituality of African Peoples: The Search for a Common Moral Discourse* (Minneapolis, MN: Fortress, 1995), 22. Paris is certain to affirm that "African spirituality is never disembodied spirituality but always integrally connected with the dynamic movement of life.... The goal of that movement is the struggle for survival ... [and] it is the union of those forces of life that have the power either to threaten and destroy life ... or to preserve and enhance it" (22).

   It remains unclear as to how he has come to define his understanding of spirituality and to what extent he sees other groups as having soul/underlying spirituality. (His definition also shares some similarities, in my view, with Paul Tillich's understanding of God as the ground of all being or with Jim Fowler's appropriation of Tillich, where he defines the focus of faith as the shared center of power.)

5. Paris, *The Spirituality of African Peoples*, 22.

6. Ibid.

7. Ibid. 25.

8. Lincoln and Mamiya, *The Black Church in the African American Experience*, 2.

9. Ibid.

10. Ibid.

11. Ibid. 3.

12. Ibid. 4.

13. Ibid. 4–5. They further point to the ways that African Americans in America are seldom treated as individuals. As history unfolds, it will be interesting to see how African American youth perceive and adapt to the communal or individual identities associated with being Black in America.

14. Ibid.

15. Ibid. 6.

16. Ibid.

17. Ibid. 2, 10. Here they are building on an earlier synopsis of the "interpretive schemes or social scientific models found in the work of past researches of the Black Church" presented by Hart M. Nelsen and Anne Kusener Nelsen in *Black Church in the Sixties* (Lexington: The University Press of Kentucky, 1975).

18. Lincoln and Mamiya, *The Black Church in the African American Experience*, 11.

19. Ibid, 12–15.

20. Ibid. 15.

21. See Gayraud S. Wilmore, *Black Religion and Black Radicalism: An Interpretation of the Religious History of African Americans*, 3rd ed. (1973; Maryknoll, NY: Orbis, 2003); James H. Cone and Gayraud Wilmore, eds., *Black Theology: A Documentary History* (1993; Maryknoll, NY: Orbis, 2003); and James H. Cone, *A Black Theology of Liberation* (Maryknoll, NY: Orbis, 1970) for examples of the histories and theology espousing and reflecting radical traditions of African American Christianity.

22. Higginbotham, *Righteous Discontent*, 16.

23. Ibid.

24. Ibid. 16, 236. See also Mikhail Bakhtin, *The Dialogical Imagination: Four Essays*, ed. Michael Holquist and trans. Caryl Emerson and Michael Holquist (Austin: University of Text Press, 1981), 293, 352, 426.

25. Higginbotham, *Righteous Discontent*, 16. Higginbotham writes, "The Black Church constitutes a complex body of shifting cultural, ideological, and political significations. It represents a 'heteroglot' conception in the Bakhtinian sense of a multiplicity of meanings and intentions that interact and condition each other. Such multiplicity transcends polarity—thus tending to blur the spiritual and secular, the eschatological and political, and the private and public" (16).

26. See Wallace D. Best, *Passionately Human, No Less Divine: Religion and Culture in Black Chicago, 1915–1952* (Princeton, NJ: Princeton University Press, 2005), 147–80 for a description of Lucy Smith and her ministry in the Chicago area.

27. Higginbotham's model also empowers us to recognize and discuss the trends in African American women's Christianity, which included everything from acts of personal piety and "a politics of respectability" as a strategy for racial progress, to fund raising, interracial dialogue, and formal resistance in woman's suffrage movements and anti-lynching campaigns.

28. This was particularly evidenced in the educational resources. Moreover my critique that the educational resources did not include an understanding of change, conversion, or transformation also includes some astonishment at the relatively low salience of salvation (however one defines it) in the youth interviews and educational resources.

29. Delores S. Williams, *Sisters in the Wilderness: The Challenge of Womanist God Talk* (1993; repr. Maryknoll, NY: Orbis, 2003); Higginbotham, *Righteous Discontent*.

30. Linda E. Thomas, "Womanist Theology, Epistemology, and a New Anthropological Paradigm," in *Cross Currents* 48, no. 4 (Summer 1998), http://www.aril.org/thomas.htm.

31. Williams, *Sisters in the Wilderness*, ix–x.

32. Alice Walker, *In Search of Our Mothers' Gardens: Womanist Prose* (San Diego: Harcourt Brace Jovanovich, 1983), xii.

33. Emilie M. Townes, *In a Blaze of Glory: Womanist Spirituality as Social Witness* (Nashville: Abingdon, 1995), 9. In addition to Townes's discussion of resistance

as an essential element of Womanist spirituality, theologian Kelly Brown Douglas also describes and defines a "spirituality of resistance" in her work *The Black Christ* (Maryknoll, NY: Orbis Press, 1994), 130.

34. Here, we also see that a Womanist spirit and spirituality entails
    - embodying sexual and nonsexual love of women and men, and one's self regardless;
    - being communally oriented—with an active commitment to the survival and wholeness of all;
    - as well as embracing/loving the creative and artistic impulses (such as dance, music, food and roundness).

35. Smith with Denton, *Soul Searching*, 162–63.

36. Williams, *Sisters in the Wilderness*, 5. Williams's articulation of the *survival/quality of life* theme in biblical narratives was and remains controversial in many African American communities and even in conversation with the more radical and militant strands of Black Liberation Theology.

37. Ibid. 6.

38. Monica A. Coleman, *Making a Way out of No Way: A Womanist Theology* (Minneapolis, MN: Fortress, 2008), 85–93. Here I note tremendous differences in the rhetoric and pragmatism between postmodern Womanist thought and earlier articulations of Black liberation theologies. For example, Coleman's work offers a dose of common sense realism in pushing us to acknowledge the reality that oppressive structures will persist and that all of our work toward justice will not be realized in this world. However, she is not (or should not be) lumped into the extreme caricatures of African American Christians as other-worldly. Instead, she holds together an eschatological hope of complete transformation with an urgency to work to resist injustice now.

39. Ibid. 86.

40. Ibid.

41. I emphasize an understanding of transformation as opposed to conversion, salvation, or even sanctification (which are historically Christian traditions). I see and understand transformation as intricately connected with the doctrines of salvation and what occurs in the act of salvation.

42. Cecil Cone, quoted in Williams, *Sisters in the Wilderness*, 155. See also Cecil Cone, *The Identity Crisis in Black Theology* (Nashville: The African Methodist Episcopal Church, 1975), 23.

43. Williams, *Sisters in the Wilderness*, 159.

44. Ibid.

45. Coleman, *Making a Way out of No Way*, 93.

46. Gustavo Gutierrez, *A Theology of Liberation* (Maryknoll, NY: Orbis, 1973), 204–5. Gutierrez also further points to the ways that conversion requires a change and conflict. He writes, "Our conversion process is affected by the socio-economic,

political, cultural, and human environment in which it occurs. Without a change in these structures, there is no authentic conversion" (205).

47. Ibid. 204–5.

48. Mary M. Townes, "Looking to Your Tomorrows Today," in *Embracing the Spirit: Womanist Perspectives on Hope, Salvation, and Transformation*, ed. Emilie M. Townes (Maryknoll, NY: Orbis, 1997), 4 (emphasis in original).

49. Parker, *Trouble Don't Last Always*, viii.

50. Ibid. 37.

51. Ibid. 48.

52. Fernando Arzola Jr., *Toward a Prophetic Youth Ministry: Theory and Praxis in Urban Context* (Downers Grove, IL: Intervarsity Press, 2008), 33.

53. Ibid.

54. How do we balance this with personal/private practices and communities of support that spiritually sustain this type of resistance and public work? Is this where other elements of Womanist spirituality and practices of African American churches can be helpful?

55. While most scholars argue against public theology as an attempt to convert persons to particular religious views or faith tradition, suspicions about religion and public life persist. Also, it is important to understand that public theology, the public engagement of issues of faith, is a modern/postmodern invention. Without the separation of our lives into public and private realms and the attempt to relegate religion (and by extension theology) to private spheres, we would not need to discuss Public Theology. However, given our history, we have developed an uneasiness about religion in the public sphere and particularly in government.

　　Even as a scholar of religion and a practitioner of Christianity, I am not always comfortable with religion in public life, because I am afraid that it will be an attempt at proselytizing or a complete disregard for any other views or beliefs. Despite my unease, there is both a tradition of bringing religion into the public sphere and a real need for us to draw upon the resources of religious traditions and communities.

56. It is important to note that my understanding of public theology is both shaped and placed into practice in my work with the Youth Theological Initiative, hosted at Emory University, Candler School of Theology.

57. Franklin was my first introduction to the concept of public moralists and public theology. He outlines his understanding also in Robert Michael Franklin, *Liberating Visions: Human Fulfillment and Social Justice in African-American Thought* (Minneapolis, MN: Fortress, 1990).

　　Elsewhere, I also draw on Duncan B. Forrester ("The Scope of Public Theology," *Studies in Christian Ethics* 17 [2004]: 5–19), who writes,

　　Public Theology, as I understand it, is not primarily and directly evangelical theology which addresses the Gospel to the world in the hope of repentance and conversion. Rather, it is theology which seeks the welfare of the city before protecting the interests of the Church, or its proper liberty to preach the Gospel and celebrate the sacraments. Accordingly, public theology often takes 'the world's agenda,' or parts of it, as its own agenda, and seeks to offer distinctive and constructive insights from the treasury of faith to help in the building of a decent society, the restraint of evil, the curbing of violence, nation-building, and the reconciliation in the public arena, and so forth. It strives to offer something that is distinctive, and that is gospel (6).

58. Robert Michael Franklin, excerpt from "A Great Ordeal" (a sermon delivered at the Fall Convocation of Candler School of Theology, Emory University on September 2, 2003).

59. This is an important distinction to make about public theology, versus any type of religion in the public square, because there are numerous examples of the interactions of religious communities and governmental agencies and policy makers to protect the rights of its members to practice as they believe or to worship where and how they want to worship. These are issues of great concern, but they are more aptly discussed as issues of jurisprudence or the separation of church and state. However, public theology or the work of the public theologian is not primarily driven by an attempt to protect the rights, and otherwise private beliefs and practices, of religious communities. Instead, Forrester notes that often the agenda of the public theologian looks like the agenda (or an agenda) of the community or world (6–19).

60. Mark G. Toulouse, *God in Public* (Louisville, KY: Westminster John Knox, 2006), 186–87.

61. Joan Chittister, "Unless the Call Be Heard Again," in *Christianity and the Social Crisis in the 21st Century: The Classic That Woke Up The Church*, ed. Paul Raushenbush (New York: Harper One, 2007), 117.

62. See my longer discussion of the legacy and practice of Black public theology in chapter 5. Also see Almeda M. Wright, "Youth as Public Theologians," in *Faith Forward*, ed. Dave Csinos and Melvin Bray (Kelowna, BC: Woodlake, 2013), 176–82.

63. James Gustafson, *Ethics from a Theocentric Perspective*, vol. 2, *Ethics and Theology* (Chicago: University of Chicago Press, 1984), 327–38. Here I am indebted to Mark G. Toulouse's interpretation of Gustafson and the connections between theocentric ethics and public theology. See Mark G. Toulouse, *God in Public* (Louisville: Westminster John Knox, 2006).

64. Almeda M. Wright, "The Kids are Alright!," *Journal of Youth and Theology* 14, no. 1 (2015): 91–110, doi:10.1163/24055093-01401008.

CHAPTER 4

1. Emilie M. Townes, "Living in the New Jerusalem: The Rhetoric and Movement of Liberation in the House of Evil," in *A Troubling in My Soul*, ed. Emilie M. Townes (Maryknoll, NY: Orbis, 1993), 85–89.

2. William R. Jones's *Is God a White Racist? A Preamble to Black Theology* (Boston: Beacon Press, 1997) has pushed us to wrestle with this in the early writing of Black theology, but it seems that the Black religious academy has left this question or turned toward humanism as the only natural response to this question.

3. See www.Faithforward.org.

4. One young poet, Adam Gottlieb, quoted from Paulo Freire in his introduction to the group. He spoke of Freire's influence on his work, not knowing the parallel influences of Freire's pedagogy in many progressive religious education and communities as well. In other words, these young people represent the perspectives of youth who are critically aware of the issues in their communities and are working for change. Yet they are the youth who do not see religious communities as a resource in the work that they are attempting to do (even if a few are actively involved in religious communities).

5. Joseph Erbentraut, "High School Poets Deliver a Powerful Message Chicago Needs to Hear Right Now," *The Huffington Post*, March 11, 2014.

6. The College Unions Poetry Slam Invitational (CUPSI) is an annual collegiate poetry slam competition. According to their website,

> Slam poetry is a form of performance poetry that occurs within a competitive poetry event, called a "slam," at which poets perform their own poems that are judged on a numeric scale by randomly picked members of the audience.
>
> Each year, ACUI produces the College Unions Poetry Slam Invitational (CUPSI) offering an opportunity for campuses with new or existing Poetry Slam programs to compete for top honors and to share their artistry and voices. And everyone is enriched by sharing poetry, embracing the value of inclusivity, and supporting a program in which "Everyone's voice is welcome." ("Poetry Slam," *Poetry Slam*, April 22, 2016, https://www.acui.org/poetryslam/)

7. See http://youngchicagoauthors.org/purpose/ (accessed July 28, 2016).

8. According to their website, http://youngchicagoauthors.org/purpose/,

> Louder Than A Bomb (LTAB) is the largest, youth poetry festival in the world. Founded in Chicago in 2001 and hosted by Young Chicago Authors (YCA), the event attracts 1000 participants from 120 schools in over 100 different Chicagoland zip codes. Imagine high school in-class and afterschool teams focused on a Literary Arts curriculum as a team sporting event—with reading & writing literacy as the goal! This is the power of the LTAB platform.
>
> Running annually from February to March, the festival attracts participants from diverse socioeconomic and cultural backgrounds. Of the four thousand young people served in Chicago through the various year-round YCA programs in writing, publication, and performance education, approximately 68 percent are African-American and 18 percent are Hispanic-Latino. More than half of those populations come from low-income households.

9. The poems were all found on the Internet, using a simple Google search for "Louder Than a Bomb." The other poetry contests were found from this search. Based on typical search-engine logic, these results demonstrate both more recent posts and posts that have received the most traffic (visits, likes, and views on YouTube, etc.). So beyond my selection for content and some balance of gender among the African American and minority poets, this sample represents young poets who are also widely viewed and/or popular with others (indicating a possible resonance of their messages and style with current youth and young adults).

10. Almeda M. Wright, "The Power of Testimonies," in Moore and Wright, *Children, Youth and Spirituality in a Troubling World*, 182–95.

11. "Say it Loud: African American Spoken Word," Smithsonian Folkways Soundscapes, 2017, http://www.folkways.si.edu/say-loud-african-american-spoken-word/struggle-protest/article/smithsonian.

12. "#LTAB 2015 Feature: Jalen Kobayashi," YouTube video, 3:53, posted April 27, 2015, https://www.youtube.com/watch?v=XtgaRPaejyM.

13. "Crystal Valentine—'Black Privilege' (CUPSI 2015 Finals)," YouTube video, 3:38, posted by Button Poetry, June 2, 2015, https://www.youtube.com/watch?v=7rYL83kHQ8Y. The poem has also been published in Crystal Valentine, *Not Everything is a Eulogy* (New York: Penmanship Books, 2015).

14. "Crystal Valentine—'Black Privilege' (CUPSI 2015 Finals)."

15. Ibid.

16. See Almeda M. Wright, "Image is Everything? The Significance of the *Imago Dei* in the Development of African-American Youth," in *Albert Cleage, Jr. and the Black Madonna and Child*, ed. Jawanza Clark (New York: Palgrave McMillian, 2016), 171–187. See also Edward J. Blum and Paul Harvey, *The Color of Christ: The Son of God and the Saga of Race in America* (Chapel Hill: University of North Carolina Press, 2012) for a larger discussion of the politics and history of the color of Jesus Christ in American history. The authors make a compelling connection between White supremacist rhetoric and the image associated with Jesus, as well as other places where the whiteness of Jesus is challenged or not the central imagery.

17. "Crystal Valentine—'Black Privilege' (CUPSI 2015 Finals)."

18. Ibid.

19. Ibid.

20. "Alexis Pettis LTAB Poem," YouTube video, 3:14, posted by Shante Wallace, March 16, 2014, https://www.youtube.com/watch?v=YBkScAoWL2c.

21. Ibid.

22. "Crystal Valentine—'Black Privilege' (CUPSI 2015 Finals)."

23. "Alexis Pettis LTAB Poem."

24. Ibid.

25. The questions remain, Why is there no encouragement or presence of "sanctified rage" in their reflections, and what, if anything, can we do to change this?

However, I stop short of insisting that this is the position all churches should support, as it too can become and attempt to justify God and could push youth back into a position of needing to defend God or losing hope in God because there does not seem to be any hope of the world changing any time soon.

26. "Alexis Pettis LTAB Poem."

27. Popular belief is that Black youth commit and attempt suicide at much lower rates than other youth. However, recent data demonstrate that this is not the case, showing instead that the rates are about equal (indicating an increase in the percentage of suicides and suicide-related injuries among Black youth and young adults). See Sean Joe, Raymond E. Baser, Gregory Breeden, Harold W. Neighbors, and James S. Jackson, "Prevalence of and Risk Factors for Lifetime Suicide Attempts among Blacks in the United States," *JAMA* 17, no. 296 (November 2006), doi:10.1001/jama.296.17.2112.

   Joe, et al. reflect on recent Centers for Disease Control and Prevention reports and note that the prevalence of attempted suicide among White and Black high school students (7.3 percent and 7.6 percent, respectively) were roughly equal. Although suicide has traditionally been viewed as a problem that affects more Whites, the rates of suicide among Blacks have increased significantly since the mid 1980s. A precipitous increase in the rate of suicide and nonfatal suicidal behavior among younger Blacks has reduced US racial disparities in suicidal behaviors. The difference in suicide rates between Whites and Blacks aged fifteen to twenty-four years narrowed from a ratio of 1.7 in 1980 to 1.4 in 2003.

28. "#LTAB2015 Indy Finals Winner: Antwon Funches," YouTube video, 3:25, posted by "YoungChicagoAuthors", April 21, 2015, https://www.youtube.com/watch?v=m-3WxTZMEno.

29. Ibid.

30. Ibid.

31. Ibid.

32. Ibid.

33. Ibid.

34. " 'Cody'-Nova Venerable," YouTube video, 3:35, posted by "Louder Than a Bomb documentary channel", April 23, 2013.

   According to the CDC, diabetes is disproportionately represented in minority communities. See "Age-Adjusted Rates of Diagnosed Diabetes per 100 Civilians, Non-Institutionalized Population, by Race and Sex, United States, 1980–2014," Centers for Disease Control and Prevention, December 1, 2015, http://www.cdc.gov/diabetes/statistics/prev/national/figraceethsex.htm.

   While the diagnosed rates of autism are lower in minority communities, the access to screening in minority communities is demonstrating an increase in the reported cases of Autism among Blacks and Hispanics. There is not enough information to adequately assess the actual prevalence of the disease in these groups.

35. In a different poem, Nova also describes the pain of a young woman having to take on different roles with her father after her mother left. See Nova Venerable, "Louder Than a Bomb extras—'Apartment on Austin' (full version), Nova Venerable," YouTube video, 2:31, posted by Louder Than a Bomb documentary channel, December 26, 2011, https://www.youtube.com/watch?v=FZMpePbF454.

36. Nova Venerable, " 'Cody'-Nova Venerable."

37. Ibid.

38. From this sample, I cannot predict how Nova would discuss systemic oppressions such as racism or violence against youth. However, I see her poem not as an anomaly or as a counterexample of fragmented spirituality, but as further evidence of the ways that youth see and expect God to work in their personal and individual lives, yet so often do not include God (even to question or blame God) in discussions of larger systemic issues. Her reflections connect back to some of the youth interviews and the absence of any God-talk in relationship to systemic issues.

39. Even as I note the different starting places and experiences of the content of the youth poems, it is important to emphasize the interconnectedness of the personal and systemic dimensions of youth suffering. Thus I am not arguing that these young people are addressing categorically different experiences of suffering, but that they are inviting us into a different starting place or offering us a snapshot of their lives, instead of a meta-critique of systems or generations of oppression. Both are helpful and part of the ways that Black youth are making sense of their experiences.

    Furthermore, as noted above in the experience of writing and performing, the individual reflections get transformed into a communal experience, such that the hearer and audience becomes equal participants in the speaking of a true word and in the possibility of translating what is spoken into action and transformation.

40. Tonya Ingram, "Unsolicited Advice (after Jeanann Verlee)," CUPSI 2013 Finals, YouTube video, 3:26, posted April 16, 2013, https://www.youtube.com/watch?v=1wmL9dgG10E.

41. Ibid.

42. Ibid.

43. Ibid.

44. Ibid., Tonya's poem raises many questions, as it represents the only reference in any of the poems I listened to or included in this work that seeks/connects religion with direct action in response to dehumanization and racism.

45. Ibid.

46. Eric Simpson "Hopes and Dreams," LTAB 2015, YouTube video, 2:57, posted March 30, 2015, https://www.youtube.com/watch?v=s8BbamE0oB8.

47. The meaning of being *god* is open to multiple layers of interpretation (as is true of all phrases in poetry). This could include parroting of language used by hip-hop

artists or a connection to the Five-Percent Nation. It is important to not primarily read this as a reworking of Judeo-Christian theological categories. However, the resonance of the praise "you can call me a God" is important for the move the poem makes in addressing the fear created by young African Americans who are powerful because of their hopes and dreams, even after death.

48. Paulo Freire, *Pedagogy of the Oppressed* (1970, New York: Bloomsburby, 2000), 68.
49. Anthony B. Pinn, *Why, Lord?: Suffering and Evil in Black Theology* (New York: Continuum, 1995), 10.
50. Ibid. 17.
51. Melvin Washington, *Conversations with God* (New York: Harper Collins, 1995), xxxi.
52. Ibid.
53. Ibid. xxxiv.
54. Ibid.
55. Ibid.
56. Ibid. xlvii.
57. Emilie M. Townes, "Introduction: On Creating Ruminations from the Soul," in *A Troubling in My Soul*, ed. Emilie M. Townes (Maryknoll, NY: Orbis, 1993), 1. Rightly understood, it was the White police officers who were on trial for beating Mr. King.
58. Ibid.
59. Townes, "Living in the New Jerusalem," 78.
60. Barack Obama, "Remarks by the President in Eulogy for the Honorable Reverend Clementa Pinckney" (eulogy, College of Charleston, Charleston, SC, June 26, 2015), https://www.whitehouse.gov/the-press-office/2015/06/26/remarks-president-eulogy-honorable-reverend-clementa-pinckney.
61. Townes, "Living in the New Jerusalem," 78.
62. Ibid. 85.
63. Ibid. 85.
64. Building on Audre Lorde, Townes makes a distinction between pain and suffering. I am not certain I agree with this move. However, it is helpful in distinguishing the places where people can feel empowered, as opposed to feeling overwhelmed by their current realities, which seem immutable. There also seems to be a helpful distinction in how *suffering* points to a totalizing condition, as opposed to *pain*, which she describes as a temporary feeling that offers an indicator that something needs to be addressed. Townes writes, "To suffer, in this structure, is totalizing and paralyzing. To experience pain is simply to be alive enough and attuned to one's situation enough to know that something is wrong and something needs to be fixed. It is only when the pain becomes constant and when there is no cure in sight that pain becomes chronic pain and the chronic pain becomes the defining condition of suffering" (ibid. 85).

65. Ida B. Wells-Barnett quoted in Townes, "Living in the New Jerusalem," 86.
66. Alexis's poem also brought to mind many reactions to the suspicious death of Sandra Bland in police custody. To be certain, there is insufficient evidence to rule her death a suicide; however, the overarching narrative and reactions that Bland "couldn't have committed suicide" negates a reality where she may have *included* suicide in the actions she could take to resist the corruption, evil, and suffering she was experiencing.

    This is a terrible question that African American youth must deal with, and that youth have to ask this question is itself a withering critique of our current cultural system. But this work requires us to be honest about mental health issues, the perpetual PTSD that Black youth are walking around with, and the reality that engaging youth in real conversations about death (not just how to avoid it or about the afterlife) is part of the conversations of youth ministry with African American youth.
67. Lyrics from "Oh Freedom!" a traditional Negro spiritual. The song became popular during the Civil Rights Movements and recorded by artists like Odetta in September 1956, on *Odetta Sings Ballads and Blues.*

CHAPTER 5

1. "Students Chant '16 Shots!' As Emanuel Visits Urban Prep," CBS Chicago, December 16, 2015, http://chicago.cbslocal.com/2015/12/16/students-chant-16-shots-as-emanuel-visits-urban-prep/.
2. However, this act of civil disobedience is also remarkable in that it demonstrates the courage of primarily African American youth in a public school setting, where they could be subject to disciplinary or academic sanctions. In spite of the possible repercussions, the students felt strongly enough about raising their voices that they did just that even in front of the mayor. We also see that the young people were not without some "savvy" and skill in organizing, in that they chanted together—making it harder for just one student to get kicked out of the assembly or punished more harshly than a collective effort to effect change. The collective action reflects the ideas/strategies of organizers for generations, such as Saul Alinsky, who notes that when one person yells "f*&^ you" at a contested official, it functions as a "personal obscenity"; however, when an organized collective yells it in unison, it becomes direct action against a corrupt system (Saul David Alinsky, *Rules for Radicals* [New York: Random House, 1971], 5–6).
3. See Jon C. Rogowski and Cathy J. Cohen, *Black Millennials in America*, report, The Center for the Study of Race, Politics and Culture, University of Chicago (Chicago: Black Youth Project, 2015), 22.

    The Black Youth Project survey on Black millennials offers a discussion of the political engagement and concerns of young African Americans over the last decade. In particular, this survey notes an increase in voter turnout among African Americans, aged 18–24 from 1996–2012. In 1996, 32.4 percent of Black Youth (18–24) voted (compared to 36.9 percent of White and 15.1 percent of Latino youth). By 2012, 45.9 percent of Black youth voted, surpassing the percentage of White youth (41.4 percent) and Latino youth (26.7) again. The largest voter turnout among Black youth was in 2008 (52.3 percent).

4. Here I reference a recent *Atlantic* article with a similar title. Emma Green explores the complicated narratives of many Black activist and church leaders in the Baltimore area. As one can imagine, she finds that the narrative is not simply one of contemporary activists who are no longer connected with the church or that churches are irrelevant. Instead, there is a more nuanced story to tell. See Emma Green, "Black Activism, Unchurched," *The Atlantic*, March 22, 2016. http://www.theatlantic.com/politics/archive/2016/03/black-activism-baltimore-black-church/474822/.

5. For example, see interview with Pastor Jeremiah Wright reflecting on young adult activism in Ferguson, Missouri and Baltimore. Daniel Christian, "Former Pastor to Obama Discusses Black Lives Matter, Role of Churches in Social Activism," *Missourian*, September 10, 2015, http://www.columbiamissourian.com/news/local/former-pastor-to-obama-discusses-black-lives-matter-role-of/article_625040ce-57eb-11e5-b630-c70fa6338e42.html See also Green, "Black Activism, Unchurched."

6. Savage, *Your Spirits Walk beside Us*, 9. While Savage contests the uncritical way that the term "Black church" is used, she also notes, "Yet the 'Black church' lives on precisely because it is the political and cultural shorthand and an all-purpose stand-in for the dearth of other Black institutions, especially in the twentieth century when large institutional responses to racial inequality were required" (9).

Here Savage raises an important quandary that needs to be further explored, such as, If institutional responses are no longer needed or respected, what then becomes the ongoing need for or connection to Black churches?

7. Christian, "Former Pastor to Obama Discusses Black Lives Matter."

8. Phil Zuckerman, *Du Bois on Religion* (New York: AltaMira Press, 2000), 174.

9. Barbara Savage, *Your Spirits Walk beside Us*, 11–12. See also examples of early texts that constitute the beginnings of Black religious studies from figures, such as Du Bois, Carter G. Woodson, E. Franklin Frazier, and others who theorize about Black churches as highly problematic institutions. While much of this negative framing of religion and church can be explained as an apologetic for esteeming Black people as truly modern, intellectual, and not wedded to "superstitions," it complicates a narrative that the "Black church" has been the progenitor of all political change and activism within African American history. In fact, the relationship has been and remains complex.

10. See Almeda M. Wright, "Varieties of Black Queer Religious Experiences," *Black Theology* 10, no. 3 (2012): 275–91, for a longer discussion of the need to de-center

the place and role of the Black Church in our theorizing about Black spirituality—particularly as the narratives and experiences of young African Americans (as well as others) speak to the significance of other experiences and cultural expressions that are not fully encapsulated in the Church or in our attempts to keep the church central.

11. We must attend to this reality, knowing that we cannot force youth and young adults to shoulder all of the responsibility for working for change and in turn bringing the church along with them. But it is also a reminder that the church must honor the work young African Americans are already doing to ameliorate systems of injustice.

12. For more information on Makayla, see Emma Brown, "This 17-Year-Old Is a Rising Voice in Baltimore's Black Lives Matter Movement," *The Washington Post*, February 2, 2016.

13. "Herstory," *BlackLivesMatter*, accessed June 23, 2016, http://blacklivesmatter. com/herstory/.

14. The participants in the Black Lives Matter movement and the many organizations that have been created as a direct spin-off (and at times in opposition to the ways that the original creators wanted their worked used) are innumerable. Part of the generativity of the hashtag has a great deal to do with the ways that social media is changing how younger people protest and share information. It also allows for a different type of activism and movement, one that does not depend on a singular charismatic (and often male) leader.

15. The Chicago-based Black Youth Project also reports on the formation of Black Scholars for Black Lives. See for example, Elizabeth Adetiba, "Meet the Academics Behind Black Lives Matter," *Black Youth Project*, April 4, 2016, http:// Blackyouthproject.com/meet-the-academics-behind-Black-lives-matter/.

For one report on Hoodie Sundays, see Paul Brandeis Raushenbush, "Trayvon Martin 'Not Guilty' Verdict Sparks Hoodie Sunday at Black Churches," *Huffington Post*, July 14, 2013.

16. See Dana Ford, "Jonathan Butler: Man behind the Missouri Hunger Strike," CNN, November 10, 2015.

17. "'This Flag Comes Down Today': Bree Newsome Scales SC Capitol Flagpole, Takes Down Confederate Flag," *Democracy Now!*, July 3, 2015, http://www. democracynow.org/2015/7/3/this_flag_comes_down_today_bree.

18. Brittney Cooper, "On the Pole for Freedom: Bree Newsome's Politics, Theory, and Theology of Resistance," *Crunk Feminist Collective*, June 29, 2015, http:// www.crunkfeministcollective.com/2015/06/29/on-the-pole-for-freedom-bree-newsomes-politics-theory-and-theology-of-resistance/.

19. Ibid. Cooper argues that "The clear Christian framing of her act of civil disobedience matters for a number of reasons. As the families of the nine slain offered their forgiveness to Roof for his heinous acts, I was incensed at what felt like a premature move to forgiveness. While I feel compelled to honor the right of

these families to grieve and process this loss in the way that makes most sense for them—after all this is first and foremost *their* loss—I also wonder about whether churches have done a disservice in making Black people feel in particular that forgiveness must show up on pretty much the same day as our grief and trauma and demand a hearing" (ibid.).

20. TeamEBONY, "[IN MY LIFETIME] Bree Newsome on Removing the Confederate Battle Flag," *EBONY*, February 5, 2016, http://www.ebony.com/Black-history/bree-newsome-confederate-flag-ebonybhm#ixzz3zvXsQTXf.

21. See "A Discussion with Bree Newsome and Jimmy Tyson at Wild Goose 2015 (PNS)," YouTube video, 50:25, July 30, 2015, https://www.youtube.com/watch?v=OkZNyRF2Qhc.

22. Ibid.

23. Ibid. See also Jesse James DeConto, "Activist Who Took down Confederate Flag Drew on Her Faith and on New Civil Rights Awakening," *Religion News Service*, July 12, 2015, http://religionnews.com/2015/07/12/activist-who-took-down-confederate-flag-drew-on-her-faith-and-on-new-civil-rights-awakening/.

24. Some would even go as far back to the police brutality against Rodney King in the early 1990s.

25. In her interview at Wild Goose, Newsome makes a nice comparison between her direct action and the sit-ins at lunch counters in the 1950s. She also frames this comparison with the reminder to resist the temptation to juxtapose "agitation" and creating tension, such that the establishment must respond with "peace." There seems to be a recent attempt to critique any direct action and agitation as being in opposition to "keeping the peace."

　　In reality, I often assert that there is a difference between peacekeeping and peacemaking, in that the latter requires actual transformation of unjust systems in order for peace to emerge. Newsome similarly notes that this version of peace, which is opposed to agitation, is most often not real peace, but simple order—and it is an order that is often established/secured by police occupation or a fear of retaliation if one chooses to challenge that order.

　　In terms of her theological framing, Newsome names Jesus as one of the "biggest" agitators to ever live, noting that the only time that Jesus was in the temple was when he was flipping things over or waking people up. See "A Discussion with Bree Newsome and Jimmy Tyson at Wild Goose 2015 (PNS)," YouTube video, 50:25, posted by Presbyterian Church USA, July 30, 2015, https://www.youtube.com/watch?v=OkZNyRF2Qhc.

26. Newsome was reciting words attributed to Paul in Philippians 1:21.

27. Unless otherwise noted, all reflections are from an informal, unpublished interview with Nyle Fort, June 4, 2016.

28. See "Nyle Fort the Young Minister at the Heart of Ferguson," prod. Fusion Media Network, perf. Nyle Fort, November 13, 2014, YouTube video, 4:15, https://www.youtube.com/watch?v=PgB26o_oDxo.

29. James Cone's *The Cross and the Lynching Tree* (Maryknoll, NY: Orbis, 2011) and Kelly Brown Douglas's *Stand Your Ground: Black Bodies and the Justice of God* (Maryknoll, NY: Orbis 2015) offer great theological treaties that parallel the theological moves that Fort and others make in the connection between contemporary race-based injustices and the state-sanctioned violence toward Jesus Christ. Other texts (and even sermon manuscripts from the nineteenth and twentieth centuries) offer this type of theological framing.

    However, Fort and his fellow organizers are making a slightly different move as they translate from a written theological reflection to the sacred practices of preaching in the midst of worshipping communities and with others (via social media).

    It is also important to note that I cannot pinpoint who organized the first seven last words such as these, as they began to take hold around the country and there are many examples of wedding the sacred worship practices and even Good Friday services with attention to issues at the heart of the African American community. For example, First Afrikan Presbyterian Church in Lithonia, GA for years has hosted a service of sacred remembrance, where they construct the services as solemn experiences, which are often accompanied by slide shows with images of Black bodies being lynched, images of Emmitt Till, MLK, Malcolm X, Medgar Evers, and their mothers, wives, and families looking on at their funerals.

    Each of these experiences of connecting the historical and contemporary suffering of Black people in the United States with the suffering of Jesus is powerful and complicated (as we note in our discussions of doing theodicy with Black youth), but it is helpful to see young adult activists and leaders continuing and expanding these traditions in ways that offer alternative lenses of reflection for Black Christianity (beyond forgiveness and personal piety)—the narrative is that even/especially in the holiest of Christian celebrations, there should be/can be a word that reminds youth and adults that there is a God who loves them and understands where they are.

30. Princeton Theological Seminary Black Church Studies (along with Shiloh Baptist Church, Trenton and other local and national churches and organizations) hosted one, and The Riverside Church in the City of New York hosted the other. *Seven Last Words: Strange Fruit Speaks*, directed by Nyle Fort, The Riverside Church, New York, February 20, 2015.

31. See Mike Hayes, "The Life And Last Days Of Jordan Davis," *Buzzfeed*. April 1, 2014, https://www.buzzfeed.com/mikehayes/the-life-and-last-days-of-jordan-davis?utm_term=.hiJaJ2lMJ#.cpzo5X3W5.

32. In discussing the need to lift up examples of Black public theology, I remember the tearful words of a young poet in Chicago who did not know that there were churches or religious people who were about the work and activism that she aspired to or who were even having the conversations that they were having in their poetry slam groups and schools. Fort also recalls teens attending the seven last words event at Shiloh Baptist Church, saying, "If church is like this, if I could do this [curse, be angry, and talk about real issues], I would come more."

33. Nyle Fort, "'I love you (too).'"—Sean Bell," *Seven Last Words: Strange Fruit Speaks*, The Riverside Church in the City of New York, YouTube video, 14:00, posted February 25, 2015, 2016, https://www.youtube.com/watch?v=hq8hFNbAVDc.

34. Ibid.

35. Nyle Fort, "Every 28 Hours: An Ode to Renisha McBride (A Sermon)," *Feminist Wire*, April 11, 2014. Preached at First Baptist Church of Lincoln Gardens, Somerset, NJ, January 2014, http://www.thefeministwire.com/2014/04/every-28-hours-renisha-mcbride/

    I quote sparingly from the full text of the sermon here, but the full text of the sermon is full of rich analysis and social commentary. It serves both as an example of Christian Social Witness and as exemplary preaching in its structure and content. The sermon also includes hard-hitting calls to right living and action in light of the revelation of God.

    > The lesson is clear: it is impossible to know who God really is without knowing who God's people really are.... Today's text isn't simply a biblical or scriptural text; itsa' today text, a right-now narrative. Today's story isn't merely a story about Simon; itsa' story about society, about the Christian Church; indeed, itsa' story about Renisha McBride and the 313 young Black boys and girls that the State sees as disposable. In light of the of Renisha McBride and the 313 precious human lives that have been lost due to a racist criminal injustice system, the question is where will the church stand? What will we the church do about Renisha? (Fort, "Every 28 Hours")

36. Early Black preachers such as Samuel D. Proctor foreground this method of sermon construction, and outlines a structure of thesis, antithesis, and synthesis. See Samuel D. Proctor, *The Certain Sound of the Trumpet: Crafting a Sermon of Authority* (Valley Forge, PA: Judson Press, 1994), 29.

37. Again, it is also important to note that Fort too is wedding traditional African American preaching and even a tradition of offering social commentary within Black sermons with new media. The aforementioned sermon was preached within traditional religious institutions, but it was further disseminated on *The Feminist Wire*, an Internet social commentary magazine, tweeted out, and shared to a much broader community than could or would have attended a traditional church service.

    This is also the case with each of the sermons by Fort I have analyzed (and many other preachers in my analysis). Therefore, the usage of new media is not what makes it stand out, but the ability to influence a different type of viewer or to enhance the spirituality of a broader swath of young African Americans is important to note.

38. As I noted in the activism of Bree Newsome, it is important to see images of African American women taking the lead in these movements. It is important to note that I made a concerted effort to highlight the intersections of Christian spirituality and activism, and in doing so I have chosen to lift up the work of

two women and two men who exemplify varied dimensions of these intersections. However, if I removed the constraints of wanting to offer a cross-section
of the types of Black youth and Christian activism taking place at this historical
moment, there are multiple examples of leadership by significant queer women,
such as the three women who created the official/original organization promot-
ing #BlackLivesMatter.

39. In some ways I am also offering another vision of a Black male seminarian and
activist, who does not represent the stereotypical "raceman" and who acknowledges the need for a diffused form of leadership in the works. Other leaders,
such as Stephen Green, whom I discuss below, align more typically with historical models. Nyle is a different model, even as he continues interweaving a Black
intellectual narrative into the radical Black religious experience. Also, Nyle is
intriguing, as one (not the only) of his sights of activism and protest is within the
religious community. He is speaking within churches and re-creating church
rituals and liturgy in an effort to reflect critically on the status quo and on the
transformation that is required.

   See the last minutes of his video interview, "Nyle Fort the Young Minister
at the Heart of Ferguson," for his assessment of the movement now and its
diffused leadership model, which rejects the place, role, and power of a single
leader (read male leader). Fort notes that this movement is diverse and even
transcends race, gender, and even creed. There is no tension for him in this articulation even as he stands firmly within his Baptist tradition and works in ministry with youth in a local congregation. (And of course, samples of his sermons
do not erase the possibility of deeper and more nuanced conversations regarding
interreligious conversations and his personal struggles/questions regarding his
faith and work in a pluralistic world.)

40. Because of confidentiality agreements of the youth interviews, none of the
named case studies are the students I included in my interview data (neither
are they contemporaries of those youth). It would have been interesting to offer
the examples of youth I interviewed at YTI as the youth activist case studies, as
they too have developed into what I would consider to be leaders and exemplars
of young African American activism as well, but that was not the agreed-upon
research protocol, and it is more important for me to honor that than to offer a
longitudinal snapshot of my sample.

41. Stephen's early activism is featured in a documentary, *7 Days Across America*,
directed by Patrick Cone, produced by Patrick Cone and Andrew Baker, written
by Patrick Cone, performed by Jeff Foxworthy, from Encouragement Foundation,
YouTube video, 1:01:55, posted April 21, 2011, https://www.youtube.com/
watch?v=WiOx5Ci9Nso.

   Steve Nawojczyk's work is also the source of a documentary, *Gang War: Bangin'
in Little Rock*, directed by Mark Levin, performed by Steve Nawojczyk (United
States: HBO Entertainment, 1994).

42. For example, the NAACP leadership model is still very hierarchical. This is in direct contrast to the narratives and models of other grassroots organizing groups and movements, such as the diffuse leadership model of #BlackLivesMatter and the collaborative models of other organizations (such as SPARK, which Quita Tinsley, mentioned below, works with). Its organizational structure, as well as continued reliance on charismatic, male leadership puts it at odds with many young African Americans and makes it seem obsolete to many youth. For example, in its over-one-hundred-year history, the organization to date has never had a woman president. There is female leadership on the NAACP national board of directors, but the face of the organization has remained male. (See http://blackamericaweb.com/2013/09/11/commentary-after-104-years-its-time-for-a-woman-to-lead-naacp/).

    Similarly, there is an ongoing critique of privileging of middle-class values and a performance/politics of respectability that permeates much of the NAACP, from its founding and W. E. B. DuBois's philosophy of the "talented tenth."

43. "Youth & College About," NAACP Connect, 2016, accessed May 30, 2016, http://www.naacpconnect.org/pages/youth-college-about.

44. The NAACP website offers a good summary of the types of actions they take up, as well as some initiated by Stephen Green. The specific work of the Youth and College Division of the NAACP is better addressed on their partner website, NAACP Connect.

45. Daniel White, "NAACP President Arrested during Chicago Protest," *Time*, December 1, 2015, http://time.com/4130843/naacp-president-arrested-chicago/.

46. David Edwards, "WATCH: CNN's Cop-Defender Gets Scolded on Air for Calling NAACP Youth President 'You People,'" *Raw Story*, December 1, 2015, http://www.rawstory.com/2015/12/watch-cnns-cop-defender-gets-scolded-on-air-for-calling-naacp-youth-president-you-people/.

47. Ibid.

48. While one should not go so far as to assert that there is a way that all Black preachers speak or preach, it is important to attend to patterns of speech, which are part of the larger embodied religious experiences of many persons of African descent. This also goes to attending to the ways particular types of Black male leadership is performed and affirmed. In addition to discussions of charisma, among leaders, there are dominant patterns of speech and performances of dress, which are part of the expected roles of African American clergy and civic leaders.

    For example, others civic leaders offer a similar performance of Black male religiosity that points to Black religion without religious content, for example, Jesse Jackson, Al Sharpton, and even King (however much of his speech was infused with explicitly Christian metaphors).

49. Edwards, "CNN's Cop-Defender Gets Scolded."

50. The AME Church still holds a firm stance on this issue, but reflecting the sensibilities of much of this generation of youth and young adults, Stephen is also willing to go against traditional church teachings to preach love and acceptance, even around this issue.

51. Stephen Green, "Trouble in Candyland," sermon preached at the Academy of Preachers, YouTube video, 9:19, posted March 14, 2013, https://www.youtube.com/watch?v=V3ZAj76Gc_w.

52. I am not referring to religious youth who do not participate in activism; I discuss that phenomenon briefly in discussing the way that youth experience fragmentation in their lack of direct action relating to issues that concern them. Here instead I attempt reflect on youth who are or have been religious, but for whom religion is not their animating force.

53. Again this is not the experience of all Black gay, lesbian, bisexual, transgender, or questioning Christian youth.

54. See her bio on *Echoing Ida*, "The Idas: Bios," *Echoing Ida*, http://echoingida.org/about/idas/.

55. See "FYRE," *SPARK Reproductive Justice NOW*, http://www.sparkrj.org/fierce-youth-reclaiming-empowering/. See also, *The Body is Not an Apology* online magazine, https://thebodyisnotanapology.com/magazine/bad-picture-monday-loving-yourself-right-now/.

56. Dyana Bagby, "Activists in Action: Youth Activist Quita Tinsley—Georgia Voice—Gay & LGBT Atlanta," *Georgia Voice*, October 21, 2015, http://thegavoice.com/activists-in-action-youth-activist-quita-tinsley/.

57. Ibid.

58. Ibid.

59. "Our Story," *Echoing Ida*, accessed July 4, 2016, http://echoingida.org/about/our-story/.

60. This too connected with my experience of growing up with a "unique" and "ethnic" name, which forced me to be ready with an explanation of the origins of my name, while my counterparts with names like Beth or Molly were never asked these types of questions. I even recount experiences of having relatives prefer to use my middle name, Michelle, until I corrected them. One softball coach just made up new names for me. I was called "Sam" for an entire season, because of his laziness and White privilege.

61. Quita Tinsley, "You Are Enough: A Letter to a Younger Me," *the body is not an apology*, April 11, 2015, http://thebodyisnotanapology.com/magazine/you-are-enough-a-love-letter-to-young-me/.

62. Ibid.

63. Ibid.

64. See N. Lynne Westfield, *Practicing Hospitality* (Cleveland, OH: Pilgrim Press, 2008), 105, for one discussion of the starting and ending place of her Womanist pedagogy. Westfield does not foreground the affirmation or reclamation of the

Gospel of Jesus as her starting or ending place, and for many Christians this may sound strange or even sacrilegious. But there is, for me, an understanding that there is more to the narrative of Jesus than the name of Jesus. It is to live and model lives that reflect the work and call of Jesus.

65. Quita Tinsley, "You are Enough: A Letter to a Younger Me."

66. John Fea, *Why Study History? Reflecting on the Importance of the Past* (Grand Rapids, MI: Baker Academic, 2013), 173.

67. This is noted above in questions about the generational differences between youth activism today and the protests of the Civil Rights Movement. The interview with Jeremiah Wright also attends to this question.

68. James Barron, "A History of Making Protest Messages Heard, Silently," *City Room* (blog), June 15, 2012, http://cityroom.blogs.nytimes.com/2012/06/15/a-history-of-making-messages-heard-silently/?_r=1; "The First Massive African American Protest in U.S. History Was Led by Children Marching against Lynching in the Silent Protest Parade," *Black Then* (blog), November 11, 2016, https://blackthen.com/first-massive-african-american-protest-in-u-s-history-was-led-by-children-marching-against-lynching-in-the-silent-protest-parade/.

69. Barron, "The First Massive African American Protest in U.S. History Was Led by Children Marching against Lynching in the Silent Protest Parade."

70. The National Humanities Center has published primary-source materials online that show a memorandum with several banners and slogans carried during the silent march. They include the ones listed above and many others with religious connotations and direct biblical quotes. *NAACP Silent Protest Parade, Flyer & Memo, July 1917*, (Research Triangle Park, NC: National Humanities Center, 2014), https://nationalhumanitiescenter.org/pds/maai2/forward/text4/silent-protest.pdf; see also Barron, "A History of Making Protest Messages Heard, Silently."

71. "On This Day in NYC's History: Black New Yorkers Rose Up," *New York Natives* (blog), July 28, 2013, http://newyorknatives.com/black-new-yorkers-rose-up-on-this-day-in-nycs-history/; see also Barron, "The First Massive African American Protest in U.S. History Was Led by Children Marching against Lynching in the Silent Protest Parade."

72. For a brief overview of the Children's Crusade see, Kim Gilmore, "The Birmingham's Children's Crusade of 1963," *Bio* (blog), February 14, 2014, http://www.biography.com/news/black-history-birmingham-childrens-crusade-1963-video.

David Halberstam (*The Children* [New York: Fawcett Books, 1999]) offers an in-depth treatment of the work of youth activism during the Civil Rights Movement, as well as a strong analysis of the interconnection of religion with their leadership. For example, this work centers on Nashville during the late 1950s and underscores the work of James Lawson, a preacher and divinity school student who taught non-violent social changes to scores of students from

American Baptist College (James Bevel and John Lewis) and Fisk University (Diane Nash and others).

This work offers the most balanced treatment of the early leaders of the Civil Rights Movement and the methods and struggles of preparing to participate in non-violent civil disobedience. It was the work of young leaders like James Bevel and Diane Nash who, as a part of the *Student Nonviolent Coordinating Committee* (SNCC), pushed forward and organized and trained the masses of high-school-aged students who took place in the days of the Children's Crusade of 1963.

73. Savage (*Your Spirits Walk beside Us*) offers a helpful historical account of the diversity within African American religion and politics. In part, Savage argues that the emergence of the Civil Rights Movement as a church movement and full of church folk was nothing short of a "miracle" (2). Savage instead argues that there persisted an array of debates among African Americans and various denominations and church leaders about what position they could take in relationship to the political issues of their time. And while Savage is not arguing for or against this interconnection, her work helps us to historically situate the ongoing tensions within social change and Christianity. In fact, her work pushes us beyond nostalgia of returning to the former glory of the church's leadership in social activism.

74. See James Cone, *A Black Theology of Liberation* (Maryknoll, NY: Orbis, 1970) and James Cone, *The Cross and the Lynching Tree* (Maryknoll, NY: Orbis, 2013).

Even as I recount the importance of Black liberation theology in the history of Black Christian Social Witness (and as a statement of this tradition), this type of interconnection did not often take hold in churches. Black theology also often makes the assumption that one must ascribe to these theological turns in order to see a connection between one's faith and a call to work in the world. In fact, in chapter 4 I argue that Black theology is but one theological framework that pushes us forward in the work of living out our faith, and the activists in this chapter hold to a wide variety of theological traditions, some well within the progressive, liberationist strand and others with more conservative leanings and understandings.

75. See Andre E. Johnson, *The Forgotten Prophet: Bishop Henry McNeal Turner and the African American Tradition* (Lanham, MD: Lexington Books, 2012) for a discussion of the early work of Henry McNeal Turner.

While Cone remains significant in academic classrooms, there are other Black liberation theologians who have received less treatment. For example, Albert Cleage contributed to models of interconnecting Black culture, oppression, and Christianity—and his work was done as a pastor, not as an academic theologian. He was attempting to outline a Black theology years before Cone and did it in the form of sermons—not academic treatises. See Albert Cleage, *The Black Messiah* (New York: Sheed and Ward, 1968); *Black Christian Nationalism: New*

Directions for the Black Church (New York: William Morrow and Company, 1972); Charles L. Howard, *Black Theology as Mass Movement: Deep Calls to Deep* (New York: Palgrave Macmillan, 2014), 5–24.

76. Peter J. Paris, *The Social Teaching of the Black Church* (Philadelphia: Fortress, 1985), xv.

77. See also the discussion above of Lincoln and Mamiya, and also Higginbotham, who challenged this perspective, noting the insufficiency of a single characterization of the Black church or its relationship with society.

78. Peter J. Paris, *The Social Teaching of the Black Church* (Philadelphia: Fortress, 1985), 2–3.

79. Gary Dorrien, "What We Don't Know about Black Social Gospel: A Long-Neglected Tradition Is Reclaimed," *Religion Dispatches*, November 9, 2015, 2016, http://religiondispatches.org/what-we-dont-know-about-black-social-gospel-a-long-neglected-tradition-is-reclaimed/.

80. Ibid. See also Gary Dorrien, *The New Abolition: W. E. B. Du Bois and the Black Social Gospel* (New Haven, CT: Yale University Press, 2015).

81. Dorrien, "What We Don't Know about Black Social Gospel." See also Gary Dorrien, *The New Abolition*.

82. Dorrien, *The New Abolition*, 484.

83. Ibid.

84. Robert Michael Franklin, excerpt from "A Great Ordeal" (sermon delivered at the Fall Convocation of Candler School of Theology, Emory University, September 2, 2003).

85. Robert Michael Franklin, *Liberating Visions: Human Fulfillment and Social Justice in African-American Thought* (Minneapolis, MN: Fortress Press, 1990), 3.

86. Savage, *Your Spirits Walk beside Us*, 30–31.

87. Higginbotham, *Righteous Discontent*, 150–84.

88. Ibid. 187.

89. Nannie Helen Burroughs, "How the Sisters Are Hindered from Helping," speech delivered at the National Baptist Convention in Richmond, Virginia, 1900. See also Higgingbotham, 151 and Dorrien, *The New Abolition*, 410.

90. Despite this success, over the years, Burroughs's work made her the target of tremendous gossiping and rumors and attempts at policing both her activism and her life. Many of the male leaders did not understand how to deal with her remaining single and refusing to allow the convention to control the properties of the Women's Convention or her training school. See Higginbotham, *Righteous Discontent*.

91. Savage, *Your Spirits Walk beside Us*, 238.

92. Ibid. 240–41.

93. Ibid.

94. In many ways, the fervor of theological reflection parallels the development of Black liberation theology and Womanist theology during the explosion of Black religious scholarship that occurred alongside the Civil Rights Movement.

95. David Halberstam, *The Children* (New York: Fawcett Books, 1999).
96. Ibid., 60–76.
97. It also thus is not surprising that part of the ongoing clashes with the Black Lives Matter movement and more establishment activism has been around the fact that the models of leadership and those in charge do not carefully reflect the "ideal" types of who and what a leader should be. And I differ in the analysis of some who purport that this is because a completely new/different leadership style and set of issues (which are foreign to Black church, etc.) have emerged; however, I assert that what has emerged is a recognition (because of social media) of the ways that women have led and are leading to effect change that others could not begin to imagine.

CHAPTER 6

1. Choosing life, as well as all language of choice, is heavily biased by Western privilege and values. It can be read as having ultimate control of a situation and systems that are built on oppression. It can also appeal to an idea that how one's life turns out is determined only by the choices one makes, simply to do right or wrong, good or evil. In reality, most of the circumstances described by the young people and which are plaguing their communities cannot be over come by just "doing the right thing" or simply by choosing well.

   However, I also appreciate the added layers of agency, which are implied in the idea of "choosing life" versus simply living. The concept of choosing life is based on the King James translation of Deuteronomy 30:19, coupled with an oft-overlooked saying of Jesus, that he comes that we might have a more abundant life. While we must be cautious of the simplistic belief that by simply making better choices we can change our lives, or which would too easily lay blame at the feet of young people for the types of lives they are living, there is also a need to remind youth and adults of their ability to act on their own behalf and to work to improve and correct systems of oppression and cycles of violence. Therefore, I offer the ideas of a way of abundant life and choosing life as both reminders that there is more than death and violence and that we have a role to play in bringing about and realizing this way of life offered by Christ.

2. Kira spoke of feeling called to *witness* to her friends at school and in her neighborhood because she was worried about their souls and what would happen to them after they died. While I was uneasy with the idea of proselytizing, her daily experiences of living in communities where violence and shootings and death were real and immediate helps frame her concern for what happens to people if or after they die.

3. Except, we see this same language in the framing of the activism and direct action strategies of Bree Newsome. In truth, my earlier suspicions were prejudices,

assuming that a conservative theological framework could not afford opportunities for direct action; the exact opposite might be true.

4. Here I refer to Miguel De La Torre, "A Liberation Ethics: Rooted in a Theology of Hopelessness" (lecture, Yale Divinity School, New Haven, CT, April 9, 2015).

5. I am not going as far as Christian Smith, Melina Lundquist Denton, and Kenda Creasy Dean, who in many ways are pushing or affirming the faith formation processes of more conservative religious traditions in the United States. Smith and Denton (*Soul Searching*) note the higher levels of religious literacy and practice among conservative Protestants, Mormons, and Black Protestants. Kenda Creasy Dean (*Almost Christian: What the Faith of Our Teenagers Is Telling the American Church* [New York: Oxford Press, 2010]) includes a chapter on "Mormon Envy," where she outlines the strength of this community in passing on their faith to young people. None are affirming the beliefs of any particular group, but they are arguing that in terms of passing on faith to a different generation, these communities do it better.

My analysis of Kira is that she stands out even among Black Protestant youth, who in larger studies tended toward more religious literacy, conservatism, frequency of practice, and significance of religion/religious beliefs. In other words, she has more fully integrated what she believes into how she is acting and responding in her community. This was truly rare in my sample of adolescents.

6. Also it is important not to focus on comparisons to efforts like Homeboy Industries and the Boston Ten Point coalition, so that we will not move too quickly toward simple solutions or ones that assert that if we can just "build" community or unity, then violence and racism and corruption will be fixed. That is not what I am advocating in this book.

For more information on what became known as the "Boston Miracle," see Christopher Winship and Jenny Berrien, "Boston Cops and Black Churches," *Public Interest* no. 136 (Summer 1999): 52–68.

The Boston Miracle was also the topic of a March 2015 Ted talk by Rev. Jeffrey Brown. See Jeffrey Brown, "How We Cut Youth Violence in Boston by 79 Percent," *TED Ideas Worth Spreading*, video, filmed March 2015, www.ted. com/talks/jeffrey_brown_how_we_cut_youth_violence_in_boston_by_79_percent?language=en.

For more information on Father Gregory Boyle and Homeboy Industries, see "Why We Do It," Homeboy Industries, accessed July 11, 2016, http://www.homeboyindustries.org/why-we-do-it/

7. John 10:10 (New Revised Standard Version).

8. These teachings became popular through the ministry and media of Oral Roberts. See David Edwin Harrell Jr., *Oral Roberts: An American Life* (Indianapolis: Indiana University Press, 1985) for a larger history of Oral Roberts's ministry. Also, the current ministry and university website are full of references to abundant life

and interconnected teachings on the belief in miracles and in material wealth and healings.

Somewhat ironically, as I began writing and researching theologies of abundant life, I was disheartened by the ways that the term was often equated with material abundance or even physical healings (faith healing ministries); but what I encountered was a surprising resonance with these ministries and theological positions, because while I do not want to espouse that everybody can be rich or healed (that is not the reality of human community and life), I was impressed by the genuine faith and limitless hope in a God who was concerned for and about the material realities and conditions of people.

9. Again, it is important to note that even in terms of correctives to fragmented spirituality, none will be "easy" fixes, without the potential of also being corrupted and used to serve a larger system of individualism that will keep youth and adults from realizing the work that they are called to, as part of the family of God.

10. Thomas H. Groome, *Will There Be Faith? A New Vision for Educating and Growing Disciples* (New York: HarperOne, 2011), 23.

11. Dorothy Bass and Craig Dykstra, eds., *For Life Abundant: Practical Theology, Theological Education, and Christian Ministry* (Grand Rapids, MI: Eerdmans, 2008), 1.

12. Groome, *Will There Be Faith?*, 23.

13. Ibid.

14. Hadiya Pendleton is just one of many African American youth murdered in the past decades. Her 2013 death sparked a movement against gun violence. See Meredith Rodriguez and Tony Briscoe, "Gun Violence Awareness: Hadiya Pendleton 'Would've Been 18,' Her Mom Notes," *Chicago Tribune*, June 2, 2015, http://www.chicagotribune.com/news/local/breaking/ct-wearing-orange-hadiya-pendleton-met-20150602-story.html.

15. Kristin Johnston Largen, "Life and Life Abundant," *Dialog: A Journal of Theology* 47, no. 3 (2008): 199–200, doi: 10.1111/j.1540-6385.2008.00390_1.x.

16. Largen's editorial is focusing, like many others who have considered the idea of abundant life, on economic issues and poverty—and while these are intricately connected to Kira's concerns about youth violence, I want to push these reflections further to focus on the questions of what it means to declare and work toward a way of abundant life, when life (mere daily living) is not guaranteed.

17. Howard Thurman, *Jesus and the Disinherited* (Boston: Beacon Press, 1976), 13.

18. Ibid. 35.

19. One critical educator, Ira Shor defines critical pedagogy as

habits of thought, reading, writing, and speaking which go beneath surface meaning, first impressions, dominant myths, official pronouncements, traditional clichés, received wisdom, and mere opinions, to understand the deep meaning, root causes, social context, ideology, and personal consequences of any action, event, object, process, organization, experience, text, subject matter, policy, mass media, or discourse. (*Empowering Education* [Chicago: University of Chicago Press, 1992], 129)

20. Quoted in Mary C. Boys, *Educating in Faith* (Lima, OH: Academic Renewal Press, 1989), 52. Coe's work is also highly connected with educational philosopher John Dewey, among others. Boys also describes the connection between Coe's understanding of religious education and the work of Paulo Freire. She points to the ways that both Coe and Freire, in very different historical and political contexts, affirm the work of education in transforming the world. See also George Albert Coe, *What Is Christian Education?* (New York: Scribner, 1929); and Horace Bushnell, *Christian Nurture* (New Haven, CT: Yale University Press, 1967).

21. Boys, Educating in Faith, 60.

22. See discussion of the educational curriculum in chapter 1 regarding the early formation of publishing houses. See also Kenneth Hill, *Religious Education in the African American Tradition* (Danvers, MA: Chalice Press, 2007).

23. Albert Cleage Jr., *Black Christian Nationalism* (Detroit: Luxor Publishers, 1972), xxxv.

24. N. Lynne Westfield, *Dear Sisters: A Womanist Practice of Hospitality* (Cleveland, OH: Pilgrim Press, 2001), 105.

25. Anne Wimberly, *Soul Searching: African American Christian Education* (Nashville, TN: Abingdon Press, 1994), 15, 20. In this text, Wimberly also offers a description of "liberation from the inside"—offering eight dimensions of liberation and pointing the varied understandings of liberation at work within African American churches and communities (15).

26. Hill, *Religious Education in the African American Tradition*, 10–14. Looking at the history of African American Christian Religious Education as a discipline and practices within communities of faith, Kenneth Hill argues that recent developments in the field point to three distinctive directions of research in African American Christian religious education: (1) formulation of a Black theology of education—that undergirds the relationship between theology and Christian education; (2) theory and practice of religious education—researching the relationship between theory and practice of Christian education in the African American church; and (3) spiritual direction—focusing on the spiritual formation, nurturing, and development of African Americans.

Hill's understanding of formation, information, and transformation resonates with the overarching framework I outline below. But there are some distinctions. In particular, Hill describes the focus of each of these tasks as the individual—however, I point to an essential transformative element of religious education as beyond the individual in order to focus on the transformation of communities and societal structures as well. Of course, transformed individuals bring about this work, but the changed emphasis is more than semantics, in my opinion.

Hill also outlines six contemporary approaches to African American religious education, each with a corresponding focus and purpose for religious education. (See pp. 120–35 for a fuller discussion.)

27. I am in no way claiming originality in articulating the purpose of religious education as formation and transformation. The terminology and idea that both are essential for religious education is espoused by several thinkers, including Boys, Brueggemann, and Hill. However, my introduction to this framework for religious education came in my work at Emory University's Candler School of Theology as a Teaching Assistant and Associate for RE 501, "Religious Education as Formation and Transformation."

28. Hill, *Religious Education in the African American Tradition*, 12–13.

29. Parker, *Trouble Don't Last Always*, 37.

30. As noted above, educational curricula designed specifically for African American urban youth do not consistently expose youth to the complex history of African Americans and/or their struggles of faith. Similarly, I found that the vast majority of the sermons sampled did not explicitly educate youth about African American history and/or their particular communal identity as African Americans.

31. This interview was conducted as part of a larger set of "diversity interviews" during the Youth Theological Initiative Summer Academy from 2003–2006.

32. Within the religious education of many African American churches, there are challenges of not sharing a complex story of faith and life with Black youth. There are also struggles helping youth push past the feelings/tensions/chasms that are in place between them and many historical narratives, such that when they hear the narratives, they still do not claim them as their own.

33. These scholars include Beverly Tatum, Janie Ward, Nancy Boyd-Franklin, Jawanza Kunjufu, and others. Others scholars also affirm the significance of narrative in general for education, as well as identity formation.

34. Anne Streaty Wimberly, *Soul Stories: African American Christian Education* (Nashville: Abingdon Press, 1994), 13.

35. Westfield, *Dear Sisters*, 118.

36. Wimberly, *Soul Stories*, 13

37. Walter Brueggemann, *The Creative Word: Canon as a Model for Biblical Education* (Philadelphia: Fortress Press, 1982), 14–15. Here he is referring to the Hebrew Bible passages of Exodus 12:26, Exodus 13:8, 14, Deuteronomy 6:20–21, and Joshua 4:6, 21. He also writes that each of these formulaic questions connect with part of Israel's educational agenda of educating the young in the "normative" claims of the community (15).

38. I often have to hold together the significance of normative claims for the formation of communities and my suspicion of how norms are formed. However, I appreciate the way that Brueggemann and sociologists such as Peter Berger reiterate the way that some normative values or stories function to provide coherence and stability for communities to exist. Peter Berger's *Sacred*

Canopy: Elements of a Sociological Theory of Religion (Garden City, NY: Doubleday, 1967) served as a foundational text in my understanding of the way that religion functions to create "world coherence and order" in the lives of so many. Also, it is from within this sacred canopy that youth can find the comfort to explore, question, and respond to the many other aspects of their lives.

39. Of course, one of the major limitations of this method is that within African American communities and Christianity there has not been as clear a process of canonization where the community agrees upon which stories are normative and which ones can/should be passed. However, within most communities of faith, there are theological traditions (operational theologies) as well as narratives of how they came to be as a community that must be rehearsed for the younger and older members alike.

    Also, our meta-narratives serve as important foundations that youth must be "nurtured" in. These narratives may not remain unchallenged or unchanged throughout the life and history of a community; however, it is from within this narrative structure (foundation/canopy) that people learn to successfully navigate worlds and eventually to push beyond these narratives to also change worlds.

40. Coleman, *Making a Way out of No Way*, 5. I also see a parallel between Coleman's discussion of "functional theology" and the "embedded theology" that many persons who were nurtured in communities of faith tacitly hold. However, there is also a key distinction for me between functional and embedded theologies. Embedded theology connotes a somewhat pejorative sense that it is an unreflective and uncritical theology—it is a theology that we passively receive from our communities or that which communities embed in us (or indoctrinate us into). However, functional theology, while having many of the same connotations—in that it may be uncritical and tacitly operating in our lives—also connotes a sense of being functional, in a therapeutic manner of empowering us to operate in a world.

    For a brief discussion of embedded theology, see Howard W. Stone and James O. Duke, *How to Think Theologically*, 2nd ed. (Minneapolis, MN: Fortress Press, 2006). Stone and Duke define embedded theology simply as "the understanding(s) of faith disseminated by the church and assimilated by its members in their daily lives" (133).

41. Coleman, *Making a Way out of No Way*, 5.

42. In other words, part of the formative task of religious education is to help youth develop the disciplines or habits that become instinctual and functional in all aspects of the youth's life.

43. Similarly, students like Kira, Marissa, Elliot, Jackie, and Charles have positive things to say about the shared practices of their churches, while they also offer critiques—again pushing for a re-imagining of shared worship practices and communities.

44. Cheryle Townsend Gilkes, *If It Wasn't for the Women* (Maryknoll, NY: Orbis, 2001), 127–38.

45. Ibid.

46. For a fuller accounting of the role of Biblical narratives and many prevalent themes within African American hermeneutics, see Cane Hope Felder, ed., *Stony the Road We Trod* (Minneapolis: Fortress Press, 1991); or Vincent Wimbush, ed., *African Americans and the Bible* (New York: Continuum, 2001).

47. I am in no way equating the centrality of the Bible within African American Christianity with the way that the Bible functions within Fundamentalist traditions. Within African American Christianity there is a broad spectrum in terms of beliefs regarding the Bible—and many varied responses to questions of inerrancy, inspiration, infallibility, etc. However, these are not the major or essential questions at the center of the practice of reading and hearing Scripture within African American churches. Instead, African American Christianity has formed a canon of scriptures that undergirds their understanding of how God works in their lives and connects them, as a community, with the Ancient Hebrew people.

48. Here I am referring to a more contemporary criticism of prayer as a "copout" or easy fix to many social issues. In many cases, prayer has been criticized as what religious people do when they do not know or do not feel like putting in the effort to affect "real" change.

49. Gilkes, *If It Wasn't for the Women*, 134.

50. Yolanda Smith, *Reclaiming the Spirituals: New Possibilities for African American Christian Education* (Cleveland, OH: Pilgrim Press, 2008), 1–6.

51. Don E. Saliers, "Singing Our Lives," in *Practicing Our Faith: A Way of Life for Searching People*, ed. Dorothy C. Bass (San Francisco: Jossey-Bass, 1997), 179–93.

52. Ibid. 190–91.

53. Ibid. 191.

54. Portions of this section were previously published in "The Power of Testimonies: Spiritual Formation and Ministry with Youth," in Moore and Wright, *Children, Youth and Spirituality in a Troubling World*, 182–95.

55. Drawing upon the language of legal proceedings and courtrooms, giving a testimony involves a witness to some set of events sharing the truth/details of the event as he/she perceived, remembered, and experienced it. Testimony in the African American Christian worship experience involves a similar type of sharing an event as the person perceived it, but usually involves an account of Divine agency working in that event, either changing it or giving the person strength to endure it.

56. Gilkes, *If It Wasn't for the Women*, 137. Gilkes includes testimonies as a pillar of Afro-Christian worship, alongside biblical references and imagination, preaching, prayer, and music. She discusses each from the perspective of Black feminists and explores how they address issues of gender within Black churches and communities.

57. Ibid.
58. See Thomas Hoyt, "Testimony," in Bass, *Practicing Our Faith*, 91–103. In the preface to this work, Bass describes one of the guiding purposes of the work as offering "reflections on practices as a way of connecting our faith with our daily lives. It also opens a path of spiritual formation. . . . The book represents a refusal to leave our beliefs in the realm of theory, insisting that they can make a difference in our lives" (xiii). The practice of testimony sharing is discussed in this context, demonstrating the ways that for generations African Americans have been practicing their faith and always remaining hopeful that God had something to say or do or some way to be connected with their everyday lives.
59. Hoyt, "Testimony," 102.
60. Ibid. 98.
61. bell hooks, *Teaching to Transgress: Education as the Practice of Freedom* (New York: Routledge, 1994), 12.
62. Wimberly, *Soul Stories*, 22.
63. Ibid. 23–24.
64. Ibid. 22.
65. Paulo Freire, *Pedagogy of the Oppressed* (New York: Continuum, 1970), 43–44.
66. Ibid. 79. Freire argues that "problem posing education, responding to the essence of consciousness—*intentionality*—rejects communiqués and embodies communication. It epitomizes the special characteristic of consciousness" (79).
67. Ibid. 79–80.
68. Ibid. 89–90. This understanding of faith in humanity also connects with Carter G. Woodson's discussion of the "miseducated" person. Woodson argues that many of the efforts to transform the conditions of African Americans in the United States resulted from other African Americans becoming "educated" in such a way that they were no longer of use to the community. Woodson argues that these "educated Negros" had come to despise their own people and did not trust that the people were capable of change. See Carter G. Woodson, *Miseducaiton of the Negro* (Associated Publishers, 1933; repr., Chicago: African American Images, 2000), 44.
69. Ibid. 90–91.
70. Educational theorist David White gives a fuller discussion of the domestication of youth as a result of compulsory education and the changes in educational systems, so that youth became disconnected from the "real work" of adult life and in a sense warehoused into a subculture. See White, *Practicing Discernment with Youth*; see also Patricia Hersch, *A Tribe Apart* (New York: Fawcett Columbine, 1998); and Christina Rathbone, *On the Outside Looking In* (New York: Atlantic Monthly Press, 1998) for other narratives about the culture of young people that develops in and around public schools, and the resulting ways that many youth become disconnected from adult worlds and/or become seen as somehow distant and alien to the processes that also affect and shape their lives.

See also Almeda Wright, "The Kids Are Alright: Rethinking Problem-Based Approaches to Adolescent Spirituality," *Journal of Youth and Theology* 14, no. 1 (2015): 91–110.

71. Writing in the 1980s, Grant borrows the idea of "somebodiness" from the practices of Jesse Jackson during the 1980s, where he encouraged youth to chant, "I am somebody. I may be poor, but I am somebody." See Jacquelyn Grant, "A Theological Framework," in *Working with Black Youth: Opportunities for Christian Ministry*, ed. Charles Foster and Grant Shockley (Nashville: Abingdon Press, 1989), 55–76, at 69.

72. This is posture is similar to the ways that dominant groups have dealt with other oppressed groups.

73. Grant outlines three assumptions at the foundation of her understanding of ministry with youth: 1. Black young people are not in process of becoming human; they are indeed human. 2. Something is wrong with Black youth. 3. Black youth ought to be Black youth (not White youth, nor adults of any race) ("A Theological Framework," 71).

74. Ibid. 69.

75. Grant references the work of Carter G. Woodson, who underscored the ways that in order for Black youth to be successful in American educational systems they had to learn to hate Black people. She also looks at more contemporary theorist Jonathan Kozol, who pays close attention to the ways that the cultures of Africans and African Americans are described in US textbooks as late as the 1980s. His other works, such as *Savage Inequalities* (New York: Harper), illuminates the tragic differences between schools in poorer communities (typically serving children of color) and school in more affluent neighborhoods, often in the same city (199).

76. Wimberly, *Soul Stories*, 24–26.

77. For the full definition of Womanist, where she also outlines the common understanding of the folk expression "womanish," see Walker, *In Search of Our Mothers' Gardens*, xii.

78. Emilie Townes, *In a Blaze of Glory: Womanist Spirituality as Social Witness* (Nashville: Abingdon, 1995), 9. Townes writes that an accusation of being womanish became a "warning about the dangers of Black girls moving beyond prescribed cultural boundaries and socioeconomic determinants. A womanish Black girl must not only be in charge, a gatherer of knowledge, but she must also be serious about her task. Who she is makes her dangerous to hegemony."

79. Much of my understanding of the interconnection of the personal and political in education emerged from my experiences in public or secular educational settings. In this section, I draw heavily on the work of "secular" or not specifically religious educators, partly because many of the conversations around critical pedagogy with youth are still taking place primarily in debates around schooling and public education. However, as noted above, in some of the earlier

strands and tradition of religious education, outlined by Mary Boys, there is an entire tradition or classical expression of religious education that also connects social transformation and religious education.

80. Freire, *Pedagogy of the Oppressed*, 81.
81. Ibid. 83.
82. Henry Giroux, *Theory and Resistance in Education* (Westport, CT: Bergin and Garvey, 1983), 5. Giroux uses "agency and structure" to refer to a focus on human agency or structures and systems within society. He argues that both must be included in any discussion of transformation and critical pedagogy.
83. Ibid.
84. Ibid.
85. Ibid. Giroux's discussion of critical theory utilizes the Frankfurt school—theorists such as Adorno, Horkheimer, and Marcuse, as well as the work of Antonio Gramscii.
86. Allen Moore, ed., *Religious Education as Social Transformation* (Birmingham, AL: Religious Education Press, 1989), 1–10.
87. Freire, *Pedagogy of the Oppressed*, 87. Freire repeatedly cautions against attempting to have only action or only reflection. He argues that without action, there is a tendency toward *verbalism* and without reflection, it is *activism*.
88. Freire defines coming to critical consciousness or *conscientização* as "learning to perceive social, political, and economic contradictions, and to take action against the oppressive elements of reality" (Freire, *Pedagogy of the Oppressed*, 35; see translator's note).
89. Freire, *Pedagogy of the Oppressed*, 87.
90. Ibid.
91. Ibid.
92. Katherine Turpin, *Branded: Adolescents Converting from Consumer Faith* (Cleveland, OH: Pilgrim, 2006), 56. Turpin is looking specifically at the ways that religious education can "address the impact of consumer culture on vocational imagination" (57).

Another dimension of translating Freirian pedagogy to a US context that Turpin does not spend a great deal of time addressing is the fact that within the US structure, there appears to be less clearly defined lines between the oppressed and the oppressor, or the process of becoming aware of these lines remains difficult. Also, Turpin is aware of the challenges of working with middle-class, and I would say European, American youth, who are indeed part of the oppressive structure. The dynamics of being part of the "oppressor group," if you will, requires a different starting point than working to transform the world from within the oppressed group. Thus Turpin is correct that raising awareness about one's role as an oppressor within an oppressive structure is quite difficult for youth to grasp, and the metaphor of conversion offers more "grace" in regards to how young people come to see themselves. However, I am hesitant to give up

Freire's language of critical consciousness and his understanding of dialogical and revolutionary education; because it reminds us of the often-urgent and life-altering ways that oppressive systems have become the fabric of our beings and how they persist in our society.

Furthermore, Turpin appears to focus on the work that individuals should do in "resisting" consumer culture or converting from consumerist faith. And while she underscores the systemic nature of consumerism, she does not fully push her work beyond empowering youth to do small acts of resistance, to also imagine means of reworking the entire system. Thus, I value Turpin's pragmatism, but I see the need to keep revolutionary ideals and possibilities in the conversation as well.

93. Ibid. 59. I agree with Turpin's hesitation to embrace Freire's revolutionary pedagogy in working with middle-class European American youth. (I recognize the many ways that seeing oneself implicated in oppressive structures and even as eagerly participating in an oppressive, exploitive system can serve to immobilize youth, as they begin to wrestle with what Freire refers to as the oppressor within them.) Furthermore, I also understand her preference for the metaphor of "conversion" in her discussion of consumer culture/faith; however, I am not sure she fully represents Freire's pedagogy, in that Freire is not naively suggesting that *simply* raising awareness catalyzes or brings about revolutionary change.

A more accurate critique of Freire could center on the fact that he does appear to focus primarily on action that results from change in awareness without giving attention to action that leads to changed awareness or changed commitments. For example, in *Education for Critical Consciousness*, Freire writes, "It so happens that to every understanding, sooner or later an action corresponds. Once man perceived a challenge, understands it, and recognizes the possibilities of response, he acts" (*Education for Critical Consciousness*, 39). Thus I appreciate Turpin's call for ongoing conversion, in that it explicitly attends to the ways that youth need to enter the process of transformation and be supported as they struggle with the dueling convictions, perceptions, and allegiances within them.

94. Both Freire and Turpin offer concrete strategies and methodologies for empowering people to engage in the process of critical reflection. Other religious educators, such as David White, also offer a model of discerning and perceiving more clearly how one should act in response to the deep passions that emerge or the places where youth experience injustice. White's method parallels with Freire's praxis model, but also includes listening, understanding, dreaming, and acting. See White, *Practicing Discernment with Youth*.

95. Westfield, *Dear Sisters*, 108.

96. Brueggemann, *The Creative Word*, 40.

97. Ibid.

98. Ibid. 41.

99. Ibid. 47

100. Ibid. 62–63. Brueggemann further argues, "New truth from God is likely to come as a cry and a protest of the weak, the powerless, the disinherited ones" (62). He lifts up the examples of ecclesiological issues and injustices, such as the ordination of women, and makes the case that the cry for a "new revelation" about women's ordination and leadership is less likely to come from those who are stake holders in the "old revelation."

101. Evelyn Parker, "Sanctified Rage," in Moore and Wright, *Children, Youth and Spirituality in Troubling Worlds,* 196–209. Parker outlines several examples of ways of tapping into the rage of Black youth and reconnecting it with the traditions. I am more hesitant to offer strategies or examples of how this rage can be used to benefit churches, etc., not because I believe that it cannot happen, but because I am cognizant that any way that I perceive or name as "appropriate" for expressing "Holy Indignation" might already demonstrate a domestication and attempt to normalize the breach youth are naming/ calling for.

102. Parker, "Sanctified Rage," 197.

103. See Jennie Knight, "Transformative Listening," in Moore and Wright, *Children, Youth and Spirituality in Troubling Worlds,* 226–40.

CONCLUSION

1. She was part of a group of teen poets from the Young Chicago Authors. They were invited to share spoken word pieces at the Faith Forward Conference on Children and Youth Spirituality, May 2015. Her poetry group arrived early and got a chance to listen in on the conversations and presentations at the conference.

2. Smith with Denton, *Soul Searching,* 270.

3. Alice Walker, *In Search of Our Mothers' Gardens,* xii.

APPENDIX B

1. This system of uniform Sunday school lessons, beginning in the late 1800s, is used across a wide spectrum of Protestant denominations, both predominately European and African American. The Committee on Uniform Series is part of the National Council of Churches in the United States. This cycle of lessons (like the lectionary calendar) also helps a church move through the majority of the Bible in a six-year cycle.

2. The cross-section of themes and dates selected enabled me to look the way that the UMI curricula, in both themes and design, is ever evolving. For example, from 2007 to 2008, the *InTeen* magazine format changed to include more glossy pages, like an actual magazine and not a newsletter (as it did in the past).

3. I reviewed all 106 lessons before deciding to use a random subsample for my discussion of the findings. Conducting a qualitative analysis of 106 lessons proved to be quite unruly, and determining patterns and trends became very cumbersome—leading to my decision to take a subsample of the 106 lessons. I also chose to select a random sub-sample of my sample of 106 lessons, because the Sunday school data is only used for setting the baseline for my understanding of sources of fragmentation in African American adolescent spirituality.

4. I used the random number generation function of Excel to generate two lists of random numbers between 1 and 13 (the number of lessons in each unit). The Excel program returned the values 2, 5, 8, 11 (which I used for the *InTeen* curriculum quarters) and 1, 3, 6, 13 (which I used for the *J.A.M.*).

   I chose to use different sets of values for each curriculum, in order to eliminate duplications in the biblical texts and possible theological themes, because *InTeen* and *J.A.M.* are using the same scripture lessons in each quarter. In this way, the subsample is not completely random, but is a stratified sample. ("Stratified sampling" refers to a method of sampling where the population is divided into two or more strata and each subpopulation is sampled, usually randomly.)

5. I will try to attend to any radical differences I note in any examples I lift up that were not included in the sample of thirty-two, so that they will not appear to be outliers or radically different from the trends I note in the sub-sample.

6. A local ministry is defined by a ministry that is mostly focused on local church membership. A national ministry is a ministry or pastor with a significant national as well as local following. This is typically demonstrated in the variety of media, evangelistic ministries, national conferences, or speaking tours the pastor participates in. I tend to also make this distinction based on the way that I acquired the sermon's audio recording—through a national website, such as YouTube or Streaming Faith.org, or from a local church visit or bookstore.

   While there are varied definitions of "megachurch" or congregation size, in this sample the distinctions are as follows: megachurch (>5,000), large church (1,000–5,000), medium-sized church (200–999), small (<200 members).

7. The national sermons are included without the explicit permission of the preacher as their sermons are available as part of public media for consumption and analysis.

8. Also, in collecting sermons from only local pastors, I was concerned that those who consented to participate in my research would only be the pastors who knew me well or were affiliated with Emory or my current church. Looking at this potential pool of pastors and preachers, I feared that I would only attract sermons from liberal, progressive, socially active, and communally oriented churches. Thus I opted to include both local pastors and a sample of national oriented ministries.

9. Christian Smith, *Soul Searching* (New York: Oxford, 2005), 51–53.

Index

absurdity, 136–137, 149. *See also* gun
    violence
abundant life, 14–15, 198–223, 228,
    235, 236, 242–246, 299n1,
    300n8, 301n16
    agency and, 206
    amidst death, 198–200,
      204–206, 299n1
    for Black youth, 15, 206–207
    critical pedagogy of, 208–223
    definition, 205, 207
    environmental, 206
    God and, 203–208, 236, 243, 245
    history of, 202
    hope and, 207
    through Jesus, 198, 243, 299n1
    Jesus and, 203, 205
    Kingdom and, 202
    material wealth and, 203, 300n8
    poverty and, 204, 301n16
    reorientation to, 207
    scarcity and, 206, 207
    security and, 206
    spiritual growth and, 202
    strategies for, 208–211, 236
    survival or, 203–204, 279n279n36
    theology of, 201, 203
    violence and, 201, 202, 206
activism, 5–6, 14, 29, 154–197, 293n41

    academics' response to, 193
    barriers to, 192–196
    Church and, 156–158, 242,
      288n9, 297n73
    counter-narrative about, 195 (*see also*
      Halberstam)
    curriculum and, 272
    faith and, 158, 160, 162, 167, 171–172,
      174–179 (*see also* Fort; Newsome)
    gender and, 195–196
    generational differences in,
      173–174, 296n67
    historical context of, 169, 173–175,
      182–192, 296n72
    language of, 174–175
    leadership types, 289n14, 292n38,
      293n39, 294n42, 299n97 (*see also*
      leadership; NAACP)
    motivation for, 30–31, 164, 166
    politics and, 14, 30, 155
    reproductive health, 177–178
    transformational, 192
    types of, 30, 155, 159–160
    un-churched, 156–158
    Womanist theology and, 181
    women and, 292n38, 298n90
    writing as, 178–179, 184, 196
    youth, 29–31, 155
    See also public theology

theodicy, 14, 122
  Black religious, 14
  language of, 122
  Pinn and, 144
  Womanist, 14
  youth and, 121, 138 (*see also* poetry)
theological reflection
  Black liberation theology
    and, 298n94
  of youth, 265n20
theology. *See* Black public theology;
    Liberation theology; public
    theology; Womanist
  of resistance, 161
therapeutic deism, 90–92
Thomas, Linda E., 104–105
Thurman, Howard, 61, 188, 204–205
Tinsley, Quita, 176–181, 195,
    224, 294n42
Tipton, Steven, 87
Tometi, Opal, 159
Toulouse, Mark G., 86, 118, 281n63
Townes, Emilie, 106, 122, 143, 147–148,
    152, 278n33, 286n64, 307n78
transformation, 279n41
  conversion and, 110, 279n41
  creative, 112–113 (*see also* Coleman)
  salvation and, 279n41
  Womanist understanding of, 112
Turner, Henry McNeal, 184, 297n75
Turpin, Katherine, 231, 308n92,
    309nn93, 94
Tyson, Jimmy, 163

UMI (Urban Ministry Inc.) Curriculum
  action and reflection in, 56–57
  call for change in, 57, 64
  call for response in, 58
  description, 49, 56
  descriptors of God in, 55
  focus of, 49–51
  fragmentation in, 55

history of, 49–50
homelessness, 51, 53
mission of, 61
personal v. social issues in, 270n34
race and ethnicity in, 60–61, 66
racism, 51
salvation in, 278n28
sexism, 53
social justice and, 51–52, 53
themes of, 51–55, 278n28

valuing
  young people, 237
Valentine, Crystal, 129–130, 283n13
Van Dyke, Jason, 154
Venerable, Novana, 136, 152, 284n34,
    285nn35, 38
Vertigo of the Valued, 78
violence, 77
  agency and, 141, 142
  blaming, 77
  domestic, 141
  as predominant youth concern, 201,
    238, 267n11
  racism as, 201, 267n111
  resisting, 199
  sexual, 160
  state-sanctioned, 291n29 (*see also*
    police)
  theodicy and, 77, 121
  witnessing, 199
  See also gun violence; schools;
    "strange fruit"
volunteering, 42–43

Walker, Alice, 106
Ward, Janie, 73–74, 273n15, 303n33
Washington, James Melvin, 144–147, 151,
    186, 188
watershed events, 164–165, 166
Wells-Barnett, Ida B., 148–149, 152, 178,
    186, 188, 190